HERMES III

POSTHUMANITIES
Cary Wolfe, *Series Editor*

78 *Hermes III: Translation*
Michel Serres

77 *The Organism Is a Theory: Giuseppe Longo on Biology, Mathematics, and AI*
Giuseppe Longo and Adam Nocek

76 *Ideal Subjects: The Abstract People of AI*
Olga Goriunova

75 *The Obsolescence of the Human*
Günther Anders

74 *Language Machines: Cultural AI and the End of Remainder Humanism*
Leif Weatherby

73 *Hermes II: Interference*
Michel Serres

72 *The Abyss Stares Back: Encounters with Deep-Sea Life*
Stacy Alaimo

71 *Prosthetic Immortalities: Biology, Transhumanism, and the Search for Indefinite Life*
Adam R. Rosenthal

70 *The Memory of the World: Deep Time, Animality, and Eschatology*
Ted Toadvine

69 *Hermes I: Communication*
Michel Serres

68 *Nietzsche's Posthumanism*
Edgar Landgraf

67 *Subsurface*
Karen Pinkus

66 *Making Sense in Common: A Reading of Whitehead in Times of Collapse*
Isabelle Stengers

65 *Our Grateful Dead: Stories of Those Left Behind*
Vinciane Despret

64 *Prosthesis*
David Wills

63 *Molecular Capture: The Animation of Biology*
Adam Nocek

62 *Clang*
Jacques Derrida

61 *Radioactive Ghosts*
Gabriele Schwab

60 *Gaian Systems: Lynn Margulis, Neocybernetics, and the End of the Anthropocene*
Bruce Clarke

59 *The Probiotic Planet: Using Life to Manage Life*
Jamie Lorimer

58 *Individuation in Light of Notions of Form and Information*. Volume II, *Supplemental Texts*
Gilbert Simondon

57 *Individuation in Light of Notions of Form and Information*
Gilbert Simondon

56 *Thinking Plant Animal Human: Encounters with Communities of Difference*
David Wood

55 *The Elements of Foucault*
Gregg Lambert

54 *Postcinematic Vision: The Coevolution of Moving-Image Media and the Spectator*
Roger F. Cook

53 *Bleak Joys: Aesthetics of Ecology and Impossibility*
Matthew Fuller and Olga Goriunova

52 *Variations on Media Thinking*
Siegfried Zielinski

51 *Aesthesis and Perceptronium: On the Entanglement of Sensation, Cognition, and Matter*
Alexander Wilson

50 *Anthropocene Poetics: Deep Time, Sacrifice Zones, and Extinction*
David Farrier

49 *Metaphysical Experiments: Physics and the Invention of the Universe*
Bjørn Ekeberg

48 *Dialogues on the Human Ape*
Laurent Dubreuil and Sue Savage-Rumbaugh

47 *Elements of a Philosophy of Technology: On the Evolutionary History of Culture*
Ernst Kapp

46 *Biology in the Grid: Graphic Design and the Envisioning of Life*
Phillip Thurtle

45 *Neurotechnology and the End of Finitude*
Michael Haworth

44 *Life: A Modern Invention*
Davide Tarizzo

43 *Bioaesthetics: Making Sense of Life in Science and the Arts*
Carsten Strathausen

(continued on page 290)

HERMES III
Translation

Michel Serres

TRANSLATED BY RANDOLPH BURKS

posthumanities 78

University of Minnesota Press
MINNEAPOLIS · LONDON

Originally published in French as *La Traduction:* © 1974 Les Éditions de Minuit.

Translation copyright 2026 by the Regents of the University of Minnesota

All rights reserved. No part of this publication may be reproduced, stored in a retrieval system, utilized for purposes of training artificial intelligence technologies, or transmitted in any form or by any means, electronic, mechanical, photocopying, recording, or otherwise, without the prior written permission of the publisher.

Published by the University of Minnesota Press
111 Third Avenue South, Suite 290
Minneapolis, MN 55401-2520
http://www.upress.umn.edu

ISBN 978-0-8166-7886-0 (hc)
ISBN 978-1-5179-0191-2 (pb)

A Cataloging-in-Publication record for this book is available from the Library of Congress.

Printed on acid-free paper

The University of Minnesota is an equal-opportunity educator and employer.

To the land

CONTENTS

Preface *ix*

Part I. Sciences

1. Translations of the Tree *3*
2. Life, Information, Second Law *33*
3. Betrayal: The Thanatocracy *65*

Part II. Philosophy

4. Descartes Translated into Statics Language: The Circle *101*
5. Leibniz Retranslated into Mathematical Language *107*
6. Auguste Comte Self-Translated in the Encyclopedia *159*

Part III. Painting

7. Ambrosia and Gold *191*
8. La Tour Translates Pascal *207*
9. Turner Translates Carnot *239*

Part IV. The Land

10. Roumain and Faulkner Translate Scripture *251*

Notes *279*

Preface

We only know things through the transformation systems of the sets that include them. At the minimum, these systems are four. Deduction, in the logico-mathematical zone. Induction, in the experimental field. Production, in the domains of practice. Translation [*traduction*], in the space of texts. It is far from hidden that they repeat the same word. The fact that there is no philosophy but of duction—excepting the variable and necessary prefix—is a state of affairs a person can spend their entire life trying to shed light on. In the ardor of joy, in the lights of seduction. In fact, our ancestors had a better word: *déduit*.[1] And the entire cycle recommences.

They left from every ancient site on the world map. Where there are places, where there are islands, boxes, black holes, pockets, nuclei, groups and fields, milky clouds and heads of pins. Galaxies in a chain and heavy little balls near the infinite. Pointy tips where some dimension is as gigantic as some other dimension is small for lakes deprived of horizon. They had never known anything except this, but didn't know and had just learned: that space is surprising. Populated, swarming, strange, and miraculous. Everywhere improbable, the heterotope. Space is pandoral. A countable heap of heterogeneous beings, from the iterated mundane to the unintuitable, from the furnace with black radiation to the trap for elements, from the Euclidean circle to unhealthy variety. Everything is new by means of suns.

They left from every ancient place located this morning on the map of the heavens, where there is no morning. Left ever since the morning of mornings (a will that this time had taken place and time), called, there and there, by the rumblings of the world, noise. Called by bell or muezzin, by Stentor's voice or the bugle for casting off, by the harmony of the spheres or the song of the Sirens, by the innumerable cheerful smile of the waters, they left, elements of the zero moment, letters on Lucretius's virgin beach, the wind of light at the burning originary explosion, young lovers in despair due to distance, him, taking his walking stick and travel bag, her, bearing the cavity of his call, a fire of olive wood under Mount Polyphemus, separated for a period of history, a finite, null, or transfinite interval, united for a period of history, resistant grains and transparent crowd; they left under the multiple dawn, their shoulders burdened with seven hundred thousand objects, their field and their plow, their sight and their spectacle, their vernacular voice and their divinities, their yellowed plans and their hope, their enclosure and their horizon, their well of desire and their bronze tower, their abyss and their pyramid, their antipodes and their ziggurats, their cardinal points and their directions of rivers, their deserts and their golden garden, their heavenly Jerusalem and their Elysian Fields, their Map of Tendre and their Mount Carmel, their bold verticality and their polar coordinates, their ecstatic orgasm and their virginity. Their messages and their silences.

All of them have come here. All of them here in one body. All of them in one point. A point swollen to confluence, streaming. On a dense heterogeneous pile. An alluvial fan, a moraine, a Mariana Trench, a trash can universe, a scrapyard. A borderless cloud. An index, a telephone book, a railroad timetable, a dictionary. A department store [*grand magasin*]. Philosophy was a pimp and procurer: a shopkeeper [*magasinière*]. The encyclopedia of disjoint spaces. Of the foreigner come to smile at the foreigner, his blood relative. Watertight, yesterday, was the compartment of slaked thirst. The pantopian spring.[2] The animal ark from which good wine will come, the old topless tower where the Babelian confusion resounds. Find the course of the ark, which has its olive branch; draw the plan of the tower, which has its labyrinth of rumblings. The ark and the tower, the box. Forge the key to the global box. Pandora as loved, the vagina of the woman who has every gift.

Ark, tower, box. Horn of plenty. So that men will no longer be hungry. The ark was bolted shut on the high seas: no one could jump over the guardrails. Amid the Democritean chaos of rain, the topside of the ship protected the assembled plural chaos for a time. Tomorrow the fire will no longer rain down, olive and dove, whence the new land with the power of the vine. Unload the cargo, no headway, at anchor. Here is the chest. And the tower was abandoned because Hermes hadn't yet carried Dionysus in his arms. Here is the index and the cask. And the box was terrifying, with its spreading cloud of fire, because no one had ever loved Pandora. That is enough. She is loved.

Open the flanks of the ark, open the tower, open the box. The philosopher is a stevedore, locksmith, docker, translator. If the woman's box spreads, if the grenade explodes, if the horn flows, and if, on this happy day, Pandora has loved him, he has renewed the face of the earth.

It is possible that science is the set of messages that are optimally invariant across every translation strategy. When this maximum is not reached, the other cultural areas would be at issue. Systems that are deductive, inductive ... remain the most stable across transport in general; beneath this threshold, the systems that are productive, reproductive ... vary, each according to its difference. Their difference is nothing, in fact, but the variation.

Hence the interest in examining the operation of translation. Not in order to define it in the abstract, but to make it function the most broadly and in the most diverse fields: within canonical knowledge and its history, along the relations of the encyclopedia and the philosophies, on the side of the fine arts and the texts that speak of exploited labor. It is no longer a question of explication, but of application.

The transformations of the message can be measured. A given law of history speaks of the states of matter, a given discussion of form and color speaks of the Industrial Revolution. Differential versions. At the limits of betrayal, a person who emits a political word ends up proclaiming a religious kerygma, and a group in power succeeds in diverting the optimally stable messages, science, so as to make them produce death: the thanatocracy.

Part I

Sciences

1

Translations of the Tree

> I prefer to listen to Leeuwenhoeks who tell me what they see over philosophers who tell me what they think.
> —Gottfried Wilhelm Leibniz, *Leibnizens Mathematische Schriften*

It is true that we are born of a woman and that we love a woman, to the point of dying from error, or to the point of dying from these women, and that we would like, hoping against hope, for reason to tell us whether this realm of emotion has a meaning. Here is the doorway we pass through where this truth, described by our gestures, our accidents, our journeys, and our joy, stops, becomes diluted, scatters, and becomes lost. Inventions by fits and starts of random lineages—caught in Markov chains. Order, necessity, logic: Jacob, Monod, and Lwoff adopted this eloquence to put an end to it and send it back to its natural site, without any guilty party, the aleatory space of noise.

Three admissions, however? Writing to Sophia, celebrating Aphrodite, telling of the desolate boredom of sexless—or almost sexless—cultures, the cultures of bacteria. Therefore, everywhere it is a question of algorithms.

Thesis: genetics transforms the idea of generation into a calculation of reproduction. Graphically, this means, on the one hand, the linear chain of individuals to individuals, gripped, with each "generation," by the forces of (pro)creation: the genealogical tree where the paths are traced from given names to given names. This means, on the

4 TRANSLATIONS OF THE TREE

other hand, that there is a main trunk on the tree, that of genotypical combinatorics, paths where the stations are not so much names as factors; or, even more buried, a path of invariance by copies and (graphic) reproductions where the stations are not so much factors as signs, where what is combined is presented not so much in formulas as in words: then, and only then, are individuals—who seemed to produce or reproduce—only adventitious branches attached to this trunk.

Translation: the history of genetics—respectively, the history of science in general—was represented, not long ago, in the forms of generation. *In principio erat X, qui genuit Y, qui genuit Z* [in the beginning was X, who begat Y, who begat Z], and so on. Theoretical productions begat each other, work by work, on a tree of knowledge with fruits of genius; and in the fruit, the seed . . . Now, the science as such has a space or a path (each "space" being only a station along the path, the path being only the sequence of spaces) on or along which things are done or undone, cut up, assembled, and redistributed, and on or along which things dilute the old figures and compose unexpected and retrospectively necessary forms or formulas—but who, then, shuffles the cards and decides the end of the rubber in the game of bridge? This is the main trunk, and the works, names, geniuses, authors, and signatures are only adventitious branches attached laterally to this chief path. The questions of continuity or of cutting up, of antecedence or of independence, of encounter and of twinships, must be counted on it and its random intertwinings. So the *history* of a science *of life* translates *the logic of heredity*: better, it translated it; it is translating it again. Please read Jacob's titles, not in parallel, but in chiasm or diagonally. The novelty regarding the history corresponds to the novelty regarding the science. From predecessor to successor, either there is a path or there is a detour, and this detour makes the entire affair. So, while the model has changed natures, the translation technique itself remains invariant. Whether the history is, or remains, something like a heredity is the only question. The same analysis holds, respectively, for the (other) histories of the (other) contemporary and previous sciences: they follow, blindly or not, the genea-*logies*. Auguste Comte did not conceal this; Marx admired Darwin, and Michelet collected plants . . .

The Visible and the Invisible

Aristotle set, against Plato, an elementary and grammatical conception of knowledge against a canonization of visual practice, Leibniz did so against Descartes, Cournot against Auguste Comte, et cetera, with every variant you could imagine and the necessary precisions. An algebra organized by logic corresponds to a geometry dominated by intuition. Even though the former group are formalists and the latter one topologists, the power of synthesis is of the same type, but the analysts are the clockmakers of a language and the aestheticians the orderers of a space. This philosophical divergence covers over, while intensifying them, the constants proper to science, its history, and its modernity. It is relatively easy to indicate regions of the encyclopedia and diachronic intervals favorable to a synopsis, and others that are favorable to a catalog or a dictionary, even if, in reducing the bird's eye view, things intertwine and are no longer so simple. What seems so, on the other hand, is the diagnosis to be made regarding the knowledge of our time: it has swung entirely toward one of the schools. Contemporary sciences are children of the first lineage: they are formalistic, analytic, referring, each and every one, to an alphabet of elements; they are grammatical, signaletic ... Their family resemblance is so pronounced that we start to dream of a *mathesis universalis,* at the very least of a common rhetoric. An Esperanto of scientists amid the prodigious bushiness of regions and their overlapping. It must be said, this generation has asserted itself against the generation of geometers. Mathematics wanted to take intuition and put an end to it: analyzing the interconnections between formalities, abandoning the description of existing idealities, blinding its visions in order to speak a sure language. Thermodynamics and information theory develop a philosophy of experimentation and the applied sciences: the old sensorium is subject to calculation. And so on: the encyclopedia is the kingdom of algorithms. Biology, the younger sibling, has just rejoined the family circle: still dualist when one could discern in the organic machine a topography to be described in mechanical (or in geometrical) terms and an impetus of energy, a power of its own (hence the polemical festivities that smeared our youth), biology became unified as soon as we succeeded in writing a few explicative chemical algorithms of this energy and power. As far as the eye can see, all the way to the steps of the social sciences, by elements, permutations, formalities, structures, codes, programs, and communication, the *Combinator* is everywhere. This Combinator distributes, lastly, the new generations of a technology (of a techno-logic) that's homologous to the state of science and has broken with the old state of knowledge as well as the previous technologies: something the biologists, above all, have perceived marvelously. Structuralism, the privileged election of a methodic framework among others of the same type, is an oblique projection of the situation: faithful, of course, but oblique; oblique, of course, but faithful.

Hence an apparent paradox. From among the children of Bourbaki, Brillouin, and Jakobson, a generation of writers seems to rise up whose method, style, and metaphors curiously belong to the Cartesian tradition, that of seeing and looking, even if their domain is to be found among contents belonging massively to the Leibnizian type, to the order of elementary pluralism, of networks, of arrangements. François Jacob, for example and among a few others, talks about the invisible and the visible (like Merleau-Ponty?) and about the synchronic space in which a certain knowledge, for a time, forms a picture. Is there really a gap between an aged set of philosophical tools and scientific contents that are impossible to grasp if these tools aren't changed? In fact, it doesn't seem that Jacob's visible is precisely the tradition's visible: we must interrogate another tradition, one that doesn't intensify, like the first one, the biases.

The categories of the visible and the invisible don't have the same function in philosophical literature and in scientific texts. Starting from the seventeenth century, for example, the botanists of the Jardin des Plantes were demonstrators of the exterior or the interior of plants—as if there were a box one left closed or decided to open. When open, it reveals itself to be full of boxes, and the requirement recommences. At a given moment, one or several boxes become an obstacle: it is impossible to see into the box, even if it is open, even if one can or knows how to open it. All this is a bit different from

Cartesian intuitionism and the dichotomous rules of the *Discourse on Method*. Jacob critiques this successive process of nested boxes as a theory of heredity (in Malebranche and others of the same era), but he adopts it for the heredity of theories: the Russian dolls. This is not contradictory, since the description of a fact does not, in principle, have anything to do with the succession of theories. Except, perhaps, if the fact and the succession find themselves, both, to be genealogies. Let's return to this form later. Second, during the time Bergson was talking about an intuition, Jean Perrin was practicing another and defined it by the opening of a new box, which itself was a real box: the closed system of thermodynamicists. Boltzmann's intuition had revealed it to be brimming with myriads of molecules. In the twentieth century, we have Pandora's science, with the same success and the same risk. And the same connection to Prometheus's fire. Contemporary biochemists are keenly aware of having brought about, in their department, the same breakthrough as Perrin's *Atoms*, in the past and elsewhere. They are right: the event is of the same order, of the same import; it has the same meaning. Even better, they refer to a common kinship. Reread the preface, in which Jean Perrin sketches his own genealogy. He stems from two lineages: the lineage of thermodynamicists, whom he calls analogists and who attained, without hypothesis, the two laws—note that the first law, that of equivalence, is a law of invariance, and that the second one, that of the increase of entropy, is a law of irreversible development— and the lineage of the atomists, whom he names the *intuitives* and who interpret the previous results. Setting forth the closed box and trying to *see* into it. Boltzmann forever ties the two paths together. It is still on the shores and edges of the divine sea, where the song of the lyric poets has been silent for two thousand years, that the drama ends and begins. The great Boltzmann dies by suicide right there, he who had united again the history of Prometheus and the history of Pandora. From this torment, our time will be born: atomic physics and molecular biochemistry. Hence Perrin: I want to see like Boltzmann. Hence Jacob: I am Darwinian, like Boltzmann. Hence Perrin: under the continuous *envelope,* the discontinuous bustles stochastically; the *edges* of the box do not say, quite the contrary, what is in the box; if I change scale, I see, on the map, the *contour* of the always disrupted littoral. Hence Jacob: under the first-order structure, reputed to be visible to everyone, I will see, to the point of no longer seeing, second-, third-, fourth- . . . order structures, and the orders of integration wouldn't be able to obey the same laws: elements (?), system, system of systems, et cetera. (Perrin: there is a mathematics of the continuous and another one of the discontinuous.) Let's draw the new littorals: the skin, the shell, the bark; the environment in the ecological sense and the internal environment (animals live inside); the cellular membrane (the border of knowledge, in Monod's sense, is again an edge) and the pollen envelope; the surface of crystals; the three-dimensional copy reduced to a linear translation . . . The image of a box of boxes cannot be resisted; the theme of its edge, massive in Perrin's preface (contour, bark, littoral, anfractuosities, metaphors repeated a hundred times), spreads out in Jacob's text to the point of unifying the history of living things. Hence Perrin: supposing atoms become visible to future physicists, what *hidden structure* remains to be seen? Hence Jacob: when one has reached molecules, nothing proves that they are the end of the story; beneath them, behind them, what new Russian doll is yet to emerge from the box?

Jacob invokes the lineage of Boltzmann, and his visible is Perrin's. But physics does not exhaust this operational theme. Geneticists' own lineage, too, defines a series of boxes: character, gene, molecule—the dolls, precisely, of the work. For the geneticists, as for him, the visible, what can be seen, is the phenotype. *The phenotype expresses in visible characters what is printed in the genotype, which is "invisible," in readable characters.* There are two ways to understand this sentence, which is pleonastic several times over. Either, like certain people, one refers to Kant: biochemistry, beneath the phenomenon, would have completely uncovered the noumenon. Besides not meaning much, the problematics being as distant as the sky is wide, this could already have been said, quite rightly, about Boltzmann and Perrin. And Bachelard may have said this, using language imprudently. Or one understands the series of pleonasms. Beneath the phenomenon, biochemistry has uncovered the "genomenon"; that is all it is possible to say. The phenomenon, visible, apparent, exhibits characteristics [*caractères*]: evident qualities, distinctive marks, particular properties, characteristic attributes, et cetera. I am only varying on "type" and "characteristic" [*caractère*], equivalent terms, on "visible" and "phenomenal," almost synonymous adjectives. The genomenon, hidden, exhibits, once discovered, characters [*caractères*]: numbers, letters, signs, elements of a code ... and I am only varying on "type" and "character" [*caractère*], equivalent terms. From one to the other, I pass from the *printed of the expressed* to the *expressed of the printed* [*de l'imprimé de l'exprimé à l'exprimé de l'imprimé*], from the *readable* to the *visible,* and *the famous gap is reduced.* This happened very simply according to the two senses of the word *caractère*: a set of signs or of distinctive traits on the one hand, a mark or engraving on the other. The first sense translates the second, and vice versa. The one is a set, and the other its element. A formed sentence designates a form (*eidos*); the alphabet of its elements decomposes it: this alphabet doesn't explain the form, which arises from a combination, but makes all combination possible, and hence all form. The first sense *reproduces* the second, and vice versa. The history of genetics consists in slowly passing from biological reproduction to textual reproduction. And therefore, from the visible to the readable. It can be seen to what extent we are far from the noumenon: the real is on the side of Gutenberg. It can particularly be seen to what extent, beyond Kant, biochemistry remains faithful to the norms of the seventeenth century, when science was nothing more than the decryption of a code and the code was reduced to a combinatorics. It can be seen, lastly, to what extent Leibniz remains the excellent reference, he who developed the entire abstract organon in which the new discoveries are at ease: the idea of a characteristic combinatorics, the theory of the (re)production of things taken at their root by the successive copies of a written or printed text; the refined description of a chain of expressive relations starting from a combinatorial sequence all the way up to a macrocosmic event; the closed isolation of a monadic element in which it is written for all time that, in phenomenal appearance, history will be such and such, without the pro-gram ever receiving impressions or lessons from experience (invariably imprinted, never impressionable); the set-based, alphabetic, signaletic methodology, the technology of sorting and filtering, selection, the systematic reduction to combinatorics, the global philosophy of communication, among other related practices. Thus the preceding sentence, strictly reducible to the principle of identity, is strictly Leibnizian. What biochemistry discovered is not the mysterious noumenon; it is, quite simply, the *universal characteristic*. It discovered it in its own region, the way logic, mathematics, physics, and chemistry did in theirs, and each of them in its turn. Biochemistry designates, like the other fields of knowledge, a global philosophy of marked elements. It suffices moreover to listen to what it says: it says *universality of the code*. These are Leibniz's words.[1]

Space and the Combinator

The historical picture drawn by Jacob suggests a synthesis, a group of invariants, a sort of formal unity, about which it can't be decided if they are due to the object, the method, or the tradition. For everything happens as though the theories successively defended regarding heredity—or rather, what the author retains of them—secretly referred to an unwritten axiomatics, one that is variable certainly, but not very much, over the course of history. In trying to develop this stable reference for itself, perhaps something is being said about the life sciences and their diachronic flow.

The question was posed just now about a certain gap between the operational theme of the visible and this contemporary nucleus of knowledge that can be named, to be brief, the readable (what there is to see, is organized, in fact, like a language, and I see, in the end, the way I speak). This gap is not reducible to the old distinction of intuition and concept, nor to other biases on the part of theories of knowledge. It is, in fact, reduced by a science that Jacob, without saying so, must set great store by. The set of notions gathered, ever since the end of the nineteenth century, under the collective name of topology constitutes our best *aesthetic* system. Henri Poincaré, in his *Last Thoughts,* had partially noted this in privileging that sense, of a rare and secret nobility, that philosophers highly scorn for shameful reasons—the sense of touch. More generally, topology can be considered a rigorous treatment of *formalities* that bear some relation (which? how?) to the most general *sensorium*. A new breed of Kant could observe, if he were in a hurry, that our algebras constitute something like an analytic; our logics, a dialectic; our topologies, something like a formal aesthetic. The buried babel of our immersions. They tend to make rigorous the intuitive notions of continuity, neighborhood, limit; they renounce quantitative evaluations; of the old definition of mathematics, they only preserve order, and therefore quality can appear as their horizon; at their beginnings, they described forms, layers, and continuous varieties, and deformed them without hole or tear; they were, they always are, a morphology and can be morphogenetic, familiar with notions like open, closed, interval, exterior, interior, adhesion, edge, or distinctions like local and global; hence sumptuous unfurlings of certain refined spaces; they take up again the ancient combinatorics and draw simplexes, graphs, networks, arborescences ... Of course, this assessment is caricatural, due to simplification. Whoever follows the history of this new mathematics—as old as Riemann, Listing, Leibniz, and maybe the Greeks—cannot fail to be overcome with a soothing laugh in rereading Bergson and Husserl, who ask so many anachronistic questions at the very moment they were being resolved, right beside them. But also by a more serious amazement. How does it happen that natural history and biology, for quite a long time, haven't equipped themselves with such an organon, the very sciences that always have to describe networks, (genealogical) arborescences, levels of combinations and situations of arrangements, forms and deformations, envelopes and developments, multiple or invaginated layers, orders in general, local and global phenomena, and so on? Whether it has to do with anatomy, embryology, classification, or even stereochemistry, it quickly appears—at least to an understanding which, I admit, is probably too far removed from these specialties—that topology is a highly appropriate system for the conceptual demands of the life sciences. They can profit from it in the same way that, in bygone times, they profited from a certain Aristotelian logic, that formerly they profited from a certain combinatorial algebra, that latterly they profited from the calculation of probabilities, that recently they profited from the algorithms proper to thermodynamics or information theory. This profit is one of the benefits of Jacob's book. It was surprising that a history of heredity should be named a logic. The formal unity we spoke about is the invariant schema of this logic. *The Logic of Life* is topologically referenced. Jacob, a geneticist, ceaselessly keeps in view *the topological form of the tree*. Of the genealogical tree. The book of Genesis, it is true, begins in a garden of plants where they, along with the animals, must be given names, and in front of a tree, where sex appears at the same time as death.

Let's look, for example, and as a crucial experiment, at one of the rare texts of the work *that does not have to do with genetics*. How does the book describe the emergence of experimental medicine, in the nineteenth century, in Claude Bernard's work? First of all, it is a question of space: the zoologist and the botanist used to travel in the world; nature was the external environment. Then they worked in museums, parks, botanical gardens, and zoos—each an island where plants and animals are gathered and compared—an island with a global treasure and laid out into places, like a taxonomy. The biologist now shuts himself up in a laboratory, a closed system in which energies are exchanged, an internal environment, if I may: the animals live inside. In the microcosm-island, as we know, the arborescent forms of classification function. What functions in the laboratory? First, analysis and decomposition. First model, first tree: Claude Bernard uses the division of labor in factories, industrial establishments, and organized companies as a guiding (ideological?) schema [189]. Second model (methodological), second tree: Cartesian division. The organism is divided into functional systems; these are then divided into organs, which are further divided into tissues, and tissues into cells. Taxonomy was the tree of the kingdom; this is the tree of the individual. The polytomic form is projected from phylo(genesis) to onto(genesis) in an invariant manner. On this invariant schema, the questions are repeated. However much one cuts up, the isolated cells, the pieces cut out, are not independent; in other words, the arborescence is not only an operator of distinctions, it is also a graph: a host of questions need to be asked regarding its *paths*. It is the same thing everywhere and always: every cartography separates, cuts up, unites, intersects. We have known this since the combinatorial art; we have found it in chemistry, with Mendeleev, in astrophysics since Hertzsprung, et cetera. Hence Bernard's watchword: decompose, don't isolate, decombine, keep the assemblage and arrangement in view. Sorry, it is no longer Descartes talking, it's Leibniz: analyze into elements, isolate, close with double locks (ligature), but combine, select, highlight the global unity; hence the literal repetition of preestablished harmony: "[each workman] makes one part independently of his fellow-worker who is making another part, without knowing what the [whole will be]. A fitter puts all the parts together in harmony" [189]. On this schema, polytomy is the horizontal operator, and synthesis, vertical, runs upstream from node to node, all the way to the general confluence. I am not certain things are any different with phylogenesis: Darwin and the genealogical tree, Darwin and the point of the cone. Thus the arborescent form has shifted, without notable variation, from natural history and its time to physical chemistry and its experiments. Now compare the vocabularies and say if the experimental practice is very far removed from a "tomic" logic: untangle the skein, separate, isolate, cut, damage, ligature, decompose into pieces, stop transmission, paralyze (analyze); the old words, in the laboratory, resonate in their very first acceptations: extracts, secretions (from *secerno*, to separate), digestion (distribution, division, classification, arrangement, order). From space to the tree, we have returned, now, to space when it is a question of the internal environment. Topology and combinatorics.

The Whole and the Parts

We lost our philosophical youth to a thousand obscure discourses. We were made to look, for example, to see if an organism was more than or better than the sum of its components or if it was equal to it. Repetitive pedagogy and what was then called committed philosophy both contributed to making us stupid. The sum being to the east and the whole to the west, the expected and crowned rhetoric had to subtly intertwine arithmetic's vertical column and the Cold War's horizontal strategy. Our lucidity consisted in lagging behind two sciences: biology and mathematics. A verbal dispute, of course:

for everyone knows that a verb agrees with the singular collective noun if the intention dwells on the totality and with its plural complement if it distributes plurality. An example: a handful of ignoramuses has destroyed or have destroyed my childhood. The amusing thing in the affair, and having gained some distance, resided in the fact that the individualists conjugated the collective in the singular while the collectivists conjugated parts in the plural. Amid these bits of childishness, no one thought to define the sum. It is true that we believed ourselves to have known for three thousand years that one and one make two; the question remained to know if "one and one" manifestly made two or more.

Ever since the seventeenth century, and even ever since the Greeks, the organism has been composed of parts, whatever they may be, big or small, visible or invisible, set out or cut out in such and such a way or differently. Adding them up into a sum gets us nowhere, except being delighted over a truly large number. The naturalists quickly understood that these parts are in interrelations that are multiple, reciprocal, varied, complete. This simple remark immediately disqualifies arithmetic in favor of combinatorics. The organism is less a set of generic elements, of independent grains, than a set of relations, arrangements, combinations, than of the parts they partition. So if there is a cardinal number to be set forth, *it is not that of the sum; it is not a transcendent ideality either. It is the cardinal number of the set of parts,* in the ordinary sense: $P(S)$. Who, except philosophers, is unaware that it is of a much higher power than the cardinal number of the sum and that it is entirely different? *Who doesn't see that the simplex it totalizes faithfully represents the scale of integrations Jacob talks about,* Jacob who is now free of the obligation he was put under to say if the integration was—yes or no—the bourgeois name of the dialectic. Here is a good case where a line of calculation and a clear and distinct schema forever close the court. These results, these solutions, to my knowledge, can be dated: in 1666, *De arte combinatoria* had obtained them. How is it possible that the polemic lasts three centuries past its end?

The Chain, the Tree, and the Network

We are acting here as the advocate of an evil devil, whose genius has been forgotten today. We may be wrong: we cannot, however, shy away from a few evident facts. We uphold, against everyone, the transhistorical permanence of a few forms and schemas. Jacob, for example, cites Fernel: matter is invariant; if it degraded, the world would have already disappeared from having been used up [20], taking time into account. This argument is from 1548. It is pre-Socratic: the Ionian physicists invoked it to justify the invariance of certain cosmic cycles and endlessly put off the due date for chaos. The seventeenth century reproduced it in different sites: regarding the quantity of motion, regarding the dynamics of living forces... In the nineteenth century, this argument was at the center of theories of energy, and Nietzsche recapitulated it to prepare the announcement of an invariant return. It has reappeared even today in Jacob's pen as well as Monod's: the invariance of the program prevents systems from drifting toward statistical disorder; it keeps the universality of the second law in check temporarily and locally. The form of the argument is stable; what changes is its point of application: matter, motion, force, energy, and information, on the one side; nothingness, stoppage, chaos, disorder, and death, on the other. So here is a preserved schema, no matter the "primitivity" or modernity of the knowledge. And, for knowledge to remain so, it does require a few reproduced invariants (translation). It would be good to compare—another example—the function held by the sun in the same Fernel (24)[2] and this text by Jacob: "To increase and multiply, to maintain the order of the living world despite the tendency of the universe to decay, organisms must be provided with energy from an external source. In the long run, it is the sun that provides energy for most living beings" (240-41). Of course, in the meantime, the god Ra or generic activator has become a yellow dwarf close to its supernova. There are shifts, but stable elements remain.

The first form of knowledge drawn by Jacob is that of a network, the global matrix of every tree. While nature always produces the similar, network paths are analogical: due to the flexibility of the similarities that are continuous from place to place, there always exists, no matter what the places may be, *at least* one path from any place to some given other place, and several most often, at the limit, all paths. Beings and things, caught in and by the network, are *at the intersection* of as many paths as you like (it suffices to make a detour), and therefore the microcosm is everywhere. Hence the theorem suitable for heredity: all combinations are possible; or rather, all possible combinations are realizable. Head of a bear, arm of a monkey, hoof of an ox, and face of a frog. Plants, piece by piece, correspond to animals; and from this, to rocks and stars. The network is constructed through full and brimming intersections, which is to say, through *products:* consequently, generation *produces* such monsters as you like through the freedom of passage for every element along the paths of analogy. Every transport is one of similitude, and similitude is universal, hence the picture's coherence (coherence and rigor being necessary but not always sufficient marks of scientificity). But we forget that similitude combines identity with difference: the network covers over and hides the latter. Furthermore, this analogical *grid,* allowing a continuous reading of the world, is distinguishable from a tree by the fact that the tree starts from a single vertex, while every point for the grid is a possible vertex. A wonderful era of genealogical pluralism, in which engendering of words and discourses, of beings and things, stemming from anywhere, was spreading without constraint. What, then, is seventeenth-century science? It consists *in fixing a point* of the network, in cutting out a chain with a single head, a tree with a single top, that point precisely, and leaving along their edges this labyrinth in which everything got lost, reason, naming, and the lovemaking of Ariadne and the Bull. *Cutting out a tree in the network* and defining its paths by their specific difference—that is, its relations. *Cutting out, in the tree, a chain.* Hence the order of composition—chain, tree, network—is the order of orders. Not in the time of progress, but in the form of knowledge.

Establishing a chain: Descartes. Fixing a grid for reading that would be neither degenerate nor trivial, one suitable for deciphering a book written in mathematical characters: Galileo. Introducing a filter amid the arrangements: Leibniz (and everything is no longer possible, to the point that only a single thing, among the possibles, is ultimately filtered through). The form of all knowledge is indeed that of a tree, the tree of knowledge; even more, the form of each science is also this form: invariance of a relation along a linear sequence, in the simplest case (mathematics, but also generation: "generation became the means by which form was *maintained through time* and the *permanence* of the species assured," 28); translation of this sequential order in two-dimensional space; tables of the art of complexions,[3] which, for the first time, mathematically formalizes the "structure" of kinship—that is, the genealogical tree. And soon everything is there that science needs, including up to this morning. If nature is written, it is coded: science consists in deciphering; for that, a grid is necessary, which is to say, a combinatorics; but, for that to be possible, the invariance of the code must be presupposed. Ever since the seventeenth century, the condition of possibility for scientific practice has been precisely the invariance of a code. God calculates and combines, yes, but he does not cheat. With the condition set out, the method follows from it; it is the art of complexions and the schemas that the method knows how to draw. Here, the rigorous network is forever substituted for the Renaissance network. Starting from there, it is no longer a question of anything but space and permutations: combinatorial topology.

Leibniz: better a Leeuwenhoek who tells us what he sees than a Cartesian who tells us what he thinks. We mustn't move a single step away from this advice. What does Jacob see, massively, all along history? What does he see, globally, in both the old and the new genetics? He sees, as is all too clear, what he never stops telling; he never stops telling what he sees. One need only listen. A brief analysis of the content: the most repeated word in his book, and by far, is the word *combinatorics* (and its family: *arrangements, complexions,* etc.).[4] It dominates the entire diachronic movement: the seventeenth-century method, the efforts at classification, the introduction of probabilities, the new algorithms, from Mendel to the chemists. By frequency of occurrence, the second most repeated is another family: that of *spatialized order,* which includes words like *chain, necklace, succession, tree, cone, pyramid, picture, network, cycle, circuit* . . . It is a question of a space organized by a schema, which is variable, composed of stations linked by paths, representing relations, which are, again, variable. Of course, these two families form a single family and refer to something like a combinatorial topology. I don't know if François Jacob is a structuralist, and I deplore the fact that philosophical journalism has so quickly devalued a good currency. For if a structure is always *some set equipped with one or several operations* to be defined for the set, what is repeated in *The Logic of Life* is indeed a structure. The history of heredity can be written, is written, as a variation on structure.

The great chain of beings. Everyone, one after the other, draws this chain, from *The Monadology* to Charles Bonnet—mineral beings, organized beings, animate beings, rational beings—by nested boxes or successive combinations. We see this uninterrupted chain "snaking across the surface of the Globe, penetrating the unfathomable depths of the Sea, leaping into the Atmosphere, plunging into celestial Space" [47, citing Bonnet]. A fundamental operator, it produces the problems, it impels discoveries or impasses, at least as much as it is a product of observation and analysis. Along the path, along the chain, it is possible, for example, to locate grains, stations, which are decisive, in which the attributions, the criteria, neighbor each other: Should divides between the chain links be defined? Does continuity, on the contrary, move along without solutions? Hence the place of asbestos, zoophytes, and other border beings.[5] This is not the first or last time that a drawn schema, intuitive model, or spatialized order causes questions to arise, orients them, and decides them: this is not peculiar to the life sciences; it may not be peculiar to science at all. The incessant dialogue of a language, an algorithm, an algebra . . . and a form, a diagram, a grid, runs across both history and the sciences, from geometry to chemistry, from the Greek world to our time. Without it, knowledge would go without practice. Here, a combinatorics acts as a language; a simple or complicated schema acts as a form: synopsis and generatrix.

The network of comparisons substitutes, in the seventeenth century, for the network of similitudes. The distinction is fine and seems almost zero, the other and the same being united, here and there, in proportions that are difficult to weigh. So let there be a station: as a universal intersection, a local synthesis, it was less a true station, which is to say, defined, than a total part. Let there be a path: it passed through each site, and all of them led to Rome, which is to say, everywhere; might as well talk about a labyrinth. The Renaissance's network was a cultural operator meant to reproduce the whole in each place, a transformer of the universal quantifier into existential quantifiers. The Romantic nineteenth century, alas, repeated this lesson, this legend. Only Leibniz, in the middle of the seventeenth century, preserves the transformation operator by which the one is the whole. The seventeenth century dissociates and cuts into the skein. It slips its technique of division between unity and totality; it knows multiplicity as such. In doing so, it founds what is called science. Hence the difference, forever established, to the point of being inexpiable, between pluralist philosophies and totalitarian philosophies. So, and as with mathematics, analysis and combinatorics correspond to the chain and the tree. Let there now be a station: "It is difficult to compare the forms as a whole. But when the network of resemblances and differences is established not from the organism as a whole, but from its parts after analysis, complexity becomes simplicity" (Jacob, 45). The station no longer reproduces the whole; as such, in isolation, the station is no longer a whole: it can be decomposed. Let there now be a path: it puts parts or pieces in communication. The idea of local totality excluded combinatorics: from the one to the whole, each level repeated the identical in its type. Analysis, on the contrary, presupposes combinatorics twice over. Downstream, for all recomposition; upstream, as the condition of its exercise, for feedback: omitting or repeating is counted. The art of complexions focuses on elements given by analysis and makes analysis possible: the method is unique. What the seventeenth century discovers is a theory of subsets; what it abandons is an exclusively set-based vision. Let there be, again, a station: has it exploded under the effect of the division? No, "each plant can be represented as an assemblage of elements in a given number and proportion. Each of these elements can vary infinitely in each of its parameters, and each variety of each element can match up with the variety of all the others in an infinite number of combinations. Botany becomes a kind of combinatorics with almost unlimited possibilities" (46).[6] Each station presents itself now as a combinatory network. This network functions like a multiple-dial padlock: each variety of each element forms a dial of the padlock, which can be turned at will, and each stop of which can be put next to every position of all the other dials. It is therefore true that each being has a combination number and that nature is coded: to each individual its sequential sentence, and the combinatorial art is the general theory of decoding—by the way, this has not changed much in our time. So there exist one or several networks distributing the open multiplicity of beings; there exists, in addition, a network that's proper to each station of one of these networks. Classifying becomes a hero's job, a safecracker's job (a boxcracker's job), strictly speaking, establishing a combinatorics of combinatorics, a global network of local networks, a language formed sentence by sentence, word by word, each word being an assemblage of letters, an assemblage read by turns on the table or the coded padlock. Nature is decoded according to nested padlocks. Hence the new form of nested boxes: the network of networks is a polytomic tree. "Classification is always a pyramid or a hierarchy made up of sets of classes at different levels, each class [of a level] including one or more subclasses [from a lower level]. Each hierarchy can function with differing degrees of complexity" (48). Of course, for deciphering to be possible, one must have a broader language than the sentences that can possibly be realized: "The combinative possibilities in the use of this or that part of a plant are then analyzed, and the part giving a greater number of [realizable] combinations than those found in nature is chosen" (49). If nature is encoded, the combinable possibilities must be broader than the real. Every discovery to come presents itself then to confirmation: Mendeleev and others have overabundantly taught us the lesson, the reading. That said, everything recommences, and the tree produces its problems, that of paths, for instance; what about their continuity—even though they weave a schema in the discrete finite? Hence Robinet: the difference is such "that it could not be smaller without one being exactly a replica of the other, nor greater without there being a gap" [46]. Here the great question of the age is translated into the living kingdom: is there union or contradiction between the treatment of the discrete in the *ars combinatoria* and the treatment of the continuous by infinitesimal calculus? The arithmetization of analysis and the theory of series are the first answers to the question, which can, in fact, be formulated: what is a path, a neighborhood, a limit? There is, indeed, a frontal moraine in the history of science.

The proof of this is the way Jacob translated this state of affairs in the physical sciences. He also asks Newton: what is a station, what is a path? This is because the force of gravity runs along the ridges of a new network, one that is stable and varies all along reversible time, in which the nodes are the planets and things in general. The sun attracts the moon and the earth, and the earth attracts the moon— each exerting force on the others. To this three-body problem, Venus is not indifferent, nor are any of the other stations; it is the *n*-body question. The network is a force field. Something circulates there *in fact,* something no longer only a logical relation: a time, an acceleration. That said, every body is of a corpuscular nature; gravity "wove a network of dependencies [between all the atoms that form the universe] giving cohesion to the world" (40). Hence this new box of nested boxes, which is the same one: the things are given in a network of networks, in a field of fields, down to the atoms, just like the beings were down to the individuals. The world is coherent, and so is knowledge. The latter deciphers the former by means of a combinatorics of masses and distances, or rather, of stations and paths. Between Newton and the naturalists, there is indeed translation, but this is only thinkable on condition of not prejudging who wrote the first text. Both of them translate, that's all. A century later, Newton having conquered the continent, Laplace completed, crowned, and systematized the seventeenth-century cosmos: the translation is reproduced. The theory of connections [103], the theory of the balance of organs, that is, the constraints imposed by one organ on all the others, and vice versa, the central idea of an invariant across such variations, and so on, remain faithful to the problem of n-bodies and its developments to the extent of ending up at the same result: *the single plan [plan] of composition,* a reference for the network of living beings, corresponds to the *fixed equatorial plane [plan]* of the solar system in Laplace and Poinsot, a reference for the world network. The time is near when the sciences together are going to tip from system to history: from cosmology to cosmogony, and from biology to *biogony.* Laplace already interprets Saturn's rings as fossils, and the slight inclination on the ecliptic of the axes of translation as a preserved archive. Along the paths of the seventeenth-century network, a new time will soon circulate, irreversible, the time of fire: solar furnace, machine boiler, animal heat.

The proof of this is, once again, the entire discourse of the biochemist regarding chemistry. The same form is transported. "Substances could therefore be classified like plants and, for this purpose, the same methodology had to be adopted" (41). Lavoisier therefore translates Linnaeus by dichotomy and "binions." No, they both import the same graphic form into their respective regions, into their native language: the same combinatorics, the same spatialization of order. Bichat translates in the other direction, proof that the direction can be inverted at will: "Chemistry has [its] simple bodies which, by ... combinations ..., form compound bodies ... In the same way, anatomy has its simple tissues which by their combinations form organs" (114). The order of nested boxes—organisms, organs, tissues, cells, et cetera—is of the same form as the order: compound bodies, molecules, simple bodies, isotopes, et cetera; it is not parallel to it, nor its contemporary. But their analogy is heuristic. Two families of networks, then, are put in place. Classification, globally speaking: a double-entry orthogonal grid, with homologous series and natural families on one side and functions and analogous properties on the other (101-2); Berthelot's tree for organic chemistry (229-30). The functions and analogous properties, which are local, draw the architecture of molecules in developed formulas; an example: Berthelot's carbon skeletons and the grafting of other functions onto this trunk (230). Chemistry deals with networks of networks. But the graphs from just now had to do with compounds; Mendeleev's graph orders simples; when Bohr draws the network of simples, chemistry again becomes a network of networks. New nested boxes and new trees. Chain, tree, and network are now found in every site: forest paths; as projection, Russian dolls. The key to all this is combinatorics, and chemistry is nothing other than a theory of permutations (274), arrangements, substitutions, in its language and in its topology. A reaction (the problematic term) is a set of exchanges. Hence the repetition of the two questions. What's the situation with the stations, with the number of them, which can be enormous (274) and whose size is the threshold of the living thing, with their repetitions, their movements, their nature, their site? Their relative position is so decisive that specificity seems to be a chapter title in analysis situs. What's the situation with the paths, with the number of them (valence ...), with their direction, with what they transport (energy bonds, 227-28), with their sense, symmetrical or dissymmetrical, irreversible or reversible (catalysis, enzyme catalysis for instance, is definitely a valve, a semiconduction, a one-way path filtered by no-entry paths), with their global forms: monotonic chains, ramified formations, helices, circuits, loops, nuclei, polyhedral solids, et cetera? Here, chemistry is strictly a combinatorial topology. What's surprising if, at the end of all this research, biochemistry has rediscovered a literal, signaletic, and alphabetic combinatorics? What's surprising about this since the set of these forms, which are transported, shifted, variable, but always present, bore within themselves, for all time, the elementary model of a coded language? It was in the form as much as in the thing—a generator of language as much as a language of the gene. The most recent of the Russian dolls is the smallest known padlock, the simplest sequence on the decryption grid. Through the genetic code, the method and the object coincide, and this identity in return sheds light on three centuries of logic or three hundred years of history.

Nested Boxes (Digression)

Regarding the double theory of preexistence and preformation, it is advisable to clearly distinguish the ideological aura and the technical solution, the reference to divine creation and the nested-box form of the germs. Take a look at astronomy: from Giordano Bruno's execution and Galileo's condemnation, the hesitations of Descartes, Pascal, and Leibniz between the models of Copernicus and Tycho Brahe can readily be inferred. This is going a little too fast and forgetting two things at least: the disregard into which all hypotheses had fallen for logical and physical reasons ever since the Greek astronomers, as Pierre Duhem has shown and, more recent, Robert Blanché; and the scientific legitimacy of the hesitation, which was only removed by Bradley's observations on the aberration of light: Auguste Comte showed this already one hundred fifty years ago. During the seventeenth century, there didn't yet exist any decisive, determining, demonstrative reason to opt for Copernicus. This is what Descartes, Leibniz, and Pascal said, and theological matters or terror had nothing to do with it; certain of them are indeed infinitistic, like Bruno, burned all the same. Scientific reason and discourse are affected less than it is believed (and more in other respects) by ideology, which is given too much prominence. Let's return to preexistence and nested boxes. You can easily find, in Malebranche for instance, the union of theology and a solution I believe to be positivistic. It exists, but the distinction does even more. For the seventeenth century was, in the sciences, a thousand times more atheistic than it is said to be, and as independent, in any case, of the reigning ideology as modernity believes itself to be. I think the solution is positivistic because the form of nested boxes is in complete accord with all the rigorous knowledge of the day and induced by it, and this is even more clearly so because the solution is not entwined with metaphysical dreams.

The question to be resolved is that of the reproduction of the similar by the similar; the question of an invariance that founds a species; the question of an invariant repeated along a chain; the question of *the continued iteration of a similitude*. But the set of knowledge reputed to be certain during the seventeenth century, a certitude we have gone back over only at the fringe, is dominated by the sciences of figure and motion, by mechanics and geometry. But again, the question of *the invariance of a form in its variably dimensioned graphic reproduction,* the question of the iteration of a relation of similitude over different sizes, is familiar to understandings practiced in Greek geometry as refreshed by Descartes and *has already been resolved* in the reference science ever since Thales, Euclid, and the *Geometry*'s sliding set squares. The nested boxes of germs are a *figure,* and this figure translates, transports, introduces into the living thing the old configuration of homothety. How is the *reproduction* of the *similar* by the *similar* possible? It is achieved in the science of space, which gives a fully equipped technique for packing the same form into increasingly diminishing dimensions, endlessly. Let's resolve, here, a question that can be formulated in terms akin to those used there, in another region, one whose knowledge we are certain of, in which the question has been resolved. It suffices to import the solution. So the nested boxes of germs are the translation, expressed in another language, of the iteration of homothetic forms in a given space. Is this solution so different from today's solution? What do we do to resolve the question of reproductive invariance? We import, no less than in the seventeenth century, techniques and forms that are effective "elsewhere," and our *program* also grants reproduction its *graphic* meaning. The differences are vast; they may not be essential.

The question to be resolved is that of the reproduction of the similar by the similar. The question is graphically resolved by geometry. From figure, let's move on to motion. All seventeenth-century mechanics is based, in experimental technology, on simple machines. From Descartes to Lagrange, it is a question of pulleys, ropes, weights, winches, blocks, and tackle: Lagrange's *Analytical Mechanics* also derives its principle of virtual speeds from this equipment. The theory of animal-machines says that the organism is a clock. How can we reproduce a motion as a similar motion? Whether it is a question of wheels moved by belts or gears, well known since Roemer and Huygens, the mechanical solution to this problem is to manufacture a form that's homothetic to a rotating circumference: the relation of motion would be something like the relation of the figure. The clock is indeed a nested box of gears, and every machine is a complex of wheels. Hence the idea of maximally complicating the mechanical model, of affirming that the organism is a clock of clocks, and this can be done as much as you like. The form of nested boxes is coherent with the two reference sciences in that these sciences respectively resolve the problem of the reproduction of the similar by the similar. And I am sure that the model of the nested-box clock has not left the understanding of contemporary biologists. So where, then, would these Russian dolls that François Jacob likes so much come from?

But suddenly, the set of the sciences comes into concourse. Who doesn't know that the calculation of *series* constitutes the seventeenth century's great new thing? Who doesn't see the microscope itself as an instrument of homothety? Who doesn't take pleasure in the spectacle of orders of infinity, an execrable model, in fact, of what infinitesimal calculus expresses? Here, from every horizon—algebra, analysis, optics—various forms of nested boxes arrive on the scene. And so now the individual carries inside him- or herself the theory of proportions, the geometry of homothety, the theorem of sliding set squares, the world table of orders of magnitude, wrongly imposed by the nascent infinitesimal calculus, the algebra of series. The proof by contradiction that this is the case—Buffon is going to use precisely this mathematics to demonstrate the absurdity of the theory (67). Of course, the theory freezes time: just as though, in the seventeenth century, the priority of invariance regarding teleonomy had been suspected. In short, the nested boxes of germs are the figure that the knowledge of the seventeenth century in its entirety adopts in natural history; this figure is homogeneous with it and faithful: they express one another. The same relation exists between the sciences here as will exist later between Darwin and Boltzmann, as exists, in fact, between Laplace-Poinsot's fixed plane [*plan*] and Geoffroy Saint-Hilaire's single plan [*plan*]. The history of science is the history of these relations: as long as one doesn't describe the global advance of the frontal moraine, one isn't doing the history *of the sciences;* one is writing monographs—monographs crushed by the various ideologies of classification.

Inherited, no doubt, from Anaxagoras's homoeomery, the nested-box form, distinct from the theology of preexistence, collides head-on with Galileo's great principle, for which Jacob elsewhere (34) states another consequence.[7] Physical preservation of physical laws cannot exist throughout reproduction of an object in homothetic reduction. On holidays, you can easily make Chartres cathedrals out of marzipan, reduced models in the windows of pastry shops; an actual-sized object made from sugar products would immediately flatten out, a surrealist spectacle fit for the fairy Carabosse. The principle is not very well-known in philosophical circles, and that's a shame. Thus the levels of integration, even as crudely thought as by the reduction of size, don't repeat the same laws: this has been true in the "inanimate" from Galileo all the way up to Perrin and beyond; it remains true for living things, as Jacob everywhere tells us, and he is right. So the nested boxes of germs, insofar as it contradicts the principle, marks, in the eyes of the scientists of the seventeenth century, the specificity of the living thing. What is not true of a clock is true precisely of an organism. Mechanists and antimechanists are in close combat here.

Lastly, I recover my main thesis. The nested-box form is a projection, another way of drawing a tree. In the simplest case, concentric circumferences correspond to a chain;[8] of course, the schema can be made as complicated as you like. Consequently, the theory is endowed with that major historical function of transporting, for the first time, the global graph on which the science of life and its combinatorial classifications in the little department, the little theater of the germ, are modeled. The form of the tree passes from natural history to genetics, properly speaking; it will no longer leave it. This form passes from the global to the local, from the visible to the invisible. It organized the phenomena; one can guess that it can be operational for the genomenon. What does the theory of nested boxes do? It opens the box. It makes out that there is a box of boxes (it does so poorly, but it still makes it out). Jacob should have been content with these Russian dolls. Poorly placed—who can deny?—but in place.

Repetition of Translation

The reader will have to pardon the monotony of the translations. The balance sheet of geology, described by Jacob (160), is the balance sheet of d'Haüy, Bravais, and Romé de l'Isle in crystallography: a double-entry grid table, even a triple-entry one. The important thing is that, on this network, a family of parallel paths transports time. But just as archives, in digging around, become rare, so the network is a cone, whether it has to do with geology (162) or paleontology (163). Hence, in Darwin, the figure of the tree. "Divergence, diversification, and dispersion. The succession of living forms throughout time can no longer be represented by a table with a single column, or even with several . . . ; the only figure capable of describing the diversification of a group is the genealogical tree. As buds give rise by growth to fresh buds, and these, if vigorous, branch out and overtop on all sides many a feebler branch, so by generation I believe it has been with the great Tree of Life, which fills with its dead and broken branches the crust of the earth, and covers the surface with its ever branching and beautiful ramifications" (164). And again: "All true classification is genealogical: that community of descent is the hidden bond which naturalists have been unconsciously seeking, and not some unknown plan of creation" (165). Lastly: "The continuity of living beings was replaced by that of the slow, tenacious and irresistible growth of the genealogical tree" (166). Jacob lays stress precisely on the two principal theses of Darwinian evolutionary theory: the importance granted by it to the number of stations, which is to say, the statistical calculation of large populations, that calculation of chances stemming from combinatorics; and the original nature of the paths, drawn by breaks and quantum jumps.

The entire book would have to be reproduced on the basis of Darwin, he so clearly and distinctly accumulates the figures we are talking about. The birth of genetics will correspond to the progressive mathematization of these trees. Weismann's tree, still descriptive, describes the germinal trunk and the grafts or somatic branches (215-16); he has the merit of defining the germinal trunk as a closed system, sheltered, protected, beyond all reach (216-17). The dichotomic tree of the calculation of chromosomes remains at

De arte because it writes the general term as $1/2^n$ (218). But Mendel's tree definitively makes a success of the combinatorial algorithm. Genetic cartography corresponds, in perfection, to the constant figures of its prehistory.

A set of stations linked by paths is called a system. It is material, since matter is structured like an interlacing—such as in crystals and molecules. It is political; Schwann indeed says that each cell is a citizen (119), and Jacob repeats this, after Wiener (199). It is living, as we have sufficiently seen. It is now mechanical. Starting from the seventeenth century, a machine is composed and divided up according to the rules of the *Method*, whose technological connotation is so strong that it has never been used anywhere but there. The only people I know who apply Descartes are auto mechanics. Being a mechanist in biology has always meant something regarding the dichotomy: *partes extra partes;* Bergson repeats this to the point of being inopportune, and he is right. In other words, the paths of the polytomic tree guiding the partition into pieces don't meet each other or go in the inverse direction. A second mechanist tradition, an enduring one among scientists but forgotten by philosophers, had led, with Newton, Laplace, and others, on the contrary, to the communication network. The mechanist now adopts the communication network and prejudges the first tree to be crude. What's the situation with paths in the new schema? The important thing is that they are looped, in circuits, in feedback. Logical relations, forces, and energy circulated through them, and now information is added to this (251, 282): the informational and homeostatic network thereby fights against the tendency to disorder. Hermes is now everywhere, in order to distribute messages, on the paths that loop back on themselves. What's the situation with stations? There is no longer any primary station, center, or hierarchy; the cone or the pyramid is at an end, in this site at least; the cause has a feedback effect in its cause. The produced station controls the producing station. The looping of the circuits interrupts, for a time, the irreversible processes and protects the network—an islet or pocket of negentropy that consumes negentropy—against the implacable universality of the second law. This is a weak protection, since death must happen, but also an adamantine protection, since the translations are faithful. These feedback processes occur at each level, from the cell to the organism, from the organism to the entirety of evolution (175-76). Thus order is found again in the order of systems, of more or less complex networks. Once again, the schema produces questions at least as much as it is their product; feedback is in the method: we haven't finished, I think, meditating, after Boltzmann, upon Wiener's and Brillouin's lessons. Once again, combinatorics appears, in information theory, at least due to Planck-style complexions. Once again, the invariant form of knowledge, interrogating stations and paths, expresses, in space (in one or several spaces), interactions, integrations, the general state of the organization. Biology finds itself plunged in an organon of communication here; by the way, since the Renaissance, has it ever left it? Its history is a continual variation on this logic. Logic of life or metamorphosis of the tree.

A mathematician would write the axiomatic system or systems of these combinatory or spatialized forms better than I would; he or she would choose them pertinently from graph theory; he or she would develop the corresponding systems. For Jacob, as I understand it, the enterprise is desirable; it is within reach of biological research; for its real object consists in forming the algorithms of the living world, that logic caught, once again, in a double-entry grid—the synchronic cross section of the integrated networks, in which the organization can be read, and the stochastic path of the genealogy, in which the trees of evolution can be read—that logic in which the old thermodynamics, information theory, the mathematics of stochastic functions, cybernetics, physical chemistry, and biochemistry converge (300). Graph theory could furnish general schemas to this convergence. That said, *volens nolens,* Jacob has shown, perhaps through recurrence, that the history of heredity is conceptualized in these same terms. Chains, trees, networks, always combinatory and always drawn, have been repeated, shifted, nested, and translated, invariant and variable, for three centuries, or in the space of three centuries, from Fernel to Jacob. What remains is their form, relatively stable, and their composition by stations and paths, ridges and vertices: system, operator, cartography. What changes: their domain of application, whose variance may range from the whole of nature to carbon derivatives, from the drift of species to the assemblage of a machine; the power of the set they organize; the name given to their stations: species, individual, organic part, tissue, cell, characters, chromosomes, genes, molecules, atoms ... and the sequence of these namings truly gives an idea of the nested dolls; their respective situations; the form of the paths and of their intertwining, globally conical, pyramidal, or on the contrary, without any dominant vertex; the flow these paths transport: logical relations of inclusion or of precedence, forces, energy, information, specificity; the direction of these transports, reversible or irreversible; the nature of the crossroads or intersections, the assemblages and choices, the loops and circuits, the connection of certain components, the local closure of certain other components, and so on. In its highest generality, the theme of an invariant across a multiplicity of variations is found. Everything happens as though there were two histories and two sciences: the transhistorical stability of pure forms and the complex transports of contents and practices. Can the laws of these transports be determined? We must get back to work.

Suddenly, I'm no longer very certain that it has to do exclusively with life, the life no longer interrogated in laboratories. Contemporary knowledge, in its totality, *is* a theory of communication. The biology of our three Leeuwenhoeks is the figure adopted, in their own regions, by this new Leibnizianism. This is not a discovery; the language has always known this, which distributed the sciences through variations on a single word, that of leading and communicating: deduction, pure theory, induction, applied sciences, production, the knowledge of the practices, translation [*traduction*], the history of texts. There is only one history, there is only one science. Aphrodite and Sophia were whispering to me: seduction. I won't write it.

2

Life, Information, Second Law

Music and background noise, archipelagos and sea. That is to say, information and disorder, negentropy and the second law. Maybe memory and matter. The different and the homogeneous, the precious and the diffuse. How do science, the old philosophy, and the new philosophy set about translating Democritus? And since the order of the terms is irreversible, chance is the source, and necessity the end.

Information Theory

Natural philosophy is called physics. Ever since Lavoisier, Claude Bernard, and Berthelot, the study of chemistry had underlain life sciences' old phenomenology.[1] At the end of the century, biochemistry became its obligatory prolegomena; it is here that decisive things happened in the recent past and are still happening. Biochemistry is, in a way, the set theory of biology: its elementary foundation, the reference of its unity, the table of its basic alphabet. But, contrary to appearance, biochemistry *is not* the important point of Monod's book: biochemistry is its departure point, the support for its reflection, the source of its examples. The point is physics.

No critic has yet noticed, and I am scandalized by this, the fact that biochemists, and Monod above all, have a "natural philosophy" intrinsic to their scientific activity. This indicates, for our surrounding culture, a few delays and discrepancies in relation to science and philosophy. Monod, it is true, sometimes refers to the great eponyms of the academic pantheon, Descartes, Kant, Hegel; but the effective operators of his work are not the tools forged in, and by, this tradition. It is a question of new tools, dating from about this century, and which you will find in Wiener, Bridgman, Schrödinger, and Brillouin—the latter, in my opinion, being one of the best contemporary theorists of knowledge. Not being aware of this is condemning oneself to fighting rearguard actions, and God knows, in France, we are past masters of this art. That said, let's retrace a well-known path: biochemistry is a chemistry like any other, at least in its methods and its epistemology; chemistry is a science by way of physics, at least since Perrin; and the philosophy of physics is information theory. Therefore, when a biochemist announces that he is writing a natural philosophy, this, *in plain language*, means that he is applying information theory—itself the *natural* philosophy of "natural philosophy"—to his own discipline. This is the first path by which to reach *Chance and Necessity*.

A few words of explanation before venturing into its waters. It was almost inevitable, first, that biology would arrive here. At the very beginning of the nineteenth century, it became evident, like never before, that the "vital principle" had something to do with heat. Together, they surpassed the mechanist explanation in the style of Descartes-Lagrange. This was true starting from Lavoisier and the vitalists. On the one hand and at the same time, the thermologies developed by Joseph Black and Fourier prepared the way for the thermodynamics of Carnot, Clausius, Maxwell, and Boltzmann, and this thermodynamics culminated in information theory, starting from Szilard and Shannon. Heat lost its mysteries and, above all, no matter what the surpassing might have been. The vital principle did so just as much, on the other hand, as soon as physico-chemical knowledge placed itself, for biology, on a path parallel to these same paths. Hence the end of the circuit and old rediscoveries: the science of living things finds itself confronted with the science of information in the same way that, during the Revolution, the science of heat and the science of "life" confronted each other. In the same way, which is to say, quite differently, as we shall sufficiently see. In the same way and differently. An example: vitalism, against mechanism, affirmed, at least implicitly, that life was something like perpetual motion of the first kind; today, it affirms that life must be something like perpetual motion of the second kind. Old and renewed rediscoveries. Which is what I wanted to demonstrate.

Second, I said that information theory constituted a philosophy of physics, one that's intrinsic to the discipline. It is remarkable, for example, that Brillouin decided to title his last work *Science and Information Theory*. For in it, we can find a complete, descriptive, quantified, normative, and foundational epistemology, expressed in language suitable for physics, of the idea and act of experimentation, of law, of precision and approximate knowledge, of the limits of what can be known (what can I know?), that is, all the classical; and all the "modern": a theory of codes, of language, of writing, and of translation. Philosophers no longer have to look for or write a manual in which an epistemology of experimental knowledge would be found: it is there. For if a theoretical organon answers *every* question with complete clarity, little by little, in and by the philosophical tradition regarding a given practice, if it answers them in a univocal and well-mastered language, I don't know what to call it except a philosophy that's natural to that region; and if this region is "natural philosophy," the preceding results present themselves once again. Physics now transports its own epistemology with it. In the past, I had reached the same conclusions regarding mathematics. There is a contemporary state of science in which the reflective goes hand in hand with the regulatory, and vice versa. Science self-monitors and self-regulates in an almost cybernetic manner. This closure over itself is one of the objects of Monod's book and is unavoidable.

"Of Strange Objects."[2] The expression, at the beginning of the book, is not innocent; at least it is not naive. If we read the adjective as meaning "weird" (You said bizarre? It's bizarre . . .), then we must close the book, or it closes of itself to comprehension. "Strange" has a rigorous sense, one without any relation to the judging subject, who is universal; "strange" means *improbable*. And "miracle" has been a scientific word since the last century, which has planed away its terror and theology. Mathematics has Renan's miracle, the theory of random functions has Borel's miracle, thermodynamics Jeans's, atomic physics Perrin's (*Les Atomes,* 274), cybernetics Wiener's, and psychopathology Pinel's (?), still thaumaturgical and not positivist. Nietzsche described the sumptuous miracle of the flowering meadow. So that it is possible, without fail, to define and assess Epicurus's miracle on his atomic model. Biochemistry, lastly, has Monod's miracle, cited everywhere, as much in the *Leçon inaugurale* as in *Chance and Necessity,* regarding molecular epigenesis (21, 92), for example, and elsewhere. In short, "strange" is improbable, rare, and the calculation of miracles proffers numbers that are in the closest proximity to zero. Hence Borel: the most improbable phenomena *never occur.* Hence Monod: the most improbable phenomena, *when they exist, reproduce themselves; they occur because they reproduce themselves;* the big question of chance and entropy is already outlined. And therefore, strangeness is quantified precisely: *at a high level of information or negentropy.* "Strange" is the echo of chance, and "object" is the echo of a necessity. The adjective doesn't qualify the noun; it quantifies it. Thus my body is improbable, miraculous in Jeans's sense. Who am I, strange me? A stranger. A stranger to the Boltzmannian world and the Spinozian world: stones fall, first kind; energy degrades, second kind—the universal law of increasing disorder. Here is a rare order and a probable world. Lifting rocks, transforming heat into mechanical work. Here, suddenly, is Camus and the postulate of objectivity. Suddenly and from the first word, through information theory. Who am I? A swell of negentropy stranger to the entropic sea. Who are you, my rare and precious one, my treasure island?

There was a time when the ontology of the living thing required that one state the criteria of its difference from the inanimate, or that one attach chain links of continuity between the two regions. As soon as biology refers to chemistry, in its practice, and to physics, in its theory, as soon as their laws apply uninterruptedly to objects that vary along a scale of size and complexity, the question loses much of its interest, and the polemic much of its virulence. There was a time when methodology separated two schools, mechanism and vitalism. As soon as the former is refined to the point of becoming cybernetics, as soon as the latter is reduced to a tautology devoid of heuristic fruitfulness, the division loses even its reason for being. On the one hand, there is no living matter; there are only living systems. On the other, every organism is a chemical machine. Hence, through a short circuit, the residual question: how are we to differentiate the given from the constructed? Not the inanimate from the living, or the latter from machines, but the natural as a whole and the artificial in its zone. And the question arises of knowing *who* arbitrates the difference. Who else but a synthesis of the two groups, a programmed computer? The question is posed in *informatic* terms. It develops in three stages: the geometry of forms; the mechanism of constructions; thermodynamics and information theory. The three groups of criteria have an increasing discriminatory power, so that the two characteristics of living things are defined or assessed by the terminal science: invariance as a quantity of information (we shall see how and why it is calculable) and teleonomy as the set of transfers of a quantity of this type.[3] Thus information theory clarifies and secures the results of the preceding sciences and reinterprets them globally; it furnishes, for the object, adequate and univocal concepts.

Invariance precedes teleonomy: this is the main theory. It is a biologist's and geneticist's theory: the genotype precedes and explains the phenotype; the genomenon is the coded secret of the phenomenon. It is a chemist's theory: the synthesis of proteins depends on DNA; the sequence of amino acids is determined by the sequence of the nucleobases. It is a physicist's theory: the program is maximally preserved against the effects dictated by the second law, whereas the teleonomic system is sooner broken by them; the death of an organism occurs within limits that are far narrower than the extinction of a species . . . In other words, only that order is compatible with the second law of thermodynamics. So it is a theory of philosophy, in the sense of natural philosophy: reverse the order and you are brought back to the absurd, which is to say, to perpetual motion of the second kind. The path described just now has been exhaustively followed. At the end of the road is a regulative law, a universal one.

It is possible, strictly speaking—I'm not saying easy—to understand that ontogenetic "life" is compatible with the second law. At each level of integration, from the cell to the global system, Maxwell's demons (themselves compatible with the second law, according to the Wiener-Brillouin proof) would function, demons that would retard, in the short, medium, or long term, this slow or lightning-fast brutal increase in entropy commonly called death. Ontogenetic life would have to be understood in terms of metastable equilibrium, à la Wiener, or in terms of negative-positive catalysis, à la Brillouin; and since the second law doesn't say anything about the quantity of time and sets forth an irreversibility having an indeterminate quantity (whereas the time of classical mechanics is a reversible quantity), ontogenetic life is indeed compatible with it, ontogenetic life, too, being an irreversibility having an indeterminate quantity of time between a few limits. The set of positive-negative catalyses, in Brillouin's sense, and Maxwell's demons would be agents of the determination of time, left indeterminate in the universal statement of the second law. So the reserves of energy, in Brillouin's sense, the differences, in Carnot's sense, the dissipative structures, in Prigogine's sense, even the metastable equilibria, in Wiener's sense, would be understood, would be made possible, by these limitations, these determinations of time, as quantity, sometimes in the proximity of zero, sometimes extended to millennia.

That said, Bridgman's operational objection remains. Talking about the entropy of a system has no meaning when one does not know how to measure this entropy. But that is the case with the organism: one must kill it or wait for death to kill it to do so, supposing it to be easy to do. On the other hand, this system is open—who can deny it?—at least onto its ecological niche. Talking about its entropy, even saying that it is low since it is a matter of a highly improbable structure, may have meaning, but measuring the entropy remains impossible, since exchange with the outside is the condition of its life. And since no niche is closed, not even Earth, and since nothing can be decided, without paradox, about the closure of the universe, we are once again in difficulty. The preceding examples presuppose the definition of walls that preserve differences, walls we know nothing about. Consequently, it is easy to establish such a conception, but it is swarming with paralogisms.

Brillouin, Wiener, and others do say that this is easy, without hiding the difficulties posed by Bridgman, but that it is far more difficult to understand phenomena that, unlike the first phenomenon, seem to completely contradict the second law: the evolutionary progression from the simple to the complex, for example, reproduction, the preservation of species, and so on. Even though ontogenetic irreversibility, leading the inexorable conclusion of the individual to its death, seems compatible with the second law, phylogenetic irreversibility seems to crash into it head-on. It's the old problem of Bergson's *Creative Evolution*; it's the old contradiction that leads many physicists (Walter Elsasser, etc.) to call for another law, whatever its name might be.

Monod's breakthrough consists precisely in making a virtue of necessity; I mean by these words uniting two difficulties—Bridgman's and the preceding one—to derive a solution from this. It *seems* easy to make ontogenesis compatible with the second law; this *seems* impossible for phylogenesis; but what seems easy crashes headlong into the condition of closure for systems. Phylogenesis is only understood in terms of what occurs in the genome; in fact, a genome is a closed system. So Bridgman's condition is fulfilled. Therefore, Monod can apply the second law. Therefore, it's in the phenomena of evolution—specifically, reproductive invariance—that the second law can *best* be applied. In fact, the second law predicts that if degradation applies to the whole of the system, it tolerates exceptions or local retardations in a part of the system. Darwinian selection intervenes here, and the solution becomes as clear as a thousand suns. The reversal is considerable, a complete turnaround, and, it must be said, pleasing. Monod shifts to the most difficult spot to have been defined by the previous problem. Saying that invariance precedes teleonomy is the sign of the breakthrough.

The book is constructed on these prolegomena: information is its directive and the second law its regulation; as though life were that precarious and dissipative equilibrium between wealth and loss. The couple information-entropy reduces the old metaphysical twinship of chance and necessity, into which men and gods used to emotionally invest their share of fate, to the objective, the calculable, the positive. Conversely, this couple forms the proper philosophical framework of measurement, experimentation, and knowledge. Between its limits, laws and paradoxes change place massively: when the tendency to disorder is the rule, the preservation of an order, whatever it may be, is a scandal. Consequently, I believe that the living thing is not, alone, strange: molecules and crystals, mountains and solar systems, are almost as strange. I say "almost," since one can count. Order is not the norm; it is the exception. The physicist has become an anarchist; background noise is his domain, and music is rare. Every object is a miracle. The old astonishment has reversed roles. We must accept this *reversal, next to which the Copernican one is child's play,* to enter into science today. The fact that it is intolerable to our cultural stereotypes and our liking for living in our own house is obvious. As Galileo would say, "And yet it moves." Today, this is translated as "And yet it is extraordinary that it moves." Law is no longer in the law, nor is humankind in the world. It is incomprehensible that the comprehensible exists.

And yet, therefore, order exists. Conservatories of chance and self-regulating systems, jam-packed with negentropy. Enzymatic catalyses, a power for elective discrimination. Cybernetic feedback delaying the due date for chaos. A molecular epigenesis simulating an enrichment (turn around Jacob's Russian dolls, and you will have Monod's multistage fireworks rocket).[4] A stability that's ancient, several times over. An evolution from the simple to the complex. That was in regard to information, the directive principle: everything seems to happen as though there were self-animation, self-command, self-regulation, self-construction, and autonomous history. This is regarding the second law, the regulatory principle: calculation consistently shows that the second law is never thwarted. Brillouin had exorcised Maxwell's demon; Monod repeats the exorcism at each stage by establishing the thermodynamic balance sheet of the process in question. And yet, therefore, information exists: but it never increases, except temporarily in local pockets of the system. The book is constructed, like an organism, on the joined opposites: the entropy–negentropy couple, the couple of fire. In passing, it eliminates the philosophies that, because they haven't carried out the reversal, would threaten to introduce perpetual motion.

Is life a property of a system? Not quite, for that statement is worthless. More precisely, there are no living things but certain systems. The organism is a system, one whose complexity is expressed by a large number, in the technical sense, and this large number precisely marks the threshold of the particular judgment. Below this threshold, there are, for example, crystalline systems. Hence the organism's high improbability, its prodigious negentropy, the miracle of its reliability—and the difficulty, undoubtedly irreducible, in knowing it punctually. Monod plays at calculating the difficulty, the way Brillouin computed the length of a telegram conveyed in pieces. It is through the quantity or enumeration that life can be said to be unknowable: the mystery and the miracle are quite simply in the numbers. That is saying more than a little. The occurrences of this quantitative theme in Jacob, Lwoff, and Monod happen in high frequency, and that is a sign. As though a certain Pythagorism has been returning ever since quanta and information. That said, a system, whatever its "power" may be, is above all a coordination complex, and Monod finds himself obligated to say "cybernetics" for "teleonomy." In this regard, there is no better text than the very middle of the *Leçon*. It describes a logic of exchange, of the cost of these exchanges that sometimes become nearly cost-free; a logic of *inter*ference: *inter*actions, *inter*mediaries ... Allosteric proteins are relays, amplifiers of signals: they establish, carry out, and optimize communication. This is a complete network of circulation: messages and code, translation and transduction, mediators and transfers, executions and cancellations, feedback and controls, responses to threshold effects, transitions, direct and indirect circuits, homeostasis and omnipossibility, self-regulation, writing and reading, et cetera. The organism is not only a communication space, but also the best-known one: the smallest in size, the most reliable, the one that obtains the maximal yield in its functioning. These maxima give a second threshold for the particular judgment: the miracle is, once again, in the numbers. Yet again, Hermes is the god of biochemists, who know better than others, myself included, what a messenger is. Who dreamed, during the seventeenth century, of a system of communication of "substances"? The lactose system or the fulfillment of the Leibnizian dream. Let an experimental monadology be rewritten tomorrow. That said, the two quantities-thresholds are, on the one hand, a quantity of information and, on the other, the set of transfers of this information. Whoever says system and living system says, in quantity and relation, invariance and teleonomy: which is what is needed to be found again. That is to say, a message and its circuits. "Life" is communication, and this can be calculated.

Let's return, for a moment, to the first route. There may be an order in the acquisition, by a field of knowledge, of increasingly strong norms, of increasingly numerous references. This order is locatable as a crossing from region to region. For biology, the path is so distinctly drawn that one begins to dream that it could become law. It forms a double loop, closed at the same point. Natural history starts from qualitative and, as they say, empirical description to progress toward mathematics through the combinatorics of classifications as well as genetic calculation in the style of Mendel. Biology takes up this loop again, point by point and place by place, by filling the gaps left by the short circuit of the first loop; points, places, and gaps to be located within Auguste Comte's classification. From Lavoisier to organic chemistry, from the latter to biochemistry, the route passes through the nearest discipline. But at the very moment the chemists were beginning to think their science was not so much an independent region as a physics, strictly speaking—that is to say, at the moment their science acquired stronger norms and references by passing to the nearest discipline—biology carried out a new step and became a refined, elaborate, and precise physics, through thermodynamics and information theory, for example. At the end of this second journey, or long circuit, Jacob and Monod envision mathematical algorithms, and the code again finds a combinatorics—at chemistry's end, at physics' end, just as observation had directly found one. The second loop, slower and circumspect at the intermediary stations, has joined the ending point of the first loop. Supposing the dream of the law were realized, one would get an indication of the future of the social sciences. Mathematized through plates, veneer, or too quickly by way of a short circuit, the social sciences would need, tomorrow, to retrace—point by point and secondly—the global loop drawn in today's prehistory, such that their mathematization or general logification would suddenly shift to the final instance. It is true that they already experienced, at least by metaphor, descriptions following the biological model; it is a pity that they haven't yet given themselves good technological or physical models, despite a few attempts, so as to mathematize only at the end of the course. So the old positivist classification would no longer be a partitioning grid of knowledge into sectors,[5] which history disrupted the very day it was acquired, but would define an order of passage for a field of knowledge irresistibly seeking maximal scientificity—just as if a science weren't truly one unless it was loaded with the trace of all the others. Science must be called a body of knowledge brimming with references. Science, then, is science of the sciences, and in an entirely new sense: a philosophy.

Positivism

Auguste Comte is the victim of an unjust fate. Positivism was a school; it is now a term of abuse. This is so for a thousand reasons, one of which is the following: it's best to condemn the author whose theories you repeat without citation. Who, since Comte in his *Cours de philosophie positive,* has covered and synthesized contemporary knowledge? Monod, among others, is therefore considered a positivist. To decide this, here is an experiment. The postulate of objectivity: the fact that there are objects, not projects, which is to say, purposes or final causes, seems to him to be the foundation of science.[6] He dates its appearance to the establishment of the law of inertia in the seventeenth century. The law of inertia defines the inanimate [*l'inerte*], which is subject to the free play of natural forces: nothing moves, nothing stops, of itself. It forbids perpetual motion. It was natural for Monod, who uses the second law as a constant criterion, to place science's prehistory as preceding the emergence of its equivalent of the first kind. But, in the fifteenth lesson of the *Cours,*

Auguste Comte says exactly the opposite. The passivity of raw bodies, he says, is an abstraction. They are, in fact, endowed with a *spontaneous* activity that is of the same nature, differing only in degree, as the activity of living things. Newtonian gravity manifestly shows, he concludes, that it is an *act* of matter. But if matter, of itself, indulges in spontaneous acts, the law of inertia is only a handy convention, at the limit a false one, and there is perpetual motion. The proof of this is that the cosmogonic model of the *Cours,* taken up from Laplace and regrettably completed, defines an eternal return; the primordial nebula is also terminal, by catastrophic projection of the system into the sun, and the global motion recommences: a cyclic model. So there are two families of systems or philosophies: those that posit perpetual motion, and those that deny it. Sometimes one detects its marks: look, for example, at how the words *spontaneous* or *motor* are used. Where is the motor? What is its status, its efficiency, its maintenance, its feeding, et cetera? From which it results that Comte, like so many others, is in the first case. Monod is in the second. And he is not a positivist.

He is one nonetheless and in the following manner. Two stakes in the discussion dominate all the rest. First, the laws of dynamics, the old dynamics and the new. Next, the question of the invariant, which is the same stake. Can a strategy of the sciences that is constant be envisioned? On this point, chapter 6 is perfectly clear: science discovers invariants. I would like its readers to reread, in their spare time, Poinsot's great *Mémoire sur la théorie et la détermination de l'équateur du système solaire,* one of the great scientific monuments of the nineteenth century, and which, as I shall try to show elsewhere, contains almost every secret of the Romantic age. Piaget refers Monod to Meyerson; it'd be better to compare him to Poinsot so as not to risk confusing invariance and identity. The comparison is superb: similar method, parallel history, homologous results. In short, Monod says that the theory of invariants he sets forth is Platonic. It would be better to call it mathematical, since it is from mathematics that Plato derived both the idea of invariance and the invariance of the idea. We should continue: the theory is astronomic; see precisely Poinsot. It is physical, and has been since the arithmetization of the vibration of musical strings in the infancy of science, and since optics, with the renewed (and proper) beginning of experimental knowledge during the seventeenth century. The theory belongs to natural history: look at Geoffroy Saint-Hilaire, Poinsot's living twin—I say "living" for two reasons, the second being that he is being brought back to life today. I am intentionally taking my examples from old history. So, and once again, the discussion will center on dynamics, which is manifestly privileged. The question here is which has priority: rest or motion, in relation to each other—the mechanical form of the same question, when centered on the invariant and variations. Here, positivism is found again. One remembers Auguste Comte's discussion and the historical table he proposed. At the end of a complex diachrony in which positions change and are exchanged, statics comes out the winner of the debate. Ever since Maupertuis, d'Alembert, and Lagrange, its equations have dominated dynamics. That's precisely what positivism is. The invariant precedes and explains the variation, which, without it, wouldn't be a disturbance of anything; statics precedes and explains kinematics; structure precedes and explains history . . . , invariance precedes and explains teleonomy. Hence Monod: if you reverse the position and say that *motion is first, then it is perpetual.* Dynamics, old and new, invariably presuppose preservations: living forces, energy, et cetera. Lacking which, we fall back into perpetual motion of the first or second kind. Hence the global framework: the theory of invariance is constitutive of natural philosophy; the second law is its regulative theory, and that is why it serves as a critical grid for reading philosophies. The first law precedes the second—and this is true of thermodynamics. So I'm willing to admit that Monod is a positivist, but then Auguste Comte isn't one any longer: for, while he may be on the same side as Poinsot, his interpretation of the law of inertia and his cosmogonic model are subject to critique. The contradiction is in the *Cours;* it is not in *Chance and Necessity.*

Idealism

It is a shame to have to endlessly go over the elementary. The definitions, today cursory ones, of idealism are all isomorphic with the definitions that could be given of error. So it is tautological to dogmatically demonstrate the errors of idealism. In fact, two idealisms can be distinguished. The first, roughly of Platonic origin, posits invariant idealities that transcend all possible experience; stemming visibly from mathematical practice, it is, *sensu stricto,* a realism—a realism of idealities. From the Greeks to our time, it has endured as its mathematical support has endured; our strongest intellectual security, it has endured because it cannot be proved wrong, as the contemporary discussions with the nominalists testify. Regardless of whether you like it, every mathematician, in their practice, is "idealist" in this or a related sense. Should you take up the gesture, you won't regret it. The second idealism, which is the true one (which is to say, probably the false one), is opposed to all realism, particularly the first idealism. Born in the modern era, it exclusively refers all possible knowledge to the subject. Hence its theorem: the world is nothing but my representation. Here, properly, is the idealism that is dying a natural death under the repeated blows of what's essential to the nineteenth century. It is dying like the philosophies of representation and at the same time as the psychological subject, the gnoseological subject, and the transcendental subject. A century and a half of critique has shown, I do believe for all time, that it had to do with a mythology. By ignoring these prolegomena, one says just anything at all or takes repetitions to be discoveries; I'm not rebelling against this in any way: believing the moon is made of cheese defines the party and I like parties; but however long it may last, you always wind up getting back to work. And, for example, in biochemistry. If Monod is an idealist, he can only be one in the first sense, for I don't see any subject or representation in his theory of knowledge, whereas I see them very well in many of his accusers. And if he is one in this way, no critique in this world would be able to show the objective falsity of this position. But, in fact, he is not even one, since his invariant in no way belongs to the kingdom of idealities, as with mathematics: his invariant, independent of the external world defined as an ecological niche, is not "elsewhere"; it is somewhere, determinable, defined, materially written like a sequence of letters. No one truly knows "where" *The Kreutzer Sonata* is, "where" the square, diagonal, and so on are; Monod knows *where* his invariant form is: it is written on the strand of DNA. Lastly, genetics was one of the first sciences to relativize for all time the activity of the individual subject. What more do you want? For ideas to lead the world? What philosophy has seriously underlain it for half a millennium?

Cartesianism

It had been a long time since a *Cartesian* book had been seen in France. The surprise and the misunderstandings provoked by Monod's work are due to the fact that the old lesson of method was covered over, in our time, by several other traditions, ones less close, in truth, to the practice of the exact sciences. Analytic strategies have, I don't know why, a bad reputation in the city and the court; they remain under the shelter of laboratories, where they retain an unparalleled effectiveness in the hands of the workers of the proof. This rupture is dramatic; it must have a meaning, one I can't see well enough to be able to speak about extemporaneously. In going over again, however, the marvelous taking apart of the lactose system, one is quickly persuaded that an analysis without any compromise or remainder remains the best path to discovery. Conversely, you can search in vain in the rigorous or experimental sciences for even a minor result gained by means of another method. A single example, and I will be converted. Who can deny that Descartes's rubric is clumsy, subjective, and minimal? In its canonical form, it has never been used much by either its author or his epigones. History shows that general analysis has never stopped refining itself, improving itself, being used as an increasingly complex strategy, and its regular success has confirmed this. Monod says this calmly, after direct use; hence the surprise. He states a *non-Bachelardian epistemology.* He believes in the simple, like Jacob, who, for his part, cites Perrin: explain the complicated visible by the simple invisible. Hence the opposition to Bachelard's *New Scientific Spirit:* read the real complex beneath the simple appearance.[7]

Who will tell the exquisite and perhaps essential complexity of the "simple natures," temporarily definitive, of biochemistry: proteins and nucleic acids?[8] In fact, what does "complex" mean? Bachelard doesn't seem to have defined this old scientific word, stemming from the combinatory art and imposed, in the nineteenth century, by the technology of electric networks and field theory: Maxwell, in his *Treatise*, cites Johann Benedict Listing: *Der Census räumlicher Complexe*. It means numerous, from the point of view of quantity; combined, from the point of view of elements; folded, intersected, intertwined, from the point of view of form and of relation. Hence, methodically speaking, the arithmetic-combinatorics-topology group is superposed on the chemistry-thermodynamics-information theory group. They correspond here to what Bachelard calls the "geometry-mechanics-electricity complex" in his description of the conceptual "syntheses" of physics. As always, the interference of ideas and means of attack is the rule—what has recently been called interdisciplinarity. That said, if the length (quantity) of the polypeptide chains or the polynucleotide fibers seemed, at first, a challenge to all exhaustive enumeration, it nevertheless remained necessary to pass through this enumeration, and not stop at the totality, to obtain an alphabet—which is to say, a science. Likewise, it remained necessary to finish the alphabet—which is to say, observing the fourth rule or axiom of closure—in order to know what one was talking about, or rather, to be able to talk. Similarly, it remained necessary to observe the rules of combinatorics to form a table of elements—that is, of the code and translation. The techniques for enumeration don't kill the syntheses: they predict the complexions, which is entirely different. I know, clearly and distinctly, what a combination of elements is, when they are set forth as such or discovered by analysis; I don't understand what a synthetic judgment is, and I strongly doubt that science has ever pronounced one. Nothing is more complex, lastly, than the folds of the chain of a protein; but what biochemist would dare say that he or she should go no further and take this complex as being complex, even if some given function is not possible except through it? Yes, the complicated constitution explains such and such a performance, and stereospecificity is that very thing; there is no doubt about it. But, that said, the analysis irrevocably follows its course and attempts to untangle the intertwining, either by means of a calculation of the minimum or by means of graph theory: isn't it a problem of path that's at issue?[9] The descriptive idea of "complex," when decomposed into quantity or number, elements and combinations, form and relations, is

LIFE, INFORMATION, SECOND LAW 49

relative: it is probably stadial, and the specificity of the levels can be debated, but whatever the stages, they are *always* traversed by the analytic process, or there is no science. What distinguishes Monod from Jacob, certainly without opposing them, is that the former highlights the process of analysis and the latter the specific difference of the levels of integration. Without opposing them, since the series of Russian dolls completes in Jacob what epigenesis does in Monod, from protomers to cells, through oligomers, proteins, and bacteriophages.

The analytic requirement isn't all the Cartesianism of the book. Here, in addition, is a philosophy of order. That is, a sequence equipped with a rule. If this law tolerates returns, whatever they may be, to predecessors, we obtain the cybernetic construction of teleonomic systems. This is an order, that of a complex: a Leibnizian logic. In Monod's view, saying that doesn't suffice because an irreversible order subsists. For proteins, that would suffice; for DNA, the rule doesn't tolerate returns, and that's why, as an aside, a closure is conceivable, thermodynamically speaking. For the phenomenon or phenotype, that would suffice; for the genotype, there is no return. The phenomenon is Leibnizian; genetics is Cartesian; and genesis precedes system. In other words, a point of departure exists, one that explains the series, which cannot be understood without it; one can, conversely, understand the sources without the successors along the sequence. But ascribing an absolute predecessor in the order and fixing an irreversibility is constructing, strictly, a "chain of reasons." Affirming that invariance precedes teleonomy is ascribing to DNA the role of a fixed point, which is to say, the priority of priorities; it is submitting to this chain. Two biological orders: that of systems with returns—the Leibnizian network; that of irreversibility—a chain in the style of Descartes. Transfers and difference.

That's not all: the couple figure-motion dominates the method, and living things are chemical machines. The Cartesian clockwork, refined as much as you like by Wiener and homeostasis, is constituted by molecular or atomic combinatorics and quantifications of energy. To my knowledge, there are no clocks anymore except atomic ones. The initial division of the set to be dealt with, purely analytic, is, as I just said, in the informatic style; mechanism is its principal horizon: the living stands out against the artificial, and it's a machine that judges, even if I program it.[10] But who am I, if not a machine with a program? The careful gradation of the criteria is revealing: geometry, first, by repetition and regularity, that is, figure (and static examples: house, rock) and mode of construction; next, kinematic examples, that is, mechanism and motion. This ends up with thermodynamics and information theory. Here is the history of science, even if unintentionally: and, if it stops at Brillouin, it definitely begins with Descartes. For confirmation: the concept of specificity, originating in biology, is entirely elucidated by the geometric forms of the molecules; the single and selected transfer, motion, is explained by the form or figure. Before being transmitted and in order to do so, information is form, and message is mark. Objects can be deformed, but not very much, and that is what remembering is: vestige, history, and specific invariance. The piece of wax is written on. Post-Cartesian variations on the figure: form, deformation, information, morphogenesis.

Method and conceptual frameworks induce a temperament, unless it is the reverse, unless this sentence is devoid of meaning. The fierce requirement for distinction and clarity leads Descartes to a strict separation of genera, regions, and disciplines. He dismisses those *mixtures* called mechanical curves, infinitesimal calculus, et cetera.[11] The space in which he moves is traversed with borders, divisions. Yes, it's a world with continents. Leibniz, conversely, laughing, cut up the sea with a sword to classify the sciences. Monod's space is Cartesian; it is a fibered, regulated, separated world. A closed system, terms without predecessors, differentiated sets, gnoseological borders, thresholds, history having sudden breaks and without prehistory, knowledge without prolegomenon or science without prescience, exclusive choices without mixture. The new new biological spirit is non-non-Cartesian.

On the Universal

Philosophy has long reverberated around Newton—through Hume, Montesquieu, Kant, and Auguste Comte, to cite only those said to be important, and to erase Saint-Simon, among so many others. It was the age of a concordat between the science of the world and the culture of the Enlightenment, that concordat always having to be destroyed, always having to be rewritten. But there are few, very few, great physical laws: those of mechanics, which were revised by relativity, the equations of electromagnetism . . . , the laws of thermodynamics. Let's imagine a comical uchronia: that of an eighteenth century—which partly existed—that would only have produced anti-Newtonians. That the concordat signifies something, that it must be debated for a long time because it isn't self-evident, this is something we are in accord about; but the discord signifies something at least just as important. I strongly fear now that far from laughing, we have to ask, regarding the nineteenth century, about a rending of this type. Starting from Sadi Carnot and all the way up to today, the theory of heat, about which Fourier said well that it is just as universal as the theory of gravity, has revealed itself to be fundamental; look at, among other things, the Industrial Revolution, the idea of history, life, information theory, energy, et cetera. The theory of heat has the same dates and the same dimensions as modernity. But what I fear, quite precisely, is that most of the philosophies contemporary with its birth, development, and recent maturity collide head-on with its laws, when these philosophies aren't foreign to them. From Comte to Nietzsche and Spencer. It is perhaps Freud's honor to have been counted among the rare philosophers to have made the theory of heat reverberate elsewhere than in the physical sciences; elsewhere, but not as far as it appears: how is a psychology to be conceived if not as a topology equipped with energetics? It is Bergson's merit to have compared the increase in entropy with that élan or impetus he called vital, which seemed to contradict it; to have transposed, into other regions, the canonical conditions of opening and of closure, et cetera. In short, finding a system that takes as its rules laws as fundamental to the physical or "natural" world as Newton's laws were during the seventeenth century doesn't happen very often. Just as though matter didn't concern philosophy anymore: matter is dead; I have no more fire.

This is because the aforementioned philosophies are rarely pluralist or regional: instead, they are totalizing systems. Consequently, could they model themselves on a law itself subject to conditions of closure? How can something that presupposes a partitioning by islands or pockets be imported into every place? Either the system is universal, and it doesn't meet with the law, or if it does meet with it, it denies it, for it is its stumbling block; or it observes its rule and consequently can no longer be constituted other than by divisions. This is indeed the case with Freud and Bergson. So the big question to be resolved is posed now in reverse: is the second law, itself, universal? Yes, but not quite in Newton's way. It is universal, if I may, in a non-continuous fashion, from place to place. There are archipelagos: here and there, among them, islets of negentropy. At the limit, posing the universe, as such, as open or closed is an antinomy, in Kant's sense, at least for the moment. In any case, it is universal in its negation, or better, in what it forbids: perpetual motion. So finding the latter somewhere in a system is a sign that it is either hyperlocal or so universal that it touches on antinomies. This criterion is nicely fruitful. As Aristotle would say, it is certain that a pile of rocks will never, of itself, make a house, even if it takes a long period of time for the house to make a pile of rocks. But it is certain, recently, that a cloud of photons has made a world. This is why it is always best to use the second law as regulatory, which is what Monod does constantly. He doesn't say it is deducible; he says it is compatible. Therefore, either it is strictly observed, and then Monod is right from start to finish, including his divisions and the things he forbids (but the choice of *science*—made outside science—ultimately reintroduces not so much ethics in general as a new Maxwell's demon); or it is not universal but merely local and must be demonstrated. No doubt, the near future of thermodynamics will answer this demand. One should be persuaded that this is the real question. The rest is literature.

Nature doesn't code the universal. Diffused across all times, diffused across all places, the universal doesn't need a memory. A law of nature doesn't require local stock; nor does it require translation to pass time, mark it, or define it. Such a law is, by nature, unwritten: you will not find it anywhere; nor is it dated. There is no Newton code; there is no place where Maxwell's equations are imprinted. Galileo is right and wrong: nature is *unwritten* in mathematical language. There is no code in equilibrium. When code exists, it is local and transitive.

Final equilibrium in the manner of Fourier and Boltzmann implies forgetting the initial conditions, along with duration. No matter the origin of history, its end is univocal, determined, identical everywhere, necessary, and this is so no matter the length of the process. Universal equilibrium, monotonic distribution, maximal entropy. Why would nature code the stages of a process in which the initial conditions don't condition the process and in which, no matter its stages, the final state is assigned without fail? That would be useless: there is no reason. Fated, the Boltzmannian world is without any memory that can be distinguished; it erases, as it goes along, the stocks and differences. It has its discrete events, without any conditioning predecessors; it is subject to that single linear line that assigns the populating of the classless place as the end of history. The length of time is of no consequence; it is enough to wait; and no matter what one may do . . .

If I don't know the why of the code, I can at least find a reason for it regarding the entropic world. It's because there are deviations from equilibrium, nonlinearities, sequences that are at least temporary and exceptional. But these chains require precisely a memory of the initial conditions, which is to say, a transported invariance, which is to say, a translation, which is to say, a code. Temporary, exceptional—these sequences are not universal in the sense of ordinary physics. They are even rare. It can be said then that nature codes the highly rare fluctuation, *incerto loco, incerto tempore* [at an uncertain place and time] (hence the absurdity of the question of the origin and its always circular logic); it codes a signal, a random combination, and thereby preserves it and brings about a chain. How can it be otherwise when the signal is not universal, when it is only a signal? Thus one glimpses that the identity of the code and chance is something like a necessity. Of course, I don't know why, but I do see that when a chain, tree, or network exists, there is need of a code and a translation for them to exist in that modality. In other words, it is useless to code the descent of heavy bodies; it is not useless to code the clinamen when the deviation or swerve repeats itself. How is a stability to be retained, even a temporary one, in the difference to Boltzmannian equilibrium? Imprint it, and then endlessly translate it.

Everything now happens as though there were two histories and two "evolutions." The first ones go, in total forgetfulness of their predecessors, toward universal equilibrium. They go there, as they say, by chance, but inexorably. The latter filter, one fine day, a certain signal by chance, code it, preserve it and therefore memorize the initial signal, and bring about the very process called evolution and history. Code, history, solid materials: analogous words. But precisely insofar as these two pairs are both subject to chance, they are subject to the same laws, and there is only one history and one evolution. Jacob states well the kinship between Boltzmann and Darwin; Monod, for his part, aligns neo-Darwinism with the second law. The exception proves the rule.

Thus one understands, once again, why Monod puts invariance before teleonomy. It's because the signal is translated, and translated by the products of its own translation, that this signal, normally erased by the lawful forgetting of the initial conditions, is truly negentropic. So, yes, the paradox is the invariance. Here, there is suddenly a material genesis of the signifier and a signaletic genesis of this half-meter cube of material space that locally escapes disorder and death. Who are you? The immemorial memory of something initial that has no reason and is forever lost. A stock of obstinacy regarding the meaninglessness, without which I myself, today, would not escape Boltzmann. A piece of remembered noise.

Chance

There is no good method, for men of science, for taking a definition of chance from philosophers. Because it is God or nothing, according to whether the thinker stands for nothing or for God. But no one can know anything about anything before and without science, once it has already thought something; so it is for philosophers to look for the definition near science. Before the seventeenth century, we lived fate and fatality; whether Stoic, Muslim, or Christian, we were subject to good fortunes and setbacks, we feared luck and destiny, we were amazed at encounters, occasions, and obstacles, we played games, dice, goose, or solitaire, we invoked the gods, themselves subject to blind powers, we died of wind, of shipwreck; the world was intentionally woven, unexpected, cruel, and necessary: we didn't know chance. It was invented as an object by the Chevalier de Méré, Pascal, and the other Bernoulli. "As an object"—that is to say, forever emptied of any subjective trace. Chance is rooted in the economics of life annuities and the prehistoric sociology of bills of mortality. Number tables replace tragedy. Chance no longer has any project; it only has combinations. This, if you like, is the postulate of objectivity. Since then, this well-formed chance has fairly abandoned the philosophies: they tolerated it as poorly as the religions did in the past, and that is a sign. Cite, I urge you, the systems that take exact account of it, and you will know why all that's left is to question mathematics, information theory, and the life sciences.

This is why, first of all, we must abandon, without regret, the traditional definition in the manner of Cournot, nevertheless one of the rare thinkers in the nineteenth century to give chance the role that rightfully belongs to it.[12] This is because this definition, too, presupposes a world, a view that obscures the matter. Causes, in the first place, and no one knows what's what with causes anymore. Next, the independence of phenomenal sequences, which is neither demonstrated nor refuted: to decide this, we would need to be able to eliminate or, on the contrary, assess every highly distant coupling—about which we know little. Whether the world is jam-packed with links or locally lacunary is a question for which we have too many or too few answers. Something like an antinomy, in the Kantian sense, undecidable for the time being. The definition is less clear than the defined: the latter allows a calculation, and the former permits hypotheses. In bracketing them, it nevertheless remains, as a residue, that Cournot copies the old relation of the favorable case to the possible cases, the encounter being the favor expected by the multiple sequences endowed with an empty intersection. And what imposes the definition is the geometric *staged scene*, in which intuition is entirely at ease: the event produces itself; the intersection of the lines geometrizes the product or gathers it into a set. A given path of the knight puts the queen in check. Therefore, nothing other than a combination on a table of elements, which is what I set out to demonstrate. So Cournot's definition doesn't say much more about it than Monod's examples: some arrangement of amino acids along the polypeptide chain, an arrangement acquired by shuffling the cards, an arrangement acquired from the table of possible arrangements. What the definition says, in addition, is an intuitive scene or, worse, a world that must indeed be called metaphysical. But science has had too much trouble or spent too much time leaving both of them in order to settle on enumeration and algebra for us to now accept this return. As often happens, the philosophical definition of an object of science shows the traces of its prehistory. To finish, I would like us to retain this happy word *case*, an accidental fall in Latin, which, by chance, in the French *cas*, is plural on the basis of the singular.[13] I would also like us to be attentive to the fact that Jacques Monod, when he shuffles the cards, mixes them, and to the fact that thermodynamics conceives randomness by means of the mixture of gases or molecules: in most cases, chance is articulated far more from mixture than from individuated independence.

Hence this first result: chance would be unthinkable—only emotionally felt—without a set, a base variety. The important thing here is the plural, the number of "factors," the pure multiplicity. The old world, always already law-abiding, fibered with ready-made sequences, is replaced by a table, any coded collection, an assemblage of terms about which, precisely, no hypothesis is made. The thing is verifiable in every site. In mathematics, this set was called "collective." Cournot's event can be called a signal, and the signal stands out, favorable—against possibilities, against a background, against background noise; there wouldn't be this stochastic agitation without the myriads of molecules. The rare information and the entropic disorder are defined and calculated from a number of complexions.

The unhappy accident itself, under the statue of Hermes, at the crossroads, is cut out from an astronomical number of combinations concerning individuals, vehicles, moments of duration: a state of flood. And the happy accident—I love you among a hundred thousand others—is a flood of states. The biologists: Jacob gives just praise to Darwin for having attained his double law because he considered large populations; Monod ushers in his neo-Darwinism, first regarding bacterial cultures, in which it is a question of large numbers, of course less large than the numbers of molecules in a gaseous mixture in a closed vessel, but before which he adopts the same attitude as physicists do before a thermodynamic system; next regarding the very elevated number of possible combinations on the code table or the table of amino acids. The fortuitous event, whatever it may be, is a figure on a background collective: this background is not a cosmos, it is a cloud; if it is vast, it is no longer mastered—it is chaos. Perhaps it is the first and last object encountered: object—objective since devoid of hypotheses; first noise heard—before all else, we perceive the myriad; last—Brillouin is going to tell us soon. The ultimate hypnagogic expanse in which Penelope abandons herself and drowns. Yes to the proliferating world. Set, large number, table, multiplicity, population, collective—its name matters little, nor does it matter who does the naming, the old Bernoulli, Boltzmann, or Kolmogorov. Chance is called a cloud.

Is it so surprising that there is pure multiplicity? Chance is not a thing, and it has no dimension, just like heat or information. If you think of it as a thing and give it dimensions, you will find a bound-together world or a god above gods, namely, necessity, its opposite: an antiphysics, a metaphysics. No, chance is number, a play of numbers. It is even written in numbers. Upon this new blow dealt to the deepest human narcissism, one was appalled that the polypeptide chain should be stochastic and the distant mutations from which we came should form a labyrinth of fortuities. A new Aphrodite, emerging from the Brownian sea. But who was scandalized, long after Buffon's famous needle experiment, at the fact that the sequence of decimals of π should also be random? And yet this sequence is the necessary, invariant, rigorous, endlessly replicated relation of every circle and every diameter, no matter their dimension and site. Choose a length and construct a circumference with that length as a radius; the secret message of this production is written without law or rule. However many times you do it, that's how many times you repeat this message. Chance is written in the code; it is written in the fiber; it is written in the numbers that are called real. Once said, once marked down, it is repeated endlessly. Who was scandalized, once again, at the fact that the prime numbers, scattered as we know in the sequence of natural numbers, are distributed there randomly, numbers that nevertheless, by multiplication—that is, by replication—rigorously produce every possible numeric series? The secret message of these sequences is stochastically written; the numbers are all products of this generator, through repetition of the appropriate rules; they are arranged in a lattice. Therefore, a circle and its diameter, as well as the sequence of whole numbers, carry within themselves a chance message, one that's no doubt irreducible, and this message is, in a sense, constitutive of their being. Hence a theorem by Monod generalized: everything happens as though a determinate, constituted, locatable, and regulated form or intertwining transported and repeated invariantly, when it reproduces a similar form, the same aleatory cloud of discrete elements. Are things any different with the physical constitution of matter? Can't one say that there are, on the one hand, intertwinings of distinguished, specific, and necessary form, such as atomic schemas, molecules, crystals, and on the other hand, under these repetitive determinations, discrete quantum complexions where uncertainty and chance, metastable clouds, reign as masters? But these complexions, according to Boltzmann-Planck, measure entropy and therefore information; this is the aleatory background message. What is an object in general? A message in a cloud plus transports on intertwining communication networks. To take up archaic distinctions once again, everything happens as though chance, since a name must be given, were the very matter that a form multiplies, repeats, or distributes. Yes, chance is, in any case, the very matter of science. Science is a general theory of communication: it studies what is transported on the intertwining—the message, the cloud, the aleatory complexion—and how this is transported. Thus the world as it is, the world as it goes, the world as it lives, the absent world of abstract formalities, is suddenly that library of Babel in which the scattered and disjected books take on recognizable, classifiable, and regulated forms: what is written in these volumes is pure multiplicity. The secret of things is that there is no secret. Open the black box, the hermetic box: Hermes was only transporting a cloud of numbers. New genesis with its numeral wastefulness. Yes, this is the final blow dealt to human narcissism, the hardest one in history, and the most traumatic. The background message is only noise, and no one sends me a sign, and there is no signal: this is true of the most rigorous of my securities, of my distant or familiar objects, of my lived or reflected body, of you whom I caress, and of the starry sky; the fact that, at the end of the reading, there is nothing to read, who can endure that? Einstein himself and his genius couldn't admit that God played dice. Naked horror. The truth. Thus we can understand that philosophers, theoretical people who enjoy the real in the form of totality, which is to say, laws, rules, relations, and history, who enjoy the real in the form of power, detest chance, the way they detest numbers and, no doubt, truth. The white-knuckled fear of leaving one's house, where one is lord and master. And myself, I'd like to see a history that would be entitled: numbers. History is ergodic.

Jacques Monod distinguishes an operational definition and another definition, an essential one, of chance.[14] Doubtless, the uncertainty of the dice throw is due to our ignorance, to the imprecision of our gestures; if we knew all the parameters of the experiment with an optimal exactitude, we would be certain, to the point of exact prediction, of the landing of a six. Hence the reduction of operational chance to lack of knowledge: this meticulous throw of the dice abolishes it. The person who says chance doesn't know or knows poorly. He stays at the surface of things; he doesn't measure. This critique has developed greatly since information theory, and ignorance is no longer a subjective category; it is, in its turn, quantified. What does this demand for a perfectly exact measurement actually mean? In a famous theorem, Brillouin shows that a perfect experiment is unattainable because it would give an infinite quantity of information and would demand an infinite cost in negentropy. The new fact, he adds, is the consideration of the price, of the cost of an observation; the seventeenth-century physicist thought he could move to the limit and consider what happens when errors are reduced to zero: we now know that this movement to the limit cannot be conceived, for it would cost an infinite price. Absolute determinism is a dream, for perfect precision about initial conditions cannot be obtained. In other words, the preceding demand surpasses the limits of possible experiment, surpasses its conditions. It is therefore demonstrable that we can never know the set of parameters of an experiment with perfect exactitude. There is residual chance, residual ignorance, in the operational definition. "What remains essential are the probabilistic conditions of statistical thermodynamics, and the brilliant discoveries of Boltzmann, Maxwell, and Gibbs represent the true meaning of experiment." The operational here refers to the essential, as though to its de jure limits. In the second definition, taken from Cournot, it is indeed a question of the independence of two sequences, and I believe I have just shown that it was never completely established, that it referred to an antinomy that is for the moment undecidable. This is because history, as well, furnishes too many examples of identifications or syntheses between series that seemed, before discovery, to have only empty intersections between one another: the movement of the planets and the fall of bodies, material mass and the speed of light, et cetera. Consequently, we are again sent back to ignorance as a de facto limit. Of the independence, I do believe that only the discretion of the numbers remains. In the first case, the discretion of the complexions remained. Our old results are once again present. But, in addition, the ordinary critique with its definitions of chance that boiled down to ignorance falls away of itself, insofar as science, or rather information theory, its natural philosophy and its gnoseology, gives a nonknown, an unknown, of rigorous appreciations. This is, indeed, the first time in history that we have held the code of the dialogue between knowledge and its dark limit. There is, indeed, in Brillouin, a theory of self-regulating knowledge. The old adequation flaps at the fringe, and this aleatory trembling makes the entire affair. A misfortune that's as numerous as the sands of the desert.

*

Once again, what is ignorance? Here is the starry sky that moral law and twenty physical laws have left forever. The Rorschach inkblot it draws is only a projection test. Is it essentially stochastic? Yes. Through the large number, crowd and collective, through the collapse of Laplacian determinism and through Brillouin's theorem. Uncertainty is the given. *Incerto loco, incerto tempore,* said Lucretius at the dawn of the era: a wind of atoms, a wind of light, a wind of stars, numerous clouds that always surpass the forms thought by me. Just like this pebble I'm holding in my hand, its singular volume, the complexions of its states, its historical erosion, so goes this sequence of amino acids in this polypeptide. I don't master the large number; uncertainty is at the heart of things; the exact infinitely surpasses the conditions of possible experiment. Therefore, the residual stochasticity of the given remains at the limits of experimentation; it founds those very limits. What should we call it if not the real? This is what, at bottom, the principle of objectivity is: not only the suppression of all finalism, not only the erasure of all Rorschach-style design on an all too beloved, all too human world, but also the edge of all knowledge, an edge washed with the waves of innumerable reality. The object, yes, is the nonproject; it is also the unknown or the unknowable, insofar as it is given to me through clouds of numbers and through noise in myriads. For having symmetrized finite and infinite too quickly, philosophy gave itself an easy time of it, an all too cowardly and all too comfortable time of it; but there is this diagonal ribbon that is both the mathematical finite and the physical infinite, the large number, which harbors the secrets of the knowledge of the world and of the experiment I can perform on it, which we must discuss elsewhere. The object is this intertwining, which I know or can know; it is also this cloud, regarding which I can only measure my information and its absence. So chance is indeed my ignorance, and I know its place and its function, and it's the object as it is, which is right here. Chance is the object of science, insofar as it is always *in front of* it: its *ob*-ject, its *pro*-blem. The background object. But I suddenly want to turn the image around: it's science itself that is the edge of chance, of the world, and of the object, the way the land (a littoral cut out contingently) will never be anything but the edge of the sea.

Science says this very thing. Here is a closed system. The demarcation is essential, and Bridgman will generalize this condition to all possible experiment. The closed system develops, and the knowledge I have of it or take from it follows this succession of states. What can I say about it at the start? Not know again, but say, only. First, I have no information about those myriad molecules (a numerical cloud) in random motion. Theory begins with this tautology of the unknown. Or rather, it begins with Socrates: what I know is that I know nothing. And theory links, quite precisely, equiprobability to the fact that I don't have any information. And therefore, its base postulate is that chance is ignorance, identically: what I wanted to prove. But both of them are linked to the number of elements in the game: what I also wanted to say. The *initial* conditions are defined (?) by this triple identity: chance = ignorance = large number. Or again, rather, the expression "having your head in the clouds" has taken on a formidable scientific precision these days. In the final state, the second law having determined the development (not its duration), there is only one state possible, the absolutely most probable one, and I know precisely it: so I know, and there is nothing more than implacable necessity, that of Carnot and Boltzmann. The fact that entropy is linked to information is the greatest discovery of history in the theory of knowledge and the theory of matter. It is, strictly, the link of chance and necessity. Here is that natural philosophy decreed by the science of information. It is inevitable.

I don't like polemic. Not out of fear and trembling, but because I know little about these rhetorical wastes of finesse and blindness, which aren't sanctioned, in the end, by four lines of reason or a single one of calculation. Second, because it is the standard rule that two adversaries in combat generally have multiple intersections, of repertoire and of practice, and especially the practice of debating, in fact, against a third that isn't seen and is the reason for the fight. Lastly, because the behavioral sciences teach us that the violence of an engagement is proportional to the mortal desperation felt by one of the combatants, or of both. I am not very sure whether polemics hasten the outcomes: there are examples where they cover them over or delay them. Amid the noise and fury inspired by Monod's book, one will recognize, in what precedes, the existence of multiple points about which agreement can be achieved: information theory, the second law, and the mathematics of chance are no longer, and haven't been for a long time, causes for war. Should we carry on regardless?

Monod is in a hurry: he is quickly done with history. Not a very common attitude in times when the explication of texts is slipping toward the vertiginous. Scholars, quite rightly, ought to know even better with what quick indifference Aristotle was done with Plato, Nietzsche with Leibniz, and so on. There are several ways to be serious. Therefore, Monod gives himself a criterion, which has created, almost everywhere, evident proofs, filters the texts through it, and then moves on. The future interests him. But it is he and he alone who is interested in philosophy, if one accepts this definition of it: it *synthesizes knowledge and present practices* (and this is where history intervenes, through the layers of heritage that are deposited today) *so as to anticipate* what there is and *what there will be to know and to do*. Historical comparison is not worth one day of trouble without this decision. Look at Jacob: he, too, anticipates; his history has an arrow. Adopt the gesture and be able to, want to, and know how to continue.

A philosopher attentive to the sciences hears, today, amid the technical information, a word of death. The death of our world and the human species. That foreseeable death that's in motion, that death that needs to be conquered quickly. That death our knowledge and our practices have carried in their flanks for about four centuries, which, since yesterday, has reached the point of its abominable birth pangs. There isn't one scientist who doesn't cry it out in the desert, where the noise is deafening. Yes, the question is indeed to survive the inexorableness of the multipliers. Yes, the solutions proposed are still of an extraordinary weakness with regard to the implacability of the questions. This defeat, which is our defeat, a collective one, cries out for help.

*

Goya: two men, half naked, are fighting to the death.[15] Disfigured, bleeding, badly cut, all skin and bones from hunger. The silt and quicksand are swallowing their bodies all the way up to the pelvis. We see that they will kill each other before dying. We see that they are going to die before killing each other. They have the choice. Goya—or the argument of the third man: the slaughterer.

3

Betrayal

The Thanatocracy

I think, I want, I hope I have forgotten, for the sake of my fleeting happiness and my distraught life, that singular kind of terror that passes through the body in what are discreetly called psychiatric hospitals. Sealed-off places, as it has been said, where reptilian anxiety and lethal rigidity spread. I never understood, from the moment this horror gripped me, the fascination these places exerted over the observers of right reason. Robin Clarke makes this fantastical alliance clear—an alliance too subtle for a lover of life.[1]

Outside the walls, you all think you've been delivered, with a free hand, complete liberty, and possessed of an alert, serene, and objective reason. You think that madness has been confined. That the madness that lies in wait for you depends on your mother and father, on the breast you didn't get, on erased scenes from your earliest childhood, et cetera. That is true, perhaps, but under the microscope. Another madness lies in wait for you, so gigantic, so immense, that you need a telescope to see it. All your ideas hide it from you, like clouds. It lies in wait for you; it takes aim at you from the heights of space and from the seafloor trenches. The open world is prey to the most hallucinatory of manias. The planet has entered, whole, the middle of Ward No. 6.[2] It has entered the sound and fury of the irrational—not the irrational of Dionysus, but that of Ares. And right reason has entered with it. This evident fact is like every evident fact endowed with the strength of the sun: impossible to look directly at it, at the height of noon. The sun and death. Read *La Course à la mort,* and you will not reawaken wise. No, you will sleep no longer. Insomniac and schizophrenic.

In Robin Clarke's work, as everywhere else, the question is posed: what would happen if some dangerous lunatic, having come to power, decided at that time to trigger nuclear apocalypse in an attack of psychotic mania? The answer is without dilemma: the end of the world and the human species. The available stock of armaments, according to the most restrictive balance sheets, far surpasses what would be needed to attain that goal. But the question is very poorly posed. It's a question only for those who accept the contemporary nightmare as constituting normal conditions. In fact, there isn't even any question; there is only an evident fact: the dangerous lunatics are already in power, since they constructed that possibility, installed the stocks, and shrewdly prepared the total extinction of life. Their psychosis is not a momentary attack, but rather a rational architecture, a faultless logic, a rigorous dialectic. Study the documents closely, observe the facts, and you'll be persuaded at once that only something like a psychiatry can truly explain the postwar segment of history. You'll be persuaded that we have lived, and do live, under Hitler's posterity: it seems proven to me that he won the war—just as it has been said that the Greeks won the war against the Romans, right after their defeat. His own particular paranoia, which was not individual but historical, overtook every state and infiltrated their foreign policy, without exception. Not one head of state today behaves differently from him in respect to strategy, armaments, and complete blindness to the ends pursued by means of these stocks. Not one behaves differently from him with regard to the diversion of science toward the ends of death. Not one behaves differently from him with regard to the packaging and presentation of that single truth to his people. Whatever the intention, whatever the ideological discourse may be, the behavior is consistent, invariable, and structural, over the entire planet, in regard to thermonuclear forces and intercontinental missiles. I am not saying there are dangerous lunatics in power—and a single one would suffice—I am saying there are only dangerous lunatics in power. All of them are playing the same game and hiding from humanity that they are preparing its death. Nothing left to chance. Scientifically.

Knowledge is born happy. It can be shared, happy, without being able to divide itself. It multiplies, of itself, the fruits of rejoicing. To wither on the stalk, like so many, in a profession that nonetheless is essentially linked to laughter and eros, you must never have received the sharp, delectable sting of a solution or an idea, never have, in fact, evaluated its thaumaturgical power, its profuse bushiness as soon as you give one. Knowledge is born happy for the attentive solitary or the team at work. In its nascent state, knowledge is happy, natively freed from all guilt. It is, perhaps, happy by nature. But in the institutions that manage, exploit, and transmit it, for the individuals crushed by it, it feeds, in fact, the death instinct. My entire youth, I thought I had deciphered, on the walls of the lecture halls or on the brows of the learned, that hideous phrase, Renan's piece of nonsense: sorrow alone is the creator of great things. How did this change come about? I don't know. How can knowledge be returned to its proper nature? It is urgent, under pain of death, to answer that question.

The history of science is an academic discipline. That it entered the university recently is a sign that it can no longer talk about anything but past eras and that it no longer has to talk about modernity. I mean by this the fact that, for the last thirty years or so, the history of science can no longer be conceived in the traditional sense. The sciences no longer have a history the way they, formerly and long ago, once did, because they now have a foreseeable direction, a foreseeable course, and a foreseeable determination.

The question went around: where is the process that was instituted in Greece nearly three millennia ago heading? That question, and others like it. The infantile answer was hidden behind sophisticated answers: if I look forward, the progress of the process is unforeseeable; if I look backward, it was bound to reach here, and history is recurrent.[3] A combination of an ignorance and a statement of the obvious, fine discourses so as not to say that nothing was being said. Those who held them saw themselves crowned with laurels. Everyone was quite content. Some had seen the progress as a river, others saw it by leaps, as needed: rupture and continuity divided two camps; you could have battled over wooden and iron inkpots and that would have changed nothing. For it is always possible to give any solution to an indeterminate problem. You didn't know the happiness of indetermination. The exhilaration of not knowing what, tomorrow morning, the intelligent colleague was going to discover. Yes, you used to have ideas as you had children—blindly. And the history of science was always a little bit that—the vague determination, the risky game, chance. The spirit of the times, the zeitgeist, slack conditions, but there was that echo of a thousand voices, the story of the apple and the indecipherable smile of intuition. No one had truly considered drawing up a map, a guide for not getting lost in the thicket of unknowing. Except for the education of children or for temporary unknowing. I am speaking of inventors, of living science. Absent the program, you played the encounter. It was not gratuitous, of course; the impulsion from behind existed, but it lacked constraints; degrees of freedom remained. Exploration in multiple directions, whatever one thinks of it, prevailed over organized, agricultural exploitation. Rather the picking of mushrooms, from every side—right, left, behind, and more—than the gathering of apples in an orderly orchard. When you had found something, you rolled in the grass, you burst into laughter in the sun, and everything was said. Then you laughed at the neighbors when they, in turn, rolled in the grass with pleasure. Above all, you laughed at the dogmatics of the sufficient condition who spoke in the past tense or the future perfect: it was easy, they would say, everything was in place for somebody to find that; anyone could have done it in his or her place and stead. Those speechifiers, for their part, had never done it; they spoke of a country in which they had never, in their lives, set foot. Envious reactionaries, generally priests in Nietzsche's sense, who had never been visited by intuition. The impotent are always astonishing storytellers. Of histories. It will be said, "You are describing the golden age; it has never existed." I'm less sure about it; at least, I'm leaving it; at least, it no longer exists.

Our sciences have lost their historical component. Because they have lost the indetermination, however weak it might be imagined, of the fields that suggested themselves to the inventive workers. This, in turn, shows that, without indetermination, the history disappears, fades away, and dies out. Replaced by programs that, for a time, freeze the future side of time. The planning brings us back into the orchard in which, in a certain manner, one always works counter to time. Everyone searches according to program and so searches for the same thing. Each program then overdetermines the program to come. And the one who truly searches is the composer of the plan—not the ones who execute it. But today, the composer, in almost every case, is the one who rules at the Ministry of Death. Thus this history of science has a direction, an orientation, a single determination. Necessary, tranquil, predictable, it goes toward Death. Demonstrably. A history of science no longer truly exists because the sciences are now overdetermined in their progress. Science has left history. It has entered a posthistorical era. It has been invaded through and through by the death instinct.

Science has gone beyond its old history; it has lost its living unpredictability. The rejoicing of the unexpected invention, the kind of rejoicing that makes you fall into the well, the secret home of naked truth, where the stars are seen in the daytime, was the sign of naivete. Whoever lived like that made peasant women laugh. I don't see why you wouldn't make them laugh—a goal, in life, that's as good as any other. As long as they laughed when the astronomer fell into their own wells. Everyone got something out of it, beneath the constellations. The old sage, without knowing it, had brought together the only two games where the parties win together, games forbidden by history and society, which only stop because the latter love the hideous zero-sum games to death. The misfortune that befell us was to have chased the peasant women from this field, falling into tiger traps that are no longer set by shepherdesses, but by carrion-eating sparrowhawks. No one, now, can be naive without becoming infantile and dangerous. As long as the well was awaiting you, you could drink cool water. The sap is awaiting you. Don't go forward any longer without watching your step. A hideous monster has gone ahead. Has led the path astray. Has marked it out, undermined it, camouflaged it. The military has rotted the future of science. And politics, its doddering godmother. And science itself, next to which the vilest whore is an intact virgin. Yes, science has begun to kill its history.

How has this happened? Everyone answers, "Through and since World War II." The war that the Nazis objectively won, since no one in the world, among the holders of power, any longer hesitates one minute to prepare, with rigor and method, the end of the world and the Holocaust. The war in which, to use the usual antiphrasis, science was mobilized en masse. As though it had ever been in repose. To discover the etiology of the evil and the crisis, this answer, insufficient, has been repeated since the origin of the Manhattan Project. We shall soon see that we must go even further back, by a century first, then by two millennia at least, lastly by all of history, in order to understand. But is understanding sufficient? Do we have enough time remaining? Let's stay here a moment. It has happened. The abduction of knowledge and its history yet to come by the powers of Death. Conjectural reasons—of economics, strategy, politics—are expounded; recent history, polemology, game matrices, and rat behavior . . . are evoked. It is right to explore reasons. What's important, nonetheless, is the thing itself. The evaluation that can be made of it. Its invariance, today. Its invariance across diverse countries and different systems. The partnership of industry, science, and strategy, once formed, wherever it may be formed, in whatever way it may be formed, metastasizes rapidly and invades space. Economic space, cultural space, space period. It's the partnership of the most certain theory and the most effective practices for the most exigent, imperious, and imperialistic finality. Better, the reasoned partnership of theoretical reason, practical reason, and calculative, predictive, final cause-oriented reason. The submission of every reason to reason. The most powerful and most productive triangle that history has ever put into place. Humanity has certainly dreamed of it, sometimes, but that it has made it function in its perfection—that is new. By means of a lightning-fast and always resumed circulation of financial means, concepts, methods, projects, performances, and refinements along this trinitarian and closed course, the growth of the flux is quasi-vertical. It's a motor. The appalling motor of the new history. It engenders itself by absorbing everything that is not it into its exponential bushing out. It is the most formidable of multipliers, in that it is the product of every conceivable multiplier: theoretical innovation, industrial mass production, strategic one-upmanship. They feed one another. This triangle is invariant everywhere since it is the obligatory channel for certain products. Whoever is in possession of this product—ballistic missile, thermonuclear bomb, orbital bomb, et cetera—has necessarily put the triangle in question into place as infrastructure. It is machine-calculable, by program and optimization. And this triangle necessarily metastasizes by its very nature in the very place it has been formed or, if you like, where it has been put into short circuit. The tree is where the fruit is. The fruit is discernible, here, there. The tree has to have been planted in that spot. Little by little, you see this fruit everywhere. The particular finality is the death of whoever constituted the same infrastructure, so the sum of the finalities turns out to be genocide. Humanity is collectively suicidal. Contrary to what you might think, this finality flatters us; it is strongly dynamic. If it were not that way, the multipliers multiplying between themselves would stop of themselves, for lack of parish priests to serve them. The major interest of the indicated metastasis is that any parish priest, looking to leave the triangle, finds himself there again, however far he may go. This necessity in the repetition defines a death instinct at the scale of humanity. The monster of the collective unconscious has reached consciousness; this would only be a small thing, if it hadn't come to reason. Which does all it can to dissimulate it. You will always find an ideology, a system called scientific, or a consensus of silence to hide the fact from you. I don't mind it being said, thought, or taught that a fact doesn't exist, isn't seen, or isn't thought unless it is constituted or made to appear by the global conditions of culture or theory, but the practice of that idea remains the inverse of the idea. Good perhaps for the historians or the epistemologists, the worst possible for a scientist, who, until someone shows me the contrary, continues to change his theory when a patent fact opposes it. Even if, later, it is said that this fact only appeared owing to such and such a change of horizon. It is one thing to see, retrospectively, the horizons change; it is quite another to change them actively, with one's nose right over the thing. The new and disquieting thing that no longer fits with anything that's already been thought. Or else continue to have confidence in the heritages that carry you. It's for them to sort things out. That would be well enough called cultural idealism. The new face of philosophic passivity. It's one of two possibilities: either a scientific theory is only scientific if it shatters on the test of the facts, or a theory is scientific when it is so true that any fact, whatever it may be, leaves it intact and feeds it. The history of science teaches, if it teaches anything, that the first option is quite probable, and that the second option properly belongs to the history of religion. So have a good theory if you want to remain blind to the facts it is ignorant of. But accept, however, that you've entered religion from that moment on. Now, every theory, today, contributes to, or everyone seems to have an interest in, hiding this patent fact that we are going to die, that all our powers and knowledge are leading us there, and all our pleasure. Yes, our pleasure. Never—I think—has our culture enjoyed so much. Never has it succeeded so well. Never has it made so many people happy. It is believed to be dead, it triumphs. The most sublime, the most heroic of our traditions are finally crowned with laurels. Wherever you go, it's the same magnificent, biblical, superhuman tableau: humanity finally divided into meritorious martyrs and exterminated enemies. Finally definitively divided. The pleasure, the enjoyment of dividing finally satisfied. And for all time. Exhilarating cultural invariance everywhere, giving one's life and enjoying the absolute power of an absolute division, an enjoyment furnished and acquired by the installation of the triangle, itself invariant across all places. *And when an invariant exists, whatever the system may be, the systems are dead, and the invariant is the system.* It triumphs in its turn and everywhere. The most impossible thing that the most imaginative utopians have dreamed of has happened—objectively—hidden beneath the forest of the old many-colored systems. The world government is in place. Everywhere the triangle is invariant, and everywhere it metastasizes. Same science, same technology, same programming—stable means for analogous ends—same growth gradient, the differences playing around the departure times. The world government is in place. *The Thanatocracy.* The government of death. The orbital bombs surround the planet the way the Boulevards of the Marshals encircle Paris. The end of history, the triumph of Reason.

First Generation

You wanted it, you desired it, you taught it to us right from our odious childhood, you who are growing old in terror and horror, unaware of what you have perpetrated. Our odious childhood of famine and bombings, of Jews burned alive and cropped-haired women. Your first piece of work. Only the first in the chain of your delights. You're afraid of our world? But who gave birth to it, who carefully led its abomination, if not you, you who were always afraid, you and those who made you, in sadness and shame? Never have you lived otherwise than by shame, suspicion, division, conquest, terror, and difference. In venom and by death. You have never lived except in the state of corpses. You have loved only death and taught it to your sons and to the sons of your daughters. Today, you'd like them to proclaim something different? You have prevented them from inventing—don't you forget it. Your mothers' breasts were swollen with gall, and you have swollen the breasts of your spouses with gall. The only places in this world where hope is known. You detested happiness and hated rejoicing. Never have you really thought things, really, in benignity. Never have you enjoyed yourself, nor the things around you, nor the thaumaturgic elation of an on-the-alert intelligence. You have never loved anything other than scrawniness, torsion, torture, comparison, and the death pangs of the other. Hell, as you used to say, as the impotent say—hell and being mired in vomiting and beating. You have never done anything except to win, trample, crush, destroy, to win at derisory games that made you tall among dwarves. You have never truly believed in knowledge except for degrees, ornaments, idiotic situations; your scientism was nothing but a pale-yellow handkerchief with which to conceal your little reactive belches. You passed on a hateful knowledge; by darkening it even more with your atrabilious secretions, you made it terrifying. Lethal from boredom, envy, and greed. Lethal. Your perverted children's games have become serious now. They used to be dangerous. They have become fatal. You won't be there any longer to see the monster you gave birth to grow immensely, well beyond the horizon, to the limits of the solar world—from where it trains its gun on us. You are retiring, ashamed down to your blood of your criminal legacy. We will spend hopeless lives extinguishing your debts and the fires you lit with your stingy torches. If we manage it. For you have so many offspring who resemble you and were trained well by you. We no longer have much time, just the short survival you left us, to move ourselves to pity over your feeble anxieties and your comic death rattles—just this minute, forgotten among the work, to tell you what we have thought of you since the last war and our odious childhood. Our childhood tarnished at Hiroshima, for all time. That's one minute too many. One word no doubt would have sufficed. That we forgive you. What else is there to do if we don't want to resemble you? Yes, you are going to die. May your hearts without resource or recourse be put at ease: scarcely some time before us. You will not die because of us; we will die because of you. I want to live. Without your cursed products, the world would be beautiful. And knowledge delectable and a multiplier of fruits to be shared, gracious and free of charge.

Second Generation

How are we to understand that science collaborated so readily with these monstrous enterprises? We mustn't count as a reason that daily cowardice on the part of the crowd of mediocres who spread vinegar within several centimeters with their power so as to satisfy their pedant's aggressiveness and defend the layout of their niche or their specialty. By fact and by nature, that is, for history and for epistemology, science owes its effectiveness to the principles set out during the positivist interlude. I mean by this the reductions that science carried out on the set of its finalities. It is known that, to succeed marvelously in a given practice, it is essential to disinvest from success itself: desire all, lose all. Science recognized that it needed to forgo questions of "why" and limit itself to questions of "how." It was by means of this contraction and a few others of the same family that it became operational. It became a tool; better, the tool of all tools. It owes its power and practical effectiveness to these operational decisions. That is self-evident, like a tautology. But then, an instrument—why? To do what and for whom? See the danger: the reduction of the questionnaire that's administered to the objects rebounds on the questionnaire's global activity. Just as science seeks to recognize how phenomena occur and not why, likewise it comes to understand how it itself functions and not why. Its object, yes, is deprived of project: science itself, suddenly, is an object deprived of project. A polyvalent instrument without end. It is free. By "freedom" I do not mean what politics or metaphysics means by the word, but what mechanics says about it. Or ordinary language. The way it is said that a woman is free when she is not involved in any *liaison,* or when she is no longer in love. Free, without *constraint,* for the taking. Polyvalence without project, yes, reduced to a finality without end, like an art, science offered itself on all sides. So, like Aphrodite in former times, it was Ares who took her and not Hephaestus, the murderer, not the blacksmith. The positivist ideology, necessary, I think, during formative times, entailed—we know it now—the most alarming of risks: leaving treasures of power deprived of program. It was inevitable that the class of invalids who enjoyed the maximum of power should steal that which ensured the maintenance of their post and offered itself without restraint, root, or horizon. Since science, on its side, had great needs—money, for example—to function comfortably, it offered itself to the highest bidder. An old story that Archimedes could have told, but that positivism has heavily aggravated. Auguste Comte had brought a whore into the world.

    That's not all. For science to become operational, it was essential to divide the labor. To split it up according to a rational production line of conditions and complexity. The specialists set about producing as if in a factory: receiving information, orders, and prepared products from upstream, delivering the outcomes downstream to have the finishing touches applied and the frames filled. A global view that the isolated worker does not have. Sectional division, well ordered, focuses attention and multiplies productivity. But, once again, effectiveness's local condition affects the global activity. The workers got used to never looking outside their niche, to no longer understanding the work as a whole. A city inhabited by extralucid regionals, blind to the totality. It had been divided so as to better rule over it. Anyone could steal the city; no one inside any longer had any idea that it constituted a coherent world. Whoever ran it did not work. And commanded. Set up programs. Rooms shuttered, laboratories sealed—a honeycombed city. Better than a factory, Auguste Comte had built a brothel. You discover too late who its boss is.

Third Generation

It was quite necessary for science—constituting a cultural variety all its own, not perhaps independent, but at least defined, locatable, new—to find someplace to live in the cultural universe, in the universe of discourse, of practices. To carve out a place for itself. A subset of Western culture, destined to become the set in its totality, destined to take up the whole place. Today, we're at the extreme limits of the global invasion of our cultural universe by this subset. The proof of this is that we have fewer and fewer concepts stemming from elsewhere to think this nucleus, and more and more concepts stemming from it to think what remains of the old shagreen skin.[4] Hence the interest of the analyses devoting themselves to the border between the properly scientific variety and the cultural set hosting that variety. These questions had been asked in the past by means of a complex strategy of conditions, determinations, and causes—that is, a philosophy of formation. How does the new variety emerge, once the social, economic, and conceptual practices are given, once the set of the other varieties is given? The answers never keep the question's promises. They are always theoretical and global; examined up close, in the concreteness of a historical example, they are undecidable: sufficiency is not reached. The effect, known, is of another order than the set of reasons; the conditioned, nonetheless given, is situated outside the combination of conditions. And this is so in the best case, which is to say, in the retroactive direction. An indetermination that, in the other direction, that of history, was called unforeseeability. Hence the idea that, with regard to the cultural world in its greatest generality, the scientific variety always presents itself, in a certain manner, as a new world. Strongly drawn over the old one by that excess itself. Since Montaigne and the complete revelation of the Earth, there has been no more newness in culture except scientific innovation. Hence the interest of the proposed cartography, since the edges of the variety remain unanalyzable to any reduction: what regions of the old cultural tissue do they border on? Recognizing these edges is a matter of urgency. In fact, it is through the rapid and totalitarian growth of this local nucleus that this bordering has become the entire edge of our culture. This bordering is the wall of our prison. It is, very exactly, what remains of the culture in the time when science has become the total cultural fact. And it is what induces the decisive determinations in science. The unpredictabilities of the past are understood, as though in return. The new variety, localized in a given spot of the cultural universe, was able to grow anarchically into every dimension of a world that reflected, for that variety, unknowing. Anarchy is no more, and growth is henceforth determined, foreseeable, oriented: determined by the edge. By the bark or the membrane.

We ought to patiently take up the thread of prehistory again and describe this edge. We no longer have much time to devote to it at our leisure, to detail what our culture has surrounded exact or rigorous knowledge with and where our culture has placed it in its own space. We must actualize the global project of taking up this thread again—go back to the first etiology and, by its means, understand the imprisonment of reason. How did our race to calculated suicide come about; what made our reason a reason of death? How did it happen that our set of reasoned practices adheres to the death instinct? How did it happen that theory borders on terror? It has been verified a thousand times that knowledge is consistently located nearest to power, to its exercise, preservation, and conquest. At its dawn, it was in the hands of the Egyptian priests and the masters the *Republic* educated along its course of study, et cetera. The theory of science is always as close as you please to the theory of the domination that it provides. And, once again, this is true of Comte: positive knowledge has political positivism as its final cause. Up until the moment when science will no longer be anything other than a mere label for political practice. Being or becoming the master, the possessor, of others and the world. Chancellor Bacon and Descartes repeated this at the rebirth of experimental knowledge. We understand today that it wasn't a question of an epistemological prescription, but of an ethnological diagnosis. Knowing is practicing an exercise that has degeneratively involuted into the ideology of command and obedience. Domination is never anything but the appropriation of legitimate death and destruction. Hence the stadial and only temporary interest of the first description. In the shadow of power, knowledge is in the shadow of death. It curls up and finds lodging in this dark cavity right at the dawn. Who led the primitive Thales instinctively to the foot of the largest tombs in history? Why were the first rigorous graphs drawn, under the fires of the sun, in the fringe of night of Egyptian death? Why did the Pythagoreans condemn to shipwreck the unfortunate geometer who divulged the diagonal's irrationality outside the spaces—already in secrecy—of the sect?[5] All the great inaugural texts of science are shot through with this wrath. Physics of hatred, atomism of dissolution. Why is the true principal moment of scientific rationality—the discovery of communication through dialogue, that is, verification and univocity—plunged in an ideology of hatred of the body and contempt for life, advocating that death is a birth, a liberation, a supreme healing? Reason is deathly sick at the moment of its emergence. Everything is in place right then, at the Greek miracle, that immense historical catastrophe where destruction and homicide transude from the logos. Reason is genocidal from its engendering. To get to the intelligible place, the land splashed with the torches of truth, an entire agonistics and an entire agony are needed. Yes, dying for that country. Geometric understanding, dispersed in lost worlds set off from ours by death, is lodged, ever since the *Meno*, in a master and slave dialectic. Science, the true one at last, tranquilly inhabits the instinct of destruction and annihilation. It becomes culturally natural that knowing requires dying. That knowing requires smashing the object to pieces. Hence the iron laws of all education. To educate is to hammer. No, the education of children was not under the control of Jupiter or Quirinus, the priests or producers, but in the hands of the military. Praise to Socrates, courageous in combat. From Loyola to the Napoleonic secondary schools, what is the difference? Always the military. Knowledge, here, was not born happy, and those who passed it on did so in anger, envy, and horror of life. Knowledge was born in the shadow of the tombs; it returns there just as criminals come back, they say, to the scene of their crime. Civilization is ill from this originary deviation, since it no longer has anything but knowledge and its dark edge. And here we ought to take up the prehistory again from the other end; letting the sun write Thales on the sand, while erasing from the drawing the Pyramidal night, letting the strangers dialogue with the Socrateses, while forever forgetting the *Phaedo* and its other tomb: our body. And for once, the return is possible, since science is a reversible history—the perpetuated return of generations to the start; it would suffice to teach our nephews, from the cradle on, that there is no knowledge without rejoicing. What society, today, could resist this sudden U-turn and heading back of an encyclopedia that has been led astray? You all rest easy; the solution is utopian. The military doesn't even need to be on watch. Look well around you: who, yes, who, well, who loves life? We are all suicidal. Seek one just man in this shuddering Sodom on the eve of the downpour of tar pitch, a just man who loves life unconditionally.

Fourth Generation

The rationality of knowledge is not so difficult to define as is commonly believed. Science is optimal communication. The virtual universality of its discourse and practices is anterior to the certainties it obtains. Only a philosophy referring to the subject, which is to say, idealistic, can overturn this order. When I say, "I love you," even in the best of cases, nothing can assure me of truly being understood. The uncertainty is insurmountable. I do believe, alas, that there is not, and never will be, verification [*contrôle*] in return. And the word is hideous in this miraculous affair. When I utter a theorem, I can assure myself without end that the message sent out is received and thoroughly accepted. Scientific truth is inherently the always offered possibility of a verification in return. The set of these verifications founds scientific rationality. And that's why Plato, and not someone else, really founded it, by means of a philosophy in which roles and counterroles engage in dialogue. Every rupture of dialogue, every gap in verification, ruins rationality. This rupture is called secrecy. As soon as there is any secrecy, science is no longer there. There is effective knowledge, perhaps, but no longer a foundational rationality.

Three kinds of secrecy or secrets can be easily distinguished. Sociopolitical secrecy, well analyzed everywhere: knowledge is in the hands of a given class; those who are outside the class do not have access to it. The secrecy internal to science itself in its sectoral functioning, less often brought to light: from cell to cell, from discipline to discipline, communication ceases to circulate. The more scientific labor is divided, the more effectively it is appropriated in its globality. The specialist is a species deprived of speech, unable to make itself understood by neighboring species. Divide and conquer: meetings and gatherings of more than three people are forbidden. Lastly, the set of secrets institutionalized by the military and industrial sectors. It is quite remarkable here that the army did nothing but apply to knowledge and research the techniques it has long used to keep messages and signals secret. The encounter is historic: the path established by Platonism is barricaded; we should no longer be surprised by the combatants in the *Dialogues* who threaten and rage. Successful communication is the enemy of aggression. War through the jamming and coding of signals is at the foundation of war in general, and it's a war against science. As soon as there is any rupture in communication, there is a major chance of combat, and zero probability of rationality.

The appropriation of knowledge is a function of the rigor of secrecy. Of the limits imposed on the space of communication. On the other hand, the more a message is coded, the less numerous are its proprietors, and, according to the substance of the message, the more powerful they are. The increasing importance of the third type of secrecy since the end of World War II—an increase measured by the installation of growing numbers of technologies of communication—has in return exacerbated the functioning of the first two, so that one witnesses a maximal strengthening of limitations of this kind. So *the foundation of scientific rationality is destroyed.* I do believe that sciences still exist, but they have been invaded by metastases of the irrational. There is knowledge, but the open possibility of verification in return has abruptly decreased, to the point of closing up. As soon as there is no more verification, no more counterrole, there is no more rationality. The network of scientific interferences as a whole no longer has the possibility of being self-verifying: but that was its very reason. Rationality needed countermasters; it no longer has anything but masters, who have the principal attribute of knowing nothing. Rationality finds itself trapped: delirious irrationality invades knowledge because it has lost its own self-verification. So the death instinct circulates freely. Here, the solution, the only one, is the liberation of knowledge— that is, the suppression of all secrecy, of every encoding.

When one is in the presence of a finite stock, the pie and its fractions, any division imposed by force or any exchange regulated by a contract, however one-sided it may be, is never, in the final analysis, anything but a zero-sum game. Let it be endlessly resumed by the parties, and, at each accounting, the sum will be drawn up as zero, with regularity. The abomination of history stems from this repetitive absurdity. Empire designated the winner of the zero-sum game. And it began again. We can no longer conceive of this process except as an irrational abjection. For we know of at least one game where everyone wins, and where, in winning, everyone, enriched, enriches the stakes. Scientific communication or exchange—the foundation of the rationality of exact, rigorous, effective knowledge—is, precisely, this very game. The proof of this is that the bushing-out multiplication of interferences, in the sense that I have given this word, within the very interior of the encyclopedic dictionary, describes its growth exactly. This growth is so strong that it has begun to have a meaning at the entropic scale, which is to say, to acquire the conditions of practical effectiveness, of actual power. The set of the networks constituted by scientists and their local situation, the elements of their knowledge, the very things explored by it and by them, this complex set is capable of complexions and connections so numerous that despite the smallness of the ratio to be established when we pass from binary units to thermodynamic units, the quantity of information, on balance, has ended up attaining values that take on a significance at the entropic scale. The smallness of the aforementioned ratio (10^{-16}) gives endless cause for thought: this smallness is the key to many questions for which, until today, we had only vaguely descriptive answers. Translating the little energies in play on a page of writing into the units of energy of ordinary work reveals a highly significant change of scale. It measures precisely the quasi-cost-freeness of an exercise that can be called theoretical, its laughable performance capacity, taken in itself and at the start. It measures the difference between theory, defined globally, and any practical exercise in the work-dimensioned world, taking the term "work" here in the double meaning of mechanics and ordinary praxis, in its dynamic dimensions and its sense of intervention in the world. When I carry a weight, push an obstacle, throw a projectile, I use and mobilize energies that have practically no relation to those, which we now know how to assess, that are mobilized in this sheet of printing. From this gap, Brillouin derives merely the idea of the quasi-cost-freeness intrinsic to most (tertiary) activities of contemporary life.[6] In fact, the discovery goes much further. Spoken language, along with writing, can be defined as the set of effective realizations of the theoretical project in general. From the perspective of the energetics generalized by information theory, working—plowing, forging, casting, transporting, building, et cetera—is a practice lodged within a scale of magnitude that differs almost infinitely (in Gauss's sense)[7] from the scale where the effectuations of theory, which are practical in turn, are lodged. In short, between what is called theoretical practice and the practice that's well named, the difference is measured by sixteen zeros. We finally know what we are talking about. That measure is an originary delay, a time lag. Upon the hominization achieved through language, or, closer to us, upon the origin of writing, humanity found itself having at its disposal a double energy game, a double program whose elements were separated by a large number, an astronomical number. No relation, in the exact quantitative sense of the word, could exist between its speech or its written form and its work. The only way to achieve this relation was, of course, to obtain an intermediary. Which was, one suspects, the other human, other humans. Slavery. Theory needed the energy quanta of biological or political violence in order to succeed in appearing at the scale of the world. Speech was an order as soon as an ordered practice was sought. It was inevitable that man would transform into a political animal, which is to say, despotic, as soon as its work was that of *Homo sapiens*. No other bridge was imaginable to cross that abyss of sixteen zeros in the energy scale. The monopoly of legitimate violence was taken by the most skillful speechifiers or the best scribes with a view to crossing the unfillable gap between the two programs, the handicap at the start of theory about the milieu to be seen, mastered, transformed. Any biological organization, in fact, includes a quantity of information that has a meaning at the entropic scale: it can rightly be defined as a gigantic machine for translating writing into macroscopic energy. So the biotope in general, humans included, imposed itself as the intermediary blindly sought; it carried energy quanta barely sufficient to overcome the handicap. Hence, and at the same time, the invention of agriculture, the domestication of certain animal species, and the beginnings of slavery: the generalized domination of the biotope. On balance: to link practice with theory, to give a first rational structure to ordinary activities, two programs had to be translated into each other, but that translation was impracticable due to the vertiginous change of scale. But there were precisely organizations that, by themselves, constituted the sought-after dictionary—living organisms. Life, then, turned out to be smack in the middle of the link between the two programs that were separated right from the origin, in nature and by quantity. *Theory had to dominate life to be in a position to dominate the world.* In order for *Homo sapiens* to subsist as such and develop its sapience, it needed to have power over the living in general. There is no finality in this—only a retrospective. The old hierarchy, reputed to be ontological, dividing the kingdoms (the word is telling) into the inanimate, the living, and, let's say, the theoretical, is nothing other than a quantitative energy scale. And we now know that a scale of this kind does not necessarily produce phenomena of simple increase: it reveals worlds that seem heavens apart in difference. In that sharply decreasing scale, the intermediate state functions as a translator of small energies into quantities capable of emerging at the entropic level. That long-standing ontology is an intuitive, dreaming, and archaic way of expressing an exact physics. Consequently, I'll say it again, the aforementioned sapience, as reduced as it may be to the earliest language or the primitive lineaments of writing, went directly, hand in glove, with those machines that could, without knowing, translate it naturally. I say, "Go," and they go. I say, "Carry," and they carry. With the other, I used precisely the fact that he or she, too, was endowed with a double program and a translation device. "Listen to" means hear, obey, execute. As far as I know, every machine for producing is only, has never been anything other than, a translating machine. Theory, insignificant in terms of energy, in order to be or become productive, in order to emerge onto the level of entropic work, finds there, given, machines perfectly assembled for that translation. Easy to produce, to procreate. It suffices to dominate them. To domesticate life in every sense imaginable. Plants, animals, humans. Women first. Granting itself the right to bend life to its designs—or to destroy it if it cannot. Theory, at that very moment, already espoused the possible annihilation of the living in general. Directed toward the world, adapting, as they say, to the environment, speech, before getting there, passed through a dangerous threshold where the inevitable monster, lurking, awaited it: the death instinct. And tomorrow's holocaust was engraved at theory's origin. Science is as dangerous as those overgrown children who never stop, their whole life long, when they dispose of some power, implacably avenging themselves for the offenses that their remarkable weakness had attracted when they were little.

Inversely, the translation ratio, gigantic when read in the other direction, measures the oppressive thickness of nature's system of defenses against the purely theoretical enterprise. A few informational bits in the face of the tens of megatons deployed by a hurricane. Which is why nature could not be, in the immediate and by a direct route, rationally transformable, why its laws were hidden; not concealed by the clever ruse of a subtle god, but inaccessible by the gap between the levels of the scale: a common language between these two orders was unthinkable. Hence that remark, often made, that physics discovered the existence of the weakest forces of interaction first—for example, the Newtonian one. The defense system has the mode of existence of a difficult translation, of a deciphering that demands centuries of research: we find the old language again. But in a single and precise equation. The system exceeded *Homo sapiens* on all sides and by a quantifiable measure, which was formerly expressed in affirming that the real exceeded the rational. The inverse position was idealism. Thus realism was indicative, and its contrary, optative. Not true or false, as in the sciences; not true or false, since they were global systems and their truth-value was not referable to any larger system; not true or false, but undecidable in themselves and by themselves; not true or false, but simply modal discourses. Ways of conjugating a verb—whether action or stative—in various modes. The moment of adequation came, the moment in which the identity, the equivalence of the real and the rational was announced in Western culture: it was, once again, a diagnosis, an ethnological or cultural diagnosis, a diagnosis of the current state of knowledge in general and theory. At that moment, no doubt, the quantity of information contained in the stocks accumulated by the heritage and bushy activity of the encyclopedias was finally going to border on the level of the entropic scale. And that is really what happened at the aforementioned time: the fanfare entry of theory into the macrocosm, into the totality of our practices, its production of horsepower while awaiting its inevitable production of megatons. The abyss of sixteen zeros was filled. Then, every philosophy set about creating endless variations on this final point, this grand finale, by describing the recurrent cycles that had brought this equation about, without suspecting for a single minute that the process was continuing with an exponential acceleration. The new state of knowledge was the crossing of this point.

The gigantic size of the translation ratio is a good measure of what fatality was for classical antiquity, the Turks, and the Christians, and of the weight carried by the ethical counsel of resignation. A good measure of the Stoic distinction between the things that depend on us and those that do not. This philosopheme has hardly any interest anymore, except insofar as it utters the pronoun "us." That said, and the West not resigning itself, the project of closing the astronomical gap on the scale of magnitude entailed a process of an incalculable duration. Hence a new measure: the immense duration to be spent to fill the rift and attain the practical effectiveness of theory over the things of the world, regulated, for their part, by the laws of macro-energy. What is history? Nothing but the birth, marked by blood and tears, of this translation that took ages to speak the very language of the world. The size of the ratio measures its duration. Hence the association, in the nineteenth century, in the same philosophy, of the project of transforming the world, since it's finally possible (What am I saying? The problem posed is resolved), and an explication of historical development through the working class. This is because at the instant of catching up, in the energy scale, the path traveled was finally measured, and the journey itself came, at least blindly, into consciousness. History, or rather prehistory, now closed, is identically the long staggering out—account taken of all the voluntary or unconscious delays brought to its success—of the acts of translation as a whole, of two levels into each other: that of information and that of dynamics, that of language and writing and that of calculated work, that of the rational and that of the real, that of the little energies and that of the energies having weight in the world we live in. A translation that took ages to appear in the broad daylight of work. Sixteen zeros, measure of the originary difference, measure of the handicap at the start of said sapience, measure of the defenses of nature and of the thickness of its former secrets when confronted with the little theoretical strategies, measure of history, of its length, of its bloody track. With the delay made up, the handicap caught up, the defenses dismantled, the prehistory closed, theory has moved forward to the entropic scale. It has the power to unleash the megatons of hurricanes. A new miracle, the second after that of the Greeks: this Greek one opened a path, the one that was no longer to be missed; it's not certain that the other one closes it. The question, now, is to master mastery and no longer nature. The misfortune is that the masters are always those of yesteryear—of former times, of yore, of eternity—and that they are there through death and for it.

Regrets, 1

Cathars, my forebears, having returned from Persia, you announced, in your old language, that the world is in the hands of the powers of evil. And you did not know, you, the first lucid ones, that it was a question neither of a religious dream nor of metaphysics. But of a historical judgment and a prediction. Of a precise prognostication, with implacable accuracy. We have fulfilled, insanely, word for word, your erased writing. We have descended into the inevitable spiral of hell. I now understand why they put you to death without pardon or recourse. You already knew, you were the first to know, that the death instinct was in power, that only an instinct wholly equivalent could dislodge it from power. And that death was equivalent to death. And that, therefore, all politics were equally hideous monopolies of legitimate death, masks of Ahriman. And you left on the roads, half naked, poor, and shoeless. Because you bore witness to the only truth that concerns us, and capable of saving us, they hunted you down to the very last one. No one who held a grain of power could bear that truth. You aroused an unswerving hatred. Your enemy—and mine—was and is death, the death that alone commands and rules. He who gives himself that adversary alone is promised to him by those who love him. They are legion, an armed crowd. They make up society. So you have been erased from the face of the earth. By the rats. The falcons. The sparrowhawks. Men. Whom you loved. Tenderly.

Regrets, 2

Love, not war. Elect the Arapesh . . . The slogan has poor chances of spreading. Come on, be lucid. Biting, attacking, and spreading vitriol take little talent—as well as the morose weakness of the choleric, the native impotence of the aggressive, the complicated overcompensations of the mediocre, the polar frigidity of the vain, smallness of stature, of intelligence and behavior, calculation of suspicions and infantile subordination to the cultural order. He who departs for combat always obeys. Claims to be courageous, while he is a slave. Drunk, drugged, moronic, insane. He follows the steepest slope, the way rocks do. "Fighting like cats and dogs" is a popular witty saying:

"a penny saved is a penny earned," for the skinflint. "Love, not war," that requires too much talent—as well as a power that is found in the people, a positive relation to life lacking in intellectuals, lacking in the middle class, the military, politicians, in those who imposed a culture of twisted sexuality: sadism, masochism, and I don't know what other mechanisms for exciting the exhausted—them. In those who teach children the pathology of eroticism so as to hide the exquisite delights of normality. For that, a calm power is needed, tranquil, will-less, stable, and serene like a tree. Tenderness. For that, knowledge is needed, as well as that vital fortune that gives everything in a smile, and kindness, that high genius of greatness in the corporeal relation. This is because Eros climbs back up the entropy, turns back up the steepest slope. And consequently, it demands the highest human ability. Artistic taste, a touch the violinist learns, a splendid sense of smell, a sensibility that's keen and unfurled like a bouquet. The only art to mobilize all the senses. The tremendous courage to lose oneself in the Other. Something the pusillanimous imbeciles, who manifestly defile all they touch, call death. Whereas its name is Resurrection. Surrection.[8] For that, the fully complete philosophy is needed—the true one, the one that has its feet on the earth and that's deciphered as "the wisdom of love"—as well as an actual perception of the omnitude of the cosmos, and the fully complete human knowledge, even if one doesn't know it and learns it then, plus the burning fire of the deeply moving. And you would like society to stop adoring hatred and death in order to take such difficult paths? It doesn't even need to repress sexuality—that happens by itself. On the contrary, if most weren't pushed into it, few would even have the slightest idea what such repression is. Come on, think about it. If the mighty of Eros were in power tomorrow, humanity would die of shame. Such a transvaluation, saving today, would oblige all the dominators in history to hide in the reeds.

Whole, Parts, Limit, and Edge

Our cursive state in return sheds light on the most important concepts in which our culture recognized itself, the typical form of the recurring situations of history. Nothing is more decisive, in this regard, than the notion of parts. Division in general, partitioning, even vague, remainder, or residue. Every situation, whether of theory, activity, or history, is local, definite, forms a tableau amid a different space. Said situation is equipped with borders, edges: it is a place that's plunged in a milieu, or the middle of a vaguer place, indefinite. No man's land, barbarism, primeval forest, wild sea, ignorance, other worlds, utopia; the white or the possible, which is rejected, perhaps, but representing, in the final accounting, *the reserve*. A withdrawal is possible from a waiting stock. A space in which to camp in case of accident. A broader theory in which the knots of theory are simply undone. Our place is partitive, like a sacred *templum;* the future comes from elsewhere, where it is in exile. It is open if and only if there are places outside the one in question right now. From which all possibility happens: loss and profit, deviation and disequilibrium, supplement and motricity, excesses of every type.

It is possible that the theory of science no longer has anything more to say about science in general than to designate the emergence, in every region, of a play of limitations, proper to each of them. Since Gödel and a few others, the limits of formalization are sufficiently well known. The maximal entropy of a closed system marks the boundary of its irreversible evolution. Brillouin's great theory on the infinite cost of negentropy for exact experimentation closes the series of approximations of measurement, observation, and objective apprehension in general. We are just about fully informed about the distortions of any phenomenon by its gnoseological interception. Every intervention strategy, in the final analysis, meets with this constraining play of limitations: whether it's a question of theoretical intervention in a theoretical field, of theoretical intervention in an objective field, or of practical intervention in a practical field. There are edges for every strategy.

Everything would happen, then, as though epistemology had to be transformed into a general theory of effective limitations. It would no longer have to know either the true or the false, which is the business of science itself, or the effective, or the coherent, or the fecundity of methods, or in general any description of functioning, but it would know the end and term of the set of processes. It is clear that an observer can stand outside a space if he or she contents him- or herself with describing its borders. "Where does he stand then?" is perhaps a real question, or perhaps only a naive image. Everything would happen, unexpectedly, as though a certain Kantianism, lost up until now in the mythologies of subjective reason, set its feet on the earth: here, the limits of the power of knowing are demonstrated, quantified, and perfectly assessable. But only a theory of edges would remain of it. And that alone.

At these bounds of power, epistemology meets with questions it was not trained to deal with. It was trained to speak of theoretical intervention in a theoretical field, or theoretical intervention in a practical field, pure mathematics, logic, or experimental knowledge, even if its discourse wasn't always pertinent. It could, well or poorly, answer the question, "What can we know, and what is said knowledge worth?" As soon as practical intervention in a practical field is dominated by scientific strategies, it encounters the question, "What to do?" Not "What should I do?" or "What should we do?"—*should* being defined by reference to cultural sets that have nothing to do with the sciences—but only "What to do?" in the light of said strategies, effective as much as you please, but reaching, them too, an edge, a pocket, a limit. It is now necessary to define the latter—and not in dream.

The set of limitations to the power of knowing meets with the set of limitations to our powers of intervention. Of intervening rationally, by means of science, in practical sets. There again, the old moralities, the old ethics, lost up until now in various cultural mythologies, are setting—and brutally—their feet on the earth. For that is what is at issue, the earth, in all precision, space, our space, and the material stocks, the terraqueous globe, time, quite simply that of history and that of our lives. The old spell of final ends has taken on a hallucinatory body for a humanity that's finally awoken (too late?): the end is there, in front, and almost inevitable, and it is really the last one, calculably. There's our limit. It is not theoretical; it is extrapolatable from our interventions. Consequently, *any future ontology can only be thought by reference to that limit,* just as epistemology can only be thought in reference to the other limits.

The rest is hollow dreams, literature, opium. If the epistemologist does not directly encounter that question—what to do?—he is not speaking about science. He is dreaming about it.

We have reached the edges of our interventions. The reason for this is simple. In every strategy, if there is a reasoned game, there is always, bound up with it, a gain and a loss. However much you reasoned by totalities, said totalities were always relative; positively, they were parts. The engagement always took place over an object cut out in time and space by means of a local and partial technology; gain or loss resulted from it, either withdrawn from or added to a stock. That was even one of the constraining conditions for the effectiveness of intervention. And for the possibilities of historical development. The oneiric game of the totality, of the all and the nothing—aesthetic, admirable, monumental, ineffective—was left to philosophy. Everything happens, once again, as though the grand dreams of Romanticism were coming true all of a sudden, as though they, too, were setting—and brutally—their feet on the earth. It isn't by accident that we say strategy, and no longer tactics. There are no more fights, combats, battles from blow to blow: the first blow makes and unmakes the entire war. We are seeing the close of the dialectic. Positively, this means that the total set of knowledge is henceforth mobilized, the remainders being minute, on practical fields in which the totality of space is concerned, with no place serving as an exit or field for planting for another renewing spring, and in which the totality of time is engaged, beyond every futurology, without a foreseeable moment for a different spring—that is, on sums of energy just about equivalent to the sums in play in the natural world. As soon as these totalities are in play, there are no more remainders; there are no more parts. The new game: a game without parts. All the stocks are engaged. Practice has at its disposal the set of the totalities that theoretically emerged in the Romantic age. It does not leave behind those remainders to which the tradition has accustomed us, by which the game could always recommence, at least elsewhere, as soon as the bank was broken, whether here or there. History was a global strategy of remainders. There are no more foreseeable remainders.

*

Game theory provides good strategic models, clear and distinct matrices, often applicable to determinate concrete situations. It gets complicated, of course, and can get lost in indeterminacy when three or more players are present. Brought to the case in question, we have known how to criticize the theory, stake out its limits, lay down conditions, and restrict its usage. In general, inventing a game—its strategies and matrices—is only of interest when it is playable a certain number of times. Whether you win or lose, the gain or loss results in an increase or decrease of your stock. The end, for the global loser, happens with the exhaustion of what he or she proposed to risk. Can you propose a game where it would be possible to play with only a single move and where all the players would risk the totality of their stock at the same time? When I say "the totality," I mean that they forfeit any possibility of survival, that the stock that's risked is their life, their ecological space, their future. When I say "the totality," I simply mean the world and history. This game, you will grant, would be perfectly absurd, or only conceivable, at the limit, for a vague population of perverse paranoiacs. And yet it's this precise game that all the living forces of contemporary reason are preparing. The other games are pregames. The calculation of probabilities has nothing to say about this gap between the nonrecommenceable unity and the totality, a calculation that invariably presupposes a collective and multiplicities. Admittedly, the set of all sets cannot be conceived; still less can it be wagered on dice. Except in military circles, where the theory of strategic games is that ruse of reason that, playing at past wars, in which things had remained open, prepares the last war in which they will disappear. *Quales artifices pereunt.* Who will remain to celebrate what great calculators and munitions pyrotechnicians they were?[9] A few survivors—hallucinating and disfigured, emerging from some Scandinavian underground gallery—will remember, with hatred, scorn, shame, confusion, and horror, those odious animals that we are. The presence of their fellow man, their odor, their noise, will leave them gasping for air, collapsing in disgust. Who could wish for them to have safeguarded a single mirror, to contemplate a distorted face related to ours?

*

Every philosophy of movement and history, of the movement of history, assigns or constructs a motor intended to produce this movement. And first of all, it's one of two possibilities: either the motor is outside the moved, or it is inside. Every moving object has a tractor, an attractor, a pusher, et cetera, or is self-moving. Knowing where to put God is the archaic and metaphysical formulation of the question: transcendent or immanent, prime mover or identical to nature. Hence the modernity of Spinoza, when nature did not yet have its own effectiveness: he brought, forever, the motor into what is moved. So that only the motor itself existed any longer. And, once again, it's one of two possibilities: either the motor is the whole of the moved, or it is localized there in a definite place. First case, nothing exists outside, and nothing inside, except the motor itself: you get the absurdity of perpetual motion, or, if you like, eternity in act. For a closed system reaches, at term, extinction. Hence Spinoza, rightly: God is substance and not motor, antihistory, or ahistorical. The motor must consequently be localized, here or there, in the moved. Inside the moved, it is not closed or shut, for, once again, it would become extinguished in the end. It needs to feed, to find around itself what we call sources. But if nothing exists outside the moved, it can only find food in the very thing it moves. If the motor is in the moved, it functions by the reserves, the stock, the capital that are present. The reservoir, a term used by Carnot and Bergson, furnishes, stroke by stroke, the supplement of energy that adds, by means of the motor, to the inertial headway. That something extra that allows going further forward. This something is a part taken from the whole: the reservoir, the capital. The entire question, consequently, turns around those parts; around the sum of stock, around the consumption of the sum.

Assessing the global stock seems impossible to me. This assessment comes up against three antinomies, concerning space, time, and the unforeseeability of the exploitable. If one says "the moved being closed, the reservoir is finite," that is not sufficient, for there do exist some very large finite things, things too big to be practically counted, that are equivalent to the infinite at the human and historical scale. For example, the sum of the sun's energy. It's not in this way that reasoning can be done. We have to describe directly how the motor functions. It is composed, as we have seen, of the industrial complex articulated to scientific research in its quasi-totality, both given military applications as final cause. This motor is the most dynamic and the most powerful that history has ever put in place. First of all, it is indeed a motor: insofar as it is the product (that is to say, the intersection) of our most effective multipliers (invention, production, innovation), it produces an inexorable movement, ceaselessly accelerated; insofar as it metastasizes rapidly and invades space: it grows, of itself, and regularly spreads from border to border without being notably transformed by the diverse conditions that rule here or there; insofar as it drives an increasingly powerful set of material, economic, intellectual, human, and political elements; and insofar as it mobilizes the most advanced innovation and makes the majority, a growing majority, of the new products and performances. The multiplication, the movement, the metastasis, the expansion, the drive, and the newness are in this place and by this place. It is a motor; and it is perhaps the motor, insofar as it homogenizes the partitions, insofar as it is invariant across the diversity of reference systems.

How does it function within what it drives? First, it draws from the reservoir, from that reservoir I said was difficult to assess. It draws energy, work, and information from it. The accelerating rotation of the flow within the triangle formed by the motor causes it to draw increasing quantities of these stocks. Parts that are increasingly total. But let's suppose that this is not dangerous, to the benefit of the impossibility of the inventory. The question shifts from one source to the other. Any given production returns to the reservoir (there is only it apart from the motor) something of what the condition of functioning took from it. The length of a possible history is roughly proportional to this relation: the weaker it is, the more chances there are for homeostasis; the stronger it is, the more the acceleration speeds up. And, once again, since the inventory is antinomic, you can bet on acceleration, but only bet—it entails a risk. A weak enough risk, on the whole, as long as you withdraw parts, as long as you reason by parts, as long as you practice on parts. On the other hand, there are quasi-entirely negentropic productions, like agriculture. Hence the real future of a neophysiocracy, at least technically speaking. Let's get back to the relation of the withdrawal and the product that's returned. It must be partitive and inscribed within certain limits. But the new products exceed them, just as much as you please. They are now *of a power that is roughly equipotent to the global energy reservoir.* History, then, is no longer played, from move to move, based on the parts, but rather based on the totality of available stock. Time is no longer defined based on the successive episodes of the game, on the promises and risks of the matches to be recommenced, but on the black expectation of the only move that is henceforth possible. Time no longer has a path, nor a definition: it no longer has but one end and one term. Our history is a suspended inchoative. That's because the motor produces the equivalent of the reservoir. It produces *world-objects.* Objects with the dimensions of the world, in the precise sense of dimensional equations: for space (ballistic missiles), for speed of rotation (geostationary satellites), for time (the life span of nuclear waste), for energy and heat. We no longer play percentages or ratios, but rather the totality of available capital, and the game is quite finished. Technically finished, temporally finished. We now know what "mastering nature" means: producing machines equivalent to it, making the natural and the artificial approximately equal. And, once again, this would not be dangerous but for the third segment of the triangle: if the totality of the product were poured, in a way I have trouble imagining, so utopian does it seem, into the stock of the reservoir. No one wants this magnificent happiness; the suicidal have said, from time immemorial and forever, that good literature, good philosophy, good science, good technology, et cetera, are not made by means of good sentiments. Fair enough, then let's not hesitate to make good literature, et cetera, by means of bad sentiment. Where the edge is found again. The affair having become this ingrained, everything therefore happens not in alliance, but amid fury. Owing to an exquisite partition, in which everyone finds his delight, but which is patently shown to have no other meaning than a lethal one by the existence of the invariant motor, the totality of the product is integrally directed toward the total destruction of the total reservoir as final cause. Look at the list of world-objects: not a one is an exception to the rule. *Humanity has neither known how nor been able to produce a single object of the physical dimensions of the world that works to its benefit.* As far as I know, humanity seems, there, to indicate its truth. I don't know whether there was an original sin, as is told with a rare consistency by the myths and philosophies, but who doesn't see, before us, the gigantic final error into which our entire past is projecting itself? In which our little gestures accumulated over millennia are summed up and consummated in a giant model. Final contradiction, final in every dimension: space, time, work, energy..., world, history... Final end. I don't see how it is possible to think anything at all, to work at anything at all, without referring to it. The condition, from now on, for all theory and all practice. But who agrees to see it?

What to do? With one's back to the wall, it's always the Stoic who speaks. The old Stoic who, formerly, attempted resignation in a world tightly woven with the natural series of a necessary fabric. Ataraxia, the limit opium of limit suffering. Hence so many opiums today, and of all sorts, in a milieu of artifacts imitating nature as closely as possible in its dimensions, its networks, and its force. Fighting? Places for combat only exist here and there, in the name of a large number of partitions. This amounts to speeding up the process, and it's not this morning that you should be in a hurry to accelerate history, if this is indeed its trajectory. At the end, it is always the same people who pay, the slaves furthest from the decision. And the decision of the supreme game precipitates all of humanity into the same place. Even if Clarke and others, me included, may be more or less wrong in our estimation, there remains a risk that you can reasonably refuse to take. That you can mathematically refuse to run. Leaving things as they are is, mathematically again, almost as great a risk. The situation is of a luminous simplicity: regardless of whether one takes on the fight, the outcome of the game is almost invariant. Try to calculate power relations when the forces put into play approach the sum of the energy available on the planet... It is a quantity that defies relation.

*

The only real possibility left to philosophy, since its only tool is discourse, is to speak at the level of one of the triangle's three components—science. The only one, precisely, that—at least in its content and behavior—is universal. And which is, in the chain, the weakest link. It is not possible for philosophy to intercept the flow in the triangle, except at that spot. Scientists of the world, unite. Sit by and do nothing as long as your specialty remains joined to the project of suicide. The interruption of work and information, this universal strike of the scientists, is bound to cut off every point of application. For a time to be determined, educated humanity—the workers of the proof—must only pose and resolve *demonstrably useless* problems. Since just about all the utility of knowledge is channeled toward death. The rest is to be closed to take inventory. And the inventory is to be done by taking the mortal limit as the reference for thought. Here the critique is no longer theoretical, subjective, and conditional, but practical, objective, and teleological. It no longer consists in seeking the conditions of possibility, in the thinking subject of a theoretical purity; it consists in diverting a practical set of information and tools from its actual end. The end is the reference: the limit where every conceivable figure of the death instinct that the quasi-finite totality of history has laboriously drawn, realized, and perfected is projected on a giant screen, on a giant mirror. The only hope that remains is this critique by means of the end, is the putting into short circuit of the knowledges and products, present and inherited from the millennia, with the final scene, the final conflict, the apocalyptic and definitive holocaust that they are preparing with the attentive meticulousness of the unconscious. This critique defines a critical point in time and history, where the history of reason's past finds itself face to face with the end of its hopes and future. The face of imminent death stares at the virtual figures of the death instinct scattered in the exercise of reason. In this critical point of the present, for a time that's still living, the deadly past, in a flash of lightning, meets the future and its hole of nothingness. The total history becomes involuted in this place, about which it can assuredly be said that if this place does not take place, our survival will be brief. In this critical point, amid the dazzle of that flash of lightning, something can and must happen: *the imminent death must kill forever, in a single instant of collective and historical consciousness, the death instinct that engenders it, and vice versa. Death to death,* philosophy's last word. We will cross this threshold; we will see that flash of lightning, or we will pass away, among the thousand suns of our infernal reason. This threshold crossed, we shall begin to speak of immortality. Of the new science.

Part II

Philosophy

4
Descartes Translated into Statics Language

The Circle

The order of reasons visibly organizes Descartes's philosophy. Its intuitive model, proposed by the author, is a chain. This is a technological image: the logicians of the Middle Ages had used it; the widely known theorem of the weakest link appears in syllogistic analysis. The image and the logical referent end up at the highly debated question of the circle: everything seems attached to the first link, the chain's fixed point, but, at the end of the accounting and the process, the fixed point of divine veracity propagates the guarantee of its stability backward through the chain, in such a way that the deductive linkage seems to close over itself, as in a feedback loop, which runs contrary to the strict order of the process. It is a question of a chain with two fixed points.

It is difficult, unless one multiplies the number of chains, to go beyond these results through logical analysis and description of the technological model. This description, strictly speaking, allows one to resolve a minor problem: that of knowing whether the preceding moment is fully used in the following one or only partly used. For a chain is not only that succession of metal rings used to anchor, moor, or dock ships. It is also a series of gestures and posts in a work or a productive process.[1] This meaning is presumed to be a contemporary one, but it seems to me to apply wonderfully to the Cartesian meditation insofar as this latter not only establishes an objective series of results independently of the one who poses them, but also leads the subject into the productive process and describes the subject, its act, and the object they create at each stage. It has recently been demonstrated, in chain technology, that a chain is highly fragile if the antecedent step furnishes the following one with just what is sufficient for its act. For the linkage to acquire a reasonable reliability, there must be an excess over this sufficiency; the preceding step must give a little too much to its successor. This is called the intermediate stock. A chain is all the more solid, it is all the less subject to stoppages, it is all the less prone to ruptures or breakdowns, when it transports much more in each point than what is required. It is not the objective image of a chain that is in play, but the flow of communication it transports. If, therefore, in Descartes, there is always more in the upstream link than what would be necessary for the downstream one, this is not a logical error; it is a maximization of security, from the technological point of view. It is an optimization of reliability via intermediate stock, an optimization that's all the larger when there are connections, crossroads, a plurality of chains. But this is a minor problem, which doesn't resolve the still-unresolved question of the circle.

Let's change technological models for a moment. In reasonably numerous places, Descartes refers to architectural metaphors. The solidity of a construction, he says, is guaranteed at its base by the digging of a foundation and the materials placed there; it is measured by its height, and so on. I propose to take this image seriously. Just as we reason about a chain (the technological image) and a linkage (the logical referent), let's reason about a construction (the image) and its referent, which is to say, mechanics and, more precisely, statics. To my knowledge, Descartes was a better mechanist than logician, and while no technical treatise on deduction can be found in his work, there are, quite the contrary, several profound reflections on simple machines and mechanical curves.

In a way, we move from the abstract to the concrete, in statics, when, after having stated the conditions for the equilibrium of a point, we state the same conditions for the equilibrium of *systems*. A detail, however, regarding the point. Let there be a circle placed on a straight line. The diameter, perpendicular to the straight line at the point of tangency, defines on the circumference a low point and a high point. Equilibrium is stable at the low point: this means that no matter the force that impels the point out of its site, an opposite force will bring it back there. This is the pendulum principle, if you like. By contrast, the high point only enjoys an unstable equilibrium: this means that no matter how small the force that distances it from its site, no opposite force brings it back; so it is precipitated to the bottom. Let's keep these two results in mind and move on to the statics of any nonpunctual body.

A building, in the Cartesian metaphor, is such a body, which is to say, a system. How might one be able to write the conditions for the stability of an entire system? Intuitively, there must be three such conditions.

1. It must form a system, which is to say, a bound-together unit; this condition of parts being bound to each other allows us to move from the abstract statics of the point to the concrete statics of bodies. The condition only says that there are bodies that are not divisible for our purposes into points. I shall call this condition the *coherence* condition. "Coherence" is a Cartesian word, which can be found in many places.
2. This coherent body, this system, is therefore composed. It holds together, as they say; how does it hold itself in equilibrium? Why is it stable? It remains so under two conditions. First, it must have a low point that is itself in stable equilibrium, in the sense I defined above. No matter what the force that tends to displace it may be, the point tends, via another force, to return to its originary site. Let's translate: no matter what my reasons for doubting may be, however big the force of my doubt may be, the force of my certainty will return me to the aforementioned point. Descartes here uses the word *force* or its equivalents, and he

experiences, at the limits and like a good statistician, by means of the greatest force possible, hyperbolic doubt. I am fairly content here with the use of the word *hyperbole*.²

3. But this condition, as you can see, is only an abstract condition, one concerning only the statics of the point, of a point, the low point. It is henceforth fixed, invincibly. Supposing that a bound-together body, that a coherent system, for example coherent and bound together by the order of reasons, only has a fixed point—the low point—and that in every other point equilibrium would only be unstable, in the sense I defined above, then the entire system would be unstable; it would fall. It would fall according to a circle around the fixed low point, which, for its part, doesn't move. Therefore, it would be necessary, and necessary absolutely, to write a second condition. Fairly far from the first point, a high point that also satisfies the condition of stability would be necessary. Without this condition, no matter what the foundation of the low point may be, the system, qua system, would not be in equilibrium. With this condition, the system would be in equilibrium. What's more, it is from this second condition that the global stability of the bound-together body stems. The first condition forbids displacement or wandering; it brings back to the center, the way a pendulum is brought back; but the second one forbids falling; it forbids the rolling; *it forbids the circle*. I am fairly content, on the other hand, that this point is called: high.³ And that regarding it Descartes wrote: *vis et lux* [power and light].

Assigning a second fixed point, which, as in feedback, would bind the system back to itself and bring it entirely to the stability of the low point, far from being a mistake, is a necessity; far from defining a circle, it forbids it. But to escape these old woods, a slight displacement of models was required. A shift from the image of a horizontal concatenation and its referent—linear and abstract logical order—to the genuine Cartesian image of vertical (*altum*) construction and its referent—the static skeleton. Everything then becomes clear, distinct, necessary, and sufficient.

On balance—you can say that again—we find linkage once more through coherence, series, nexus: since the two points, high and low, in their turn, define a straight line, a chain, the axis of cohesion and of stability of the global chain, which can always be called a system for more demonstrative reasons; we also find geometry again. For, in Descartes, there is no other treatment of statics than the geometric order of reasons, that is, of proportions. It is sufficient to look at his simple machines. Statics, which is to say, geometry, still dominates kinematics. The situation is the same in Spinoza: his *more geometrico* is a *more statico,* indissociably.[4] One needed to wait for the invention and welcome of infinitesimal calculus for statics to become, rather, a particular case of kinematics or dynamics, and for rest to become a limit case of motion. Auguste Comte has indeed told these histories. And it is quite simply from this state of mechanics, a state anterior to the Pascalian or Leibnizian revolution, that the illusion arises—the belief that time is discontinuous for the Cartesians. One went and looked for this illusion behind the method, more or less stated, but, above all, taken up again after d'Alembert and Lagrange, that motion was a succession of equilibria. Quite the contrary, the entire Cartesian treatment of mechanical curves shows that he thought it was continuous.

In any case, the statics solution to the problem of the Cartesian circle is only a remarkable episode in the treatment of the fixed point, which dominates the seventeenth century. It is possible to find chains with *two* fixed points elsewhere: for Huygens, in *Horologium Oscillatorium;* for Réaumur, in his essays on thermometry; and, as far as I know, in all of post-Keplerian cosmology. What a significant error for the philosophies of the Copernican Revolution to have always forgotten the *second* point. The one that is not the sun. There is a point that is the sun; there is a second one that is not the sun.

5

Leibniz Retranslated into Mathematical Language

System and Morphology

Leibniz's philosophy is systematic. What makes showing this state of affairs difficult is the widely recognized existence today of several ideal or pure types of systematic form, the coexistence or rather encounter of at least two of these types during the seventeenth century, and their blending within the author's texts or projects. The historical weight of his work is due in large part to the complex connection of a deductive formalism, stemming from the mathematical sciences and culminating in a renewal of them, and a theoretical morphology, stemming from new mathematics and suitable for describing totalities like those of life. In other words, systematic form is safe either when algebras and logics are of concern or when topologies are of concern. Perhaps we must understand that Leibniz produced two systems (at least) in one; we definitely have to admit that he used combinatorics (initially a technique of manipulation, later elevated to the status of a universal doctrine) as an organ of connection—connection between a universal analytic and a universal aesthetic, for "system" in the first sense is equivalent to an analytic, and the rigorous morphology is equivalent to an aesthetic.

There is system, first, on the ancient model of Euclid's *Elements,* when the discourse is presented *more geometrico* [following a geometrical manner], after the manner of Spinoza or, more obscurely,

Descartes. A coherent corpus of propositions is rigorously deduced from a small number of propositions set forth beforehand and from them only, according to an irreversible chain. This is the axiomatic project, about which it can be debated whether it is a method, in the heuristic sense of the word, about which it can be said, at least, that it was, that it sometimes is mere clothing or rhetoric among other bits of mere clothing or rhetoric. Is this the case with Spinoza? Many have claimed this, including Leibniz, who have nonetheless never shown, as d'Ortous de Mairan demanded, where the paralogism is. Leibniz is the first to carry out this project, the first to correctly state the general conditions of the effective enterprise he supposes. In saying this, he reinvents formal logic and discovers, in its globality, a new landscape: mathematical logic and, to put it quickly, the new mathematics and the philosophical debate reinvigorated by it not too long ago. Hence his position in relation to the rhetorics of the dogmatists of the seventeenth century: he didn't produce any definitive text in which his philosophy would be concretized in and by a single formal system; on the contrary, he produced many, under variable headings, leaving the doctrinal core unscathed and invariant. The latter remains single and stable across the transformation of the order of statements. There is only one theory of numbers, but there are as many systems of numeration as you like: it suffices to change bases. Hence the solution to an old problem of the commentary, which was no doubt impressed by the order of reasons, the Spinozan *mos* [manner], and the reference to the Euclidean monolith, which had nevertheless long been plucked clean: the system, it said, is aimed at and not in any way realized; it remains in the planning stage; it is only a dream (and Diderot did say "dream" in place and stead of "system" out of precaution, critique, honesty). The proof is that it was never written, or if it was, it was in a thousand forms and presentations that attest that Leibniz had hesitated, clothed, and failed in a design that, if it had succeeded, would have taken on the Euclidean manner. Answer: the effective, operational, and formal conditions of any system in general are, first of all, set forth by him, not all of the conditions certainly, but at least forever; the proof is that the scientific nineteenth century, from the reopening of the field of formal systems onward, with one voice granted the paternity of its first designation to Leibniz and not to others. Descartes is the forefather of a geometry that has almost vanished; the *calculus ratiocinator* is the original attempt of our living mathematics, precisely conversant with what a system is.[1] The fact that, on the other hand, the monadology, or the philosophy of substantial communication, has been redrawn a hundred times shows that a scenographic series can express an invariant ichnography in multiple ways:[2] Leibniz according to the orders of Reason. Is not the one who does the clothing the one who believes the monk has only one outfit, which is charged with making him what he is? Harlequin, for his part, has a thousand outfits and has never seen but one country over the course of his travels. There were times, happy ones, when one was unaware that there were a number of *mores geometricos* [geometrical manners]. That said, the Leibnizian system is comparable to the Euclidean ideal in that it knows, beforehand, how to cut up the elements. There exist, primitively, *stoicheía* [elements] in general. The cutting up varies according to the region where the system is going to be constructed, but the elementary set is present. The primitive is a term. Pluralism is not primarily an ontological decision; it is a method; the endless argument over the oneness of being or its multiple dispersion is undoubtedly undecidable, or it conceals any attitude one might like, including political ones; its operational character remains: pluralism is a set-based strategy. In the final analysis, it is science itself, the possibility of mathematizing, at least of reasoning, articulating, and producing. Set, elements, and relations. Music: notes and intervals are the first givens, in the old sense of *systema* and *diastema* in the *Timaeus* [35b–36b]; combinatorics: any notes whatsoever and variations or reciprocal situations; algebra: letters and operational symbols; geometry: points and respective sites; language: depending on the level of attack, sounds, letters, words, sentences, or languages themselves if one is seeking the original linguistic core, and again, the meanings for a given sign or the definitions for a cut-out word; theory: the set of truths that are analytically finite or of infinite decomposition; and so on. God's understanding is the game space of possibles. The elementary world is constructed by cutting up, while remaining elementary: atoms, forces, life principles, monads. Theorem: these monads are both the veritable atoms of nature and, in a word, the elements of things. This must be read: monads are to the nature of things what notes are to combinatorics, letters to written languages or sounds to words, points to geometry, truths to the logic of certainty, and so on: *stoicheía*. Not that monads *are* points, notes, atoms . . . ; they are natural elements, *the way* the others are linguistic, mathematical, musical . . . elements. And so, first, cutting up into parts without parts taken to be simple and primitive; not that they *are*, absolutely speaking, simple and indecomposable, since it can be shown, just as much as you might like, that they sometimes envelop multitudes; but they are *posited as* simple. *Substantiae vel suppositi* [substances or suppositions]. Thus we learned, in the seventeenth century, to recognize, at the start, elements and relations, about which hypotheses can or cannot be made, in all clarity. Of course, this in no way has anything to do with arbitrariness: the sufficiency of the hypothetical level depends on the object, on its region as much as on the system to be constructed. Second, establishing a *catalog*. Leibniz devotes himself feverishly to this other moment of systematizing activity. Because giving oneself elements and relations is not everything, when possible one should draw up a list of them by sets, and when this isn't possible, due to their number, even their infinity, they should be ordered along a scale as is seen in the *Monadology*. The *De arte combinatoria*, right at the very beginning of the work, calculates and forever closes the lists of possible variations for the domain of the discrete finite, whatever the content might be; this victory has never been forgotten, except by French philosophers, for it is a victory over Descartes: here, the enumerations *are* complete and the reviews *are* general, the guarantee that nothing was omitted or repeated having been secured by a mark. Hence the tremendous blossoming of the synoptic enterprise for the combinator: the exhausting pursuit of the closure of every possible list. Here are alphabets, linguistic ones, signaletic ones, numeral ones, the global project of the alphabet of human thoughts computed up to the maximum limit; chains, interspersed with subtotals; maps, in which the sciences are likened to seas and continents, *de continente et contento* [of container and content];

projections, in which the multiple anamorphosis will end its scenographic cycle in the horizon of an ichnography; harmonic tables, double entry, equipped with a law of closure, the mother idea of the idea of the matrix; registers, medical ones, demographic ones, bills of mortality, inventories, classifications, plans, programs, dictionaries, encyclopedias ... What would a system be if it weren't, first and at the minimum, a *sum*? What would a philosophy be if it let anything at all escape? What would a theoretical man be if he didn't take pleasure in the totality of the real? What would the *ars inveniendi* [art of invention] be if it weren't first *ars inventoriendi* [art of inventory]? A new opposition to Descartes: repudiating or accumulating, tabula rasa or banquet.

First, cutting up and attaining elements, pluralism of pluralism; compiling catalogs next, sum of sums, sometimes left open and closed when possible, equipped with a broad or strict order. Few (or no) readers have analyzed those lists of definitions that proliferate in the unpublished texts: these lists are generally better formed than a cursory inspection would have you believe; they are also meant to reform a language that resists rational calculation and therefore resists decision. Many, on the contrary, were surprised by this nonfinite mass: as though Leibniz hadn't warned them of the status of truths of fact; that their analysis is interminable is shown *in fact* by these collections, just as this was shown by those numeral pyramids whose base is lost beyond everyone's sight—even God's. So far, we have elementary sets and sets of groupings having weak or high complexity, since their variation stretches from the harmonic triangle to the encyclopedia of the sciences and arts. Pluralism is a set-theoreticism, in its propaedeutic state. The system, then, remains to be built once its materials are gathered. Hence the third stage: selecting from the catalog or catalogs. Leibniz canonized the activity of sorting once, methodically, in his combinatorics and another time, metaphysically, in the game space of the divine understanding. At the extremity of all the conceivable filters, or of some of them, suitably chosen, remains a small number of elements and relations, of principles and terms, starting from which, by a path that's determinate, distinguished, deductive, well-formed, defined, rapid, economical, optimal, the whole or part of the whole can be repeated. This, then, is "system" in the ordinary sense: it is not difficult to see that it depends on the selection, the filter, the choice of the terms-principles at the start and on the order by which a sum is repeated. This is the ordinary activity of every axiomatics. Never forget the author's two constant affirmations, which seem to be, but are not, contradictory: that he always starts from the things themselves and that everything is deducible from a small number of prior definitions, ideally reducible to identity. Everything is in the starting and in the prior: an axiomatic system is never, all things considered, anything but a repetition. In it, one goes back to the start, but the return, the detour, and the ruse prepare a short circuit thanks to which one suddenly lays hands on an entire country it would have taken one's life to travel meter by meter: the labyrinth and its thread, Ariadne and the method. So there are not two origins, but rather simply two ways to lay it out. In comparison to the summation of knowledge that knows a thousand routes, there exist one or several good routes. Pluralism distributes the things as they are; its axiomatics is a repetition that's selective, economical, and tachygraphic. Contrary to what is ordinarily believed, system equals speed. The formalism, lastly, is in no way in opposition to the real, except in the case of a grave misinterpretation. It is a technique of *compendium* that envelops a maximum of reality. This is the global paradox of mathematics, which is ideally pure and endlessly applicable: a language that is both at the limits of monosemy, hence the guarantee of a quasi-perfect communication, and jam-packed with polysemy, hence the promise of a multivocal exportation. We are not deceived by it, and we do not deceive anyone with it, and yet it can say anything. Leibniz is a formalist. He sought, his entire life, the universal language, which is to say, the language of languages: he understood that the mathematical language of his time wasn't yet formed. He constructed a number of deductive systems. He never lost his passion for the things of the world. He canonized the whole of these attempts in a metaphysics in which calculation is equivalent to creation, in which the vast plenitude of the real is expressed by a maximally pure discourse, and in which substances—being of infinite complexity and in their hopeless solitude—communicate perfectly. Yes, preestablished harmony is a theory that is isomorphic with the paradox of a noiseless message transporting—no one knows how—the entire clamor of the real, incomprehensibly comprehensible.

So here is a first global view of systematic activity; there is a second one, as we have seen: difficult to dissociate from the first one, and yet different. Let there be a collection of any propositions whatsoever, for example, for us, the set of the author's writings, or for him, and as he said, human thoughts. If it is always possible to draw a path, or better, to designate an already open path between one of the propositions and any other and, inversely, a return from the second one to the first, whichever proposition it may be, we are in the presence of what mathematicians call strong connectivity. When Leibniz says "system" and readers or commentators use this term, they are blindly aiming at this precise phenomenon. Not always, of course, and in the rest of the cases, they are aiming at the first sense. "System," then, signifies strongly connected variety, which is to say, entirely decomposable into strongly connected components. We have already tried to describe this state of affairs by means of what are called true graphs, which is to say, schemas depicting the strong connectivity. Its vocabulary has thrown off many, even though it uses the Leibnizian language of path, route, plan, and cartography, which is to say, both the author's most authentic language and that of topology: it happened that, by a miracle of history, Leibniz had invented analysis situs, and that this analysis, in return, served us as a methodological guide, in the sense of a travel guide, suitable for exploring the sites he had opened.

The difficulty lies in the fact that we must be clear about the word *system* twice. Leibniz attained the two senses. The first one gives him a face the nineteenth century began to draw as soon as it became aware of its own knowledge and which was left for us to complete: pluralism, set-theoreticism, theory of multiplicities; logicism, formalism, theory of formal languages and of deduction; algebraic formalism, initiation into concepts that, though not named differently in his work, were fairly new: application, structure; theory of vernacular languages and of well-formed characteristics; dictionaries, lastly, in the sense of a sum and in the sense of communication. The second sense reveals another face, besides this latter one, now familiar. The theoretician of morphology. What does this mean? Everywhere, here, are direct descriptions of what could be called varieties. The critique of Cartesian extension, of mechanistic explanation, of the world of atoms in the style of Epicurus or Gassendi projects them together onto a locally empty morphology occupied in a scattered and chaotic manner. The morphology that replaces it, considered to be more faithful to the real, is described a hundred times and with an inestimable precision: inexhaustible division, compactness, locally iterated nested boxes, replications, continuities, and sets that are everywhere dense. Leibniz intuits exactly what the following are: an accumulation point, a neighborhood (he uses this term), and a limit. He proposes continuous transformations, without gap or jump or rending; he draws connections. Philosophical writing, he says, must be drawn *per linearum ductum* [by means of lines], which cannot be translated in any other way than by graph theory. It isn't by chance that the question of freedom appears to him as the figure of a labyrinth, or that he treats it as analogous to the question of the continuous: we might say apart from a homeomorphism. It isn't chance if the lexicon of topography comes under his pen quite naturally. He was led to it by both projective geometry and differential geometry. Seeking, on the other hand, the general conditions of diffusion, he writes a global morphology of interaction, for which the *Monadology* forms the canonical example; he loves to draw this morphology on fluid models. Conversely, he treats of rupture, sites of discontinuity; he radicalizes closures: the monad is *without hole* or doors. At the extreme consequences of the infinitesimal organon and the calculation of variations, he ensures that rigorous knowledge attains, and for all time, a general theory of *edges:* first, in order to classify the varieties, hence the definition of a line as the edge of a surface and a surface as the edge of a volume, but above all to characterize each variety and the laws that traverse it; the principle of the maximum and the minimum, the optimization canonized in the metaphysics of creation, is an application of the universal determination by edges, of a theory of ultrastructure; preestablished harmony is demonstrably another such application; hence a thousand examples, repeated a thousand times: drops of oil and of water, sphericity, right angle, the fall of heavy bodies, straight lines or brachistochrone ones, techniques for filling game spaces, architecture ... This final example is interesting: it factually shows the construction, the structure, in the seventeenth-century sense, of an optimal system determined by both the greatest descent of heavy bodies, therefore requiring an invariant core of right angles and vertical lines, and by the best occupation of space in the assigned limits, something drawn by the plans, topography, scenography, and ichnography; multiple determination by edges. Thus God is the grand architect; he knows the two senses of the word *system*, and his creative word unites them. On balance: when one knows what a fold [*pli*] is, when the whole meditation revolves around this form, from duplication to complexity, from multiplicity to envelopment, when one knows what *between* means, from the drawn path to nested boxes, when one carefully distinguishes the local and the global, giving the adverb *everywhere* a technical sense and the word *universal* a nonobscure one, when one knows what an accumulation, a continuum, and a border are, when one knows how to finely describe the states of the full and even to draw or model its phenomena, when one knows how to dream rigorously about the alveoli of a beehive ... one isn't very far from a morphology. And now a renewed Leibniz appears, laden with a new mathematics, with a topology or a graph theory he did not obscurely dream, but rather established lucidly and applied immediately to the things of the world.

What clutters the terrain and prevents seeing it is the traditional and puerile quarrel over words that are no doubt laden with affective and cultural values, over words that are exchanged and shared in order to define oneself sectorally by an opinion and find security in a place of your own in lieu and stead of calculating. In fact, in the texts on the multitudes of the full, Leibniz describes and distinguishes these multitudes as being as material, mechanical, organized, and spiritual. The aura of these namings can obscure the context and maintain several wars of religion: there are the upholders of the fishpond and the upholders of the fish, the way elsewhere there are those of the chicken and those of the egg. The important thing to see here, turning our backs on these archaisms, is the morphological treatment of the varieties so named, the modalities of the description. Hans Reichenbach, for example, and Norbert Wiener managed to isolate, in analogous texts, a relativistic theory and a general physics of communication. It is easy to extricate a well-formed "aesthetic" of a considerable methodical power. The history of science, in general, has little trouble pulling a pertinent invention from the ideological jumble once the invention has *already* taken place between historian and document, and the invention sheds light on the document in return. It is only a question of recognition. Thus Louis Couturat locates De Morgan's laws in a forgotten calculus. It is not the same here, because the document is an invention ahead of us. The document uses a morphology that announces our topological structures precisely and that adapts to varieties it is possible to encounter in the phenomena of life. I didn't say this morphology wasn't applicable to other regions; I am only saying that it is faithfully expressive of said phenomena. And it is clear enough that Leibniz wanted things this way: all nature is full of life, everything is full in nature, and this is how these plenitudes, this continuity, these invariants that are stable across continuous and continual variations, these geneses joined with preservations, these reciprocal interactions, and so on, should be described. Doubtless there is no other definition of meaning than the play of respective situations. Since these documents, the old analysis situs has conquered refined spaces, has described situations of an exquisite complexity: thus one can be surprised to the point of scandal at the fact that the seventeenth-century lesson has not been followed or read along its proper grain. How does it happen that we don't yet have an anexact morphology, one having a topological support, of the varieties presented by anatomy, embryology . . . by the local, elementary, or general mechanisms of the living thing? The synthesis, however, the one Leibniz intuited, and the application are clearly possible. We are behind by a science in both our knowledge and the author's. It follows that recurrent history, here, does not come to the aid of the historian of science's riskless victories and that we are blinded to the clearest texts. But let's continue: the project of a rigorous-anexact morphology of the varieties of the living thing is, quite naturally, not separable from an aesthetic, in the traditional sense.

Topology is, or includes, an aesthetic, just as the logico-algebraic set is, or includes, an analytic. As soon as Leibniz is in possession of the two senses of the word *system,* he announces Kant's distinctions, laterally, and our science, directly. In short. How does it happen that we don't yet have a refined description of the spaces of perception (such perception, at a given moment, operates in the intersection of multiple varieties), of the repertory of gestures, of coenesthesia, intropathy, proprioception, of the body schema, of behaviors that are practical, artisanal, occupational, gymnastic, artistic, of every pathological attitude of the lived body, and of its relation to the environment? The weaver doesn't immerse his hands in the same variety as the mason, the wrestler, or the pianist; the claustrophobe doesn't move about in the same topic, in the same "space" as the mime, and so on. How does it happen that we are unaware, even though we know it, how does it happen that theory is ignorant of the fact, even though it is ready to know, that we are immersed in precisely describable and highly differentiated varieties and that the individual is distinguished, no doubt, and determined, perhaps, in and by an original intersection of said varieties, affirmations extrapolated from what Leibniz said about its site? I don't see any reason to close these domains to mathematical treatment. So, the three-century-old prevision indicates a synthesis between mathesis universalis and a physics of the individual.

Leibniz wrote at least two systems: an analytic and a morphology. No contradiction separates them; there is no longer any opposition between our two forms of mathematics, but rather complementarities. Just as he preferred to compute possibles and construct a theory of decision to invest his options in a choice made by inclination, he, at a stroke, gave a well-formed organon of intuition and an architectonic of formal idealities.

System and Synthesis

Leibniz's system is a synthesis between universal mathematics and the metaphysics of the individual. This sentence is from Dietrich Mahnke:[3] it is both exact and inexact, for it masks the theory of communication. This latter is decisive for the synthesis. The commentators most often grant this definition but have reservations regarding the success of a union considered to be either an inaccessible horizon or a reassuring illusion, not only in the author's texts, but in principle: the union would signify the accord of the understanding and existence, of the monadology and the monad, of reason and freedom, or, by a slight shift, of culture and nature, which is to say, the reduction of a gap that, to the eyes of a certain modernity resolved to maintain this gap, intensified, in its nascent state, lucidly, is precisely productive of both science, in the real, and of philosophy in dream. Leibniz never stops affirming that he has succeeded in these conciliations. If this is false, his system is not rigorous; if this is true, it has to do with a dream. A double failure, be it in the eyes of the seventeenth-century thinkers or in the eyes of contemporaries. Another reservation: he has not given a definitive universal mathematics for science; he has not given a decisive metaphysics. He also doesn't brag that he has done so: he merely says that he has achieved their accord. We must therefore stay at the level of synthesis and demonstrate its effectiveness. We must take him at his word and, as he advocated, calculate. Let two texts be chosen, each expressing one of the two themes. On condition of showing that the second one is linked to it. The eighth paragraph of the "Discourse on Metaphysics" defines, constructs, and exhibits the/an individual substance. This paragraph is, apparently, at a maximum distance from a mathematics: let us discover it there, underlying and decisive for the metaphysics of the individual. The discovery of the harmonic triangle gives its inventor the idea of a mathematical synopsis as ample as that occasioned for Pascal by the arithmetic triangle; this discovery is, on the other hand, one of the originators of infinitesimal calculus. The discovery is, in appearance, as distant as you please from a metaphysics and a theory of the individual: so let us show its connection to the *Monadology*, which is to say, to the Leibnizian discourse on individuated substances.

FROM THE METAPHYSICS OF THE INDIVIDUAL TO UNIVERSAL MATHEMATICS
("DISCOURSE ON METAPHYSICS," PARAGRAPH 8)

It is a question of distinguishing the actions of God from those of creatures, in other words, of defining their respective share of responsibility, freedom, determination, will, behavior, and efficacy. On the horizon looms the problem of evil and sin, which is to say, the monumental *Theodicy*, and the question, very popular in those days as in our own, of the invariance of the forces present and at work in the real, which is to say, a philosophy of dynamics. Leibniz keeps his distance from Malebranche, about whom it is known that he accorded all the efficacy to the Creator, and from the continued conservation of an initial quantity of motion in the Cartesian mode. In order to maintain this distance, he first renounces a certain theological lexicon: the notion of individual substance replaces the figure of humankind who is the image of his Creator and therefore originarily determined by the *fiat*. In a way, the Hellenic tradition is taken up again, beyond the dogmatics of Christian inspiration; it is not chance that made Alexander rise from the dead when the text was constituting the individual in its full singularity and found itself needing to resurrect an example, Alexander the Great, whose teacher was precisely Aristotle and who, alas or inevitably, was such an individual's image, and not the Malebranchian Adam whose creator and model was God. Hence, as an aside, a text structured like a creation, outside biblical theology, since it moves from an intellectualist architecture in the Aristotelian style to the appearance of a singular subject jam-packed with predicates, life, and universe: how the royal individual surges up, Alexander the statesman as a paradigm. In order to maintain the same distance, Leibniz, second, literally changes subjects. The question asked requires dividing actions—whatever they may be—into divine actions and human actions by attributing them to two well-separated subjects; this requirement inclines the answer; it irresistibly impels one to distinguish real acts, those of God, and contingent acts, a veritable efficacy and an apparent, occasional causality. The text shifts the dichotomies: the acts and behaviors are divided into actions and passions (which inclines to the answer, in its theological form: the creature is capable of action, the first theorem of the "Principles of Nature and Grace"), and the attribution is unified, since actions and passions properly belong to individual substances. The question asked was not sincere; it implied an answer. The operation of shifting is not any more sincere; it contains the opposite answer. We pass from the creationist prejudice to the ontological prejudice. What remains invariant in the two ways is the problem of predication. As a good formalist, Leibniz will treat this problem while seeming to turn his back to any decision about the content. Hence composition: the elements of a grammar of attribution lead first to a nominal definition of individual substance; the fact that several predicates are attributed to the same subject, and that this subject isn't attributed to any other, allows for the recognition of the defined entity but doesn't in any way show its possibility; the real definition is discovered only when the whole of the operation is founded in the nature of things; the doctrine of inherence allows stating it; lastly, *the proper noun* of the individual Alexander concretizes this synthetic construction of the monadic real, through a singular example. The theory is well-known: vestiges, traces, and marks of the past, present, and future—for personal history and its multiple connections to the world stage—are written forever in this concentration of contingency and eternity that is his million-voiced soul, which Leibniz's God placed, as he did for every soul, at the center of everything, like the echo of a sound.

It indeed is a question of a metaphysics of the individual. Singular, exemplified, existing in act(s), denominated *rightly* (actions and passions belong to it in its own right), the individual is constructed synthetically starting from a *grammar of common nouns,* from a logic of predication and inherence, from a theory of definition, from a general organon of truth, the identical, the virtual, and the necessary. Here it is now plunged in the multiserial physical connection of things, overflowing on all sides the apparent insularity of its finitude by circles propagated on the fluid fabric of the universe starting from the single concrete (solid) notion enveloping-developing the infinity of its predicates in expanding series. This is an ontological and therefore metaphysical translation: of the logical theory in terms of which all singular judgment is universal, what belongs to the individual not being the particular; of the physical theory regarding the continuity of all communication in general; every closed system (and there only exist concretely closed systems, the monads) *reproduces and produces* in its department the totality of totalities; the individual is indivisible, its partitioning is coextensive and cointensive with the world it expresses. It is not a locality of the world and history; the only reality exceeds the physical. The text is silent about universal mathematics.

No, universal mathematics traverses the text entirely; this mathematics articulates its demonstrations and gives it its structure. To say "the individual" is to use the existential quantifier: there exists a being such that ... and here is this being. But it appears among a massive use of the universal quantifier: an analysis of content shows fifteen occurrences of it. The first sentence: "God does *everything*"; the last sentence: *"from all time* in Alexander's soul, there are vestiges of *everything* that has happened to him and marks of *everything* that will happen to him, and even traces of *everything* that happens in the universe, even though God alone could recognize them *all.*"[4] At a first reading, the path goes from God to God, from his production to his knowledge, *salva universalitate* [to save universality or with universality preserved], from creationism to monadology via the individual substance. It likewise goes from one universal quantifier to another, to a crowd of others, specified in genus, via the existential quantifier, from totality to totality via unity.[5] It can be noted, moreover, that the question of predicates—nominal and real definitions—is accompanied by indefinite quantifications of the order of "several" and "some." Leibniz's philosophy, as a coherent pluralism, is projected here in something like a reduced model: the multiplicity in it is the fabric where the relations of the one and the universal play. Elements (generic), sets, totality—this is not only the list of the categories of quantity as it occurs in the degenerate discourse of the Kantian critique; it is the table of the first terms of a mathesis universalis in the Leibnizian sense as well as our own. A synthesis, in Mahnke's sense, between mathesis universalis and the monadic ontology is produced as soon as the sole concrete reality resides in a unity described and thought in the middle of its set-based links with the multiple and its integral links with the universal. The bare thought of the singleton, even if it were the only real entity, is in no way constituted, an alphabetic stuttering or silent ecstasy, and is not expressible without the architecture of these relations; this is why expression, which explains the emergence of all language, is precisely the one-multiple star. This is equally true of the monadology, as a discourse on the monad, and of general science, as a cycle of regional monadologies. This is true, again, of our set theory, our elementary mathematics or elementary logic, our particle physics, which is reduced to babbling without its unitary symmetries, our physics of "elements," our molecular biochemistry, our grammars in general, alphabet-based disciplines, well-formed cells of the encyclopedia, monadologies in their respective genera. And the word *monadology* itself was taken up again in astronomy by Milne and Whitrow. As soon as there is science, which is to say, faithful and noncontradictory construction starting from a table of any elements, the system of monadology returns and imposes itself, variably transcribable for the disciplines cited, virtually transcribed by them, in such a way that a comparative epistemology could be constructed with minimal cost: the models are there; their structure has three centuries of patina. Which we must talk about elsewhere. Therefore, the simple cannot be known or spoken without an organon of the complex: it would be better to name it simplex. And this organon, in return, is not constructible without it. In Leibnizian language, the substantial *one* is that without which neither the thing nor discourse can exist, but nothing can be stated outside the processes of multiplication and division of said individual. It is both the whole of these operations and their limit, the place without place where they are born and exhausted. On the network: unity, multiplicity, and totality finely articulate the concrete, the real, and its faithful expressions. Monadic existence takes (does not take) place on the fabric of the mathesis. After all, synthesis, in Mahnke's sense, is but the definition of science in general.

Let's return to the quantifiers, which cadence the text, form the picture, and institute the fabric. Let's erase, for the moment, the background of the discourse in which they take place:

First moment: God does or makes everything; he only makes ... (there exist) individual substances; what is such a substance?[6]

Universality, restriction on this latter, existence. *Talis . . . qualis*, quality, the sign of a real existent, in Leibniz as well as for us, who say, "There exists a being such that..." The individual-totality relation is put in place as a limit framework. It must be filled in the conclusion. Hence a calculation *de continente et contento*. What is the relation between the content and the container? In other words, what is inherence? In the final analysis, the monad is indeed the absolute of the content and the absolute of the container: atom and world.

Between these two limits, the second moment traces a decrease among the multiplicity, a decrease toward the abstract nominal: "several, no, not enough."[7] Hence a certain subject, *quidam*, the indeterminate, the common noun. There is indeed a calculation, and almost a functional one: abstract knowledge and nominal definitions are poor, no doubt necessary, certainly not sufficient, and this can be measured, so to speak, by the quantity of information. If the quantity is low, we remain in generality, the commonality of the notion, the abstract. The proof is the third moment, which, conversely, indicates an increase among the multiplicity; starting from the sequence "not everything, not determinate enough, not the other qualities nor everything...," which concerns the accidental, information is maximized to attain the sequence: "complete, consummate [*accomplie*], sufficient" to attain the totality.[8] There is indeed a calculation, an extensive and intensive one: a container is to be filled all the way to brimming, all the way to its maximum. Poorly filled, with the minimum of information, is the common notion, the formula, the formal; sufficiently full is the real. Hence the importance, in Leibnizian language, of the words *full, complete, entire*, including in notions like entire reason or full cause. How is this completion realized? In the series of predicates, defined in the language of inherence. The individual subject, defined nominally as that which cannot serve as a predicate, is filled, that is, defined really or constructed in fact or even created, as soon as its predicates, in an infinite series ordered by a law or reason, are summed up completely, that is, understood in two aspects: in their deductive linking and their comprehensive totality. A double reason determining fact. Each of the predicates belongs to the aforementioned series, develops or expresses its law. But, as an intersection or node, such a predicate belongs to one or several other series of the world; it therefore carries one or several other laws, which it expresses or develops; it is marked with one or several other determinations. However simple it may appear, it is always a product in the sense of intersection; in other words, the line of the predicative series developing an individual and enveloped by this individual traverses the fabric of the universe; each point of its warp meets a point of the weft, is inherently part of the weft. In the complete sum of the predicative series, the individual totalizes these projections of the universe in the form of vestiges, traces, or marks, these inscriptions of something else and of everything that its own predicates are. The universal completion is a double totalization of a series of series, which is to say, a harmonic table. Hence Leibniz commenting on Pascal: double infinity and monad. This is indeed the maximum of completion possible, which is expressed by the repetition of the universal quantifiers, at the end of the text, when the proper noun appears. When such an individual exists, he or she is such that everything is in him or her; and every existent is individual and universal in this way. The relations of the existential quantifier and the universal quantifier are precisely in place. Here is the required synthesis. It occurred just a bit ago regarding the science aspect; now it has occurred on the side of Alexander, the paradigmatic concrete individual. What God alone understands, he is alone in possessing (he is alone in understanding it, that is, in enveloping it, and the active-passive relation, the first problem, is resolved in the actual-virtual relation); what God alone knows, Alexander practices, amid the confusion of his fated choices.

At the same time as it produces, in its nominal-real-named subject curve, the individual existing in fact, the text is a calculation, and a calculation that groups every characteristic commonly stated of universal Mathematics. Something that's all the less surprising because there is production or creation only through the calculation. Therefore this calculation is: *de quantitate et qualitate,* and even *de quantitate et mensura* [of quantity and measurement] (theorem: the construction of the qualitative real is a quantitative completion), *de continente et contento, de maximis et minimis,* of the indeterminate and the determinate, of the one, the multiple and the whole, of the finite and the infinite, of the virtual and limits, of the general and the sufficient, of chance and necessity. And this paragraph of the "Discourse" is in no way exceptional: as an exercise, the reader can free these logico-mathematical forms from every Leibnizian text dealing with a metaphysics of the individual. Corollary: all this lets us understand with the greatest clarity the reason the true offers itself to us more easily than the complete real, which belongs to God alone. Let $A = B$ be proved. If $B = pqr$, then p, q, r can be located in the sequence of predicates of $A = abpcdeqmnrst$ ... well before the exhaustion of its infinite series. The true is only a selective filtering in a completion whose totality is not in our power. It is true that we must sometimes go very far in the analysis, but the discovery and the demonstration don't require exhaustion. They are in our power, and the real is in our acts and our virtualities. Mathematics says all this unambiguously.

FROM UNIVERSAL MATHEMATICS TO THE METAPHYSICS OF THE INDIVIDUAL OR MONADOLOGY

Several opuscules treat the harmonic triangle and compare it to Pascal's arithmetic triangle, the former of which appeared for the first time in *De arte combinatoria*: the *Historia et origo calculi differentialis*, the *Nova algebrae promotio*, the *Compendium quadraturae arithmeticae*, et cetera. The discovery dates from the years 1672–1673, when the system was still in formation. Leibniz showed himself to be particularly proud of it and said as much to his correspondents, such as Oldenburg. It seemed to him that his schema realized a mathematical synthesis as strong as that of his predecessor: a synopsis of the rules of the combinatorial art, the theory of numerical orders, algebra through the determination of binomial coefficients, the *ars conjectandi* [the art of conjecturing] through the questions regarding parts, and analysis through the summation of series; on the other hand, he presents his triangle as one of the first intuitions of infinitesimal calculus. In short, it has to do with a table that unites or traverses the entire mathematical encyclopedia of the day. It is not mathesis universalis formally speaking or theoretically formulated; it is one of its *realizations,* one of its *figures.* The fact that this triangle seems to us now to be a minor result has no relevance: the synthesis realized in it was, for the time, full and complete; a horn of plenty from which all the wealth of rigorous discourse could be drawn. A figure of the mathesis, it prefigures the *Monadology.* In examining it, these two figures, expressions, or models merge in the table. The metaphysics of the individual is realized in it, like the mathesis, without requiring much effort to extract it: it suffices to let it speak in its language. The translation is immediate.

Let there be a table in which the harmonic triangle and the arithmetic triangle are united, as shown in figure 1.

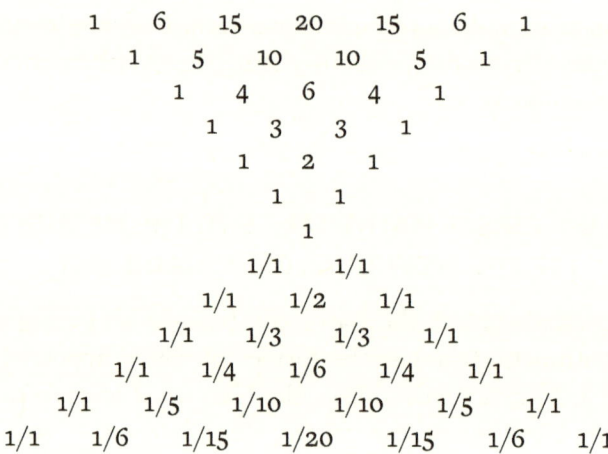

Figure 1. *The harmonic triangle and the arithmetic triangle united in an hourglass shape.*

It contains *every* number, natural and rational; it *produces* them according to a simple reason. It represents them, as a pyramid, according to a plan that gets lost in the infinite beyond our eyes (*Theodicy*): it subsists without end in that number abyss of sleeping parts (*De rerum originatione radicali*). It is a question of an aggregate, well-linked together, but not unique or necessary: the numbers, as a whole, could be represented differently, and in a thousand other ways, even an infinity of ways; this way is simple, elegant, *placet harmoniam oculis subjicere* [it is pleasing to lay harmony before the eyes], says another opuscule about a synopsis of the same type; this way is beautiful, maybe the most beautiful, because the most complete and the most brimming, which is why it is called harmonic, but it is not the only necessary way; a pond, a fishpond, a collection of numbers, among other ponds. This aggregate is constituted of series; this table is a series of series; it is an order of coexistents, like space, an order of orders of succession, like time; it is an order of orders like a spacetime. Any number, just like a given existent of the world or of a current state of the world, is an intersection or node of infinite series, to be read according to the lines, according to the columns, according to the transverse directions, by diagonals or tiered sequences; it is analyzed by these law-abiding sequences: there would be nothing to say about this number without them, which endlessly provide its predicates, which designate it as even, triangular, natural, combined, added up, divisible, and so on. It is multidetermined by several predicative laws that govern the totality of the table; it therefore has dealings with each sequence, with every sequence, with the infinite totality of the table, which then is its own ichnography; as the current term of a multiplicity of series, it finds itself here the bearer of the law of each of them and all of them: the law of even numbers, natural numbers, combinations, and so on is written in the envelopment of this number, and this writing is indeed scenographic; everything is there, but *quodammodo* [in a certain way]. Yet, each number is different from all the others, at least by position or situation, and none is omitted from the synopsis: individualized, discernible, it nevertheless has every conceivable relation with the aggregate as a whole; it envelops these relations in its own constitution; it contains them as its own definition. Supposing one knows all of them, one could read the totality of series of the table in it: the arithmetician is the god of these numbers, the way the creating God is the calculator of things. In other words, this number is what it is, originally and primitively, through the set of its operational relations with the other numbers: single, but caught through and through in the middle of the arithmetic fabric, the network, the lattice. The table, the aggregate of series, exhibits one or two infinite repetitive series of units, set *at the edges* of the triangle, as though along the generatrices of a cone (of vision) and crossing at the vertex, at the intersection-point of view of the two nappes. Said units are generic, elementary in the strict sense; they engender the entire table through immediate operations. As Leibniz wrote regarding another triangular figure, that of binary numeration: *sufficit unum* [one is sufficient]. They are simples that enter into compounds: figures of monads, veritable atoms of the schema. And each number is reducible, through the same operations, inverted, into the units. But each singular series refers to one of the latter as though to its dominant monad, whether the sequence is cut up according to lines, columns, or other directions that would be diagonal or transverse. Each subaggregate of the table is equipped with its directive unit. The dominant monads, in their border region (every dominant monad is defined at a limit), form series, as we have seen, which are themselves referred to or intersected (produced) at the single unit that is the vertex, which, at the edge common to every edge, dominates the dominants and thereby the entire table. But again, this latter unfurls and develops infinitely two triangles (two pyramids or two cones) put into relation in and by this very unit. The first triangle is composed of units or aggregates of units, an aggregate of aggregates and a series of series, a figure that's expressive of the world of things; this triangle is distributed by Leibniz into subsets or parts, pond, army, fishpond, fish . . . down to the individual substance reputed to be indecomposable. The second triangle decomposes, unfolds, and takes apart the segment (0, 1), which can indeed be called generic in comparison to the triangle of the world, which is to say, exhibits the infinite plurality (just as inaccessible as the infinity of composition) of affections and relations inside the unit itself; it is the figuration of the vestiges and traces inherent to the individual, deposited in layers, which are covered over and to be uncovered, as numerous as those of an unerodable palimpsest which would have been written on for all eternity. So, the global synopsis is "harmonic" in its purest sense; it shows the set of complex unit-multiplicity relations through what one scarcely dares to name a symmetry, as complicated as you like. It sums up, at least, the first thirteen paragraphs of the *Monadology* and, at most, the *New System of the Communication of Substances*. One dominant unit and one alone brings about the punctual relation between the individual and the world, between the infinite varieties buried in the monadic unit and the aggregative multiplicities of units, respectively decomposed and composed according to laws that are same and other, identical and different, invariant and variable, inverted, turned around as in a mirror whose focus would be this vertex common to every interiority, to every exteriority. The dominant of the dominants has its site at the point of harmony: vertex, limit of all limits, edge of all edges, point of view and ichnography of all scenographies, constitutive and comprehensive unit. The segment (0, 1) is suitable for sequences of numbers; it expresses them in its partitioning; it represents them faithfully. In other words, it is easy to read *natural series* in *harmonic series,* or, in Caesar's or Alexander's soul, the Rubicon, Darius and Porus, death by dagger or by malaria. The unit is divided the way the aggregate is composed: the unit is a world in its department and by its partition, as powerful as the complex of things. So here we find explicated the harmonic connection of the soul and the body, of the individual and the world. Explicated—that is, unfolded—by sequences of simplicities: the upper part of the table forms every relation of the simple to compounds; the lower part develops the relations of the simple to its own parts; the table as a whole exhibits the relations between the parts of the simple and the complexes of simples, passing through the originary unit. The harmonic connection is never explicated in any other way. Hence whatever you like regarding representation and perception, universally regarded as corollaries of harmony and defined—like harmony itself—by the relations between the multiple and the one. The iterated sections of the segment (0, 1) appear without any reference to the triangle of compounds; these sections nonetheless faithfully repeat the numbers of the first table. The monad automatically deciphers, in itself and for itself, a universe that is, at a stroke, its closed interior, its own account, and the extensive whole of the exteriority. If the partitioning is expressive of perception, if it draws the map of the world in a siteless site, there is no need to go very far on the second triangle to attain refined and ultrarefined differences, just as inapperceptible as the minute perceptions.[9] However far one advances, one only finds a finite part of them; the virtual proliferates below, present, passive, and actualizable. The monad is inaccessibly full of affections sufficient to represent a nature that's full and compact like it is: the inherence of every number suitable for deciphering. The monad is imprinted-expressing, but never impressionable. It could be said, later, that the segment (0, 1) is equipotent to the continuum (the set of real numbers). Leibniz couldn't say this because he only used rational numbers. But he does see it, blindly. His doctrine, right in the middle of the seventeenth century, causes the great Platonic problematic of the *Parmenides* and the questions posed by contemporary mathematics to be exchanged. From these two plenitudes, on the other hand, it follows that history or time could never end, for the table overflows any effective drawing, and also that, since the monad contains the number of this transcribed immensity, no one can see how the monad could die or be born. There are only envelopments and developments, increases and decreases. The harmonic triangle is something like the little theater for which the arithmetic triangle represents the big theater, in which the compound, the probable, and summation rule: it fills, in the spot one wants, the gaps in the discrete composite; it is everywhere in the macrodecor—as though its tip could be put in every point marked by units. Thus the aggregate is not juxtaposition, the mechanics of a mill; it is set up as tightly woven, dense with harmonic wells. The fabric of space and time, the orders of the composite in general, just like the fabric of the determination that's interior to the singular unit, is woven with sequences without terms to the left and the right, locally without rending or gap. Better still, and decisively, the series or orders, ruled by their law or reason, and therefore all of them universally by the principle of reason, arrive at, whether via downstream or upstream, a term, an origin, the unit, identity, the one identical to itself, and therefore at their limit and universally at the principle of identity, itself multiply broken down into units identically unfolded into repetitive series at the limit of each order; so, this term, this unit, and this origin are immediately relative. I mean: they are generically absolute and relative in the crossed development of geneses. For the series of each order continue infinitely, whether on the one side or the other side of the unit; they plunge into the other order. For the same series turn around, become inverted, in this point, so as to be able to continue and repeat their reason. For the same sequence endlessly says the same thing in its order, then the same thing in another order, so radically other that the order is quite simply the inverse of the first one (as when the East and the West are exchanged, according to the hypothesis proposed to Clarke, as though Ptolemy were right here and Copernicus right there), besides being its homogon in the order of size all the way to the virtual.[10] Everything is always and everywhere the same thing, and no matter its alterity, here pushed to the point of opposition, except for the degrees of size and perfection, even when the world vanishes into the soul and I blossom out into the things of the world. The unit, the identical, is the respective common edge of the same and the other, the pole or harmonic pivot where the multiple, to be able to iterate its message, takes on a transposed or contraposed figure, gets lost, and is found again in incommensurable dimensions. The fixed variant of absolute variation. The soul is the border, the limit where the body stops, and the edge where the body is left behind, the body's adherence; the world is, rigorously speaking, the outside of the monad, which is a closed being. Thanks to the identity of the serial laws and the impossibility of their ending, the world and the soul each state the same reasons and transcribe the same inscription. And the monads communicate in the same way. They carry the same inverted number at the crossing of the boundary.

Monadic philosophy is of a transparent rationality. One can read, on the numeric prism, the ordered, scattered, recomposed light of its laws, the continuous and the discrete, the one and the multiple, the same and the other, the old Parmenidean discourse and its contradictions in their place. How can we not understand, upon its dazzling inspection, the union of the principle of identity, the principle of reason (series), and the logic of the probable, a union determined by the first triangle? However, this union seemed to be a stumbling block for the commentary. It would be discourteous to go any further. The reader can enjoy choosing, as an exercise, a proposition of the system and play it using the stops of this organ. Here are two: the easiest one, the question of freedom or predetermination, solvable by the labyrinth and the knot of series; the most provocative one, that of love, where the joy found in the joy that the other finds in me superabundantly demonstrates that the elective communication has its key in the elation of the harmonically inverted numbers.

Just as music is an account that no one takes account of, the Leibnizian metaphysics of the individual is buried in the numeric register whose endless discourse we have just heard. This is what was to be demonstrated.

Encyclopedia and First Philosophy

The *De rerum originatione radicali*, from November 1697, forms a cycle.[11] It starts with the world and finishes with the world. It is a cycle, formally, when the world is a concept; it is one really, since it tries to constitute things and unfold their history. It institutes, on the other hand, an infinite open series. It starts upstream of the things, *praeter Mundum* [beyond (or before) the world, 149]; there is no limit to the left, in the infinity of iterations of the prerequisite; it finishes downstream of the history of the world, *nec unquam ad terminum progressus* [thus, progress never comes to an end, 155]; there is no limit to the right in its envelopment-development. The words *progressus, terminum,* from the end, correspond to the words *originatio, regressus* [go back, 149], from the start. The world is an open series without any internal origin or assignable goal, a chain without a fixed point. If the world is a series, its law must be enveloped inside it, for the law of a series is internal to it and not external; it is even its general word, its flowing word, a certain way of reading and writing each of its words: the law of the world is *written* on any state whatsoever of its time, the way the development of the monad is written on and in the monad, the way it is written in Caesar's soul that he will cross the Rubicon and in Alexander's soul that he will vanquish Darius and Porus, the way it is written in any state (*status*) whatsoever of a moving object that its kinematic trajectory will pass through such-and-such point, this or that state. A mathematical chain, a mechanical chain, chains of history. And, therefore, a state of the world is copied out based on the preceding one, the way a given exemplar of the book Euclid's *Elements* is copied out (*descriptum*) based on the preceding one, and so on, ad infinitum. The world is a series, but perhaps the elements of the sequence are identical since endlessly transcribed. So physics, like metaphysics, is governed by the principle of identity; the physical law of the series would be: the whole effect is equipollent to the full cause. On balance, there is a cycle, an infinite open series, a quasi-fixed and immobile repetition. The philosophy of history already recapitulates its possible forms.

The *De rerum* has a total encyclopedic recapitulation as its support. Leibniz everywhere states his ideas of full cause, complete reason, consummate and sufficient notion; in his dense and brimming world, nothing exists and nothing acts unless it is complete in completeness. If he imposes fullness on the world, beings, and relations, he also practices it for himself and plunges his system into it. Here, for example, the whole of knowledge has a hand in speaking about the totality of the world and of history. And first and foremost, the logico-grammatical sciences, the knowledge of discursive formality. It is (recently) traditional to immoderately translate the title of the fragment as "radical origin"; "immoderately" because the nineteenth century, Germany in particular, has plunged us fully, since Rousseau, let's say, into a problematic of origin and into a demand for radicality. The fact that Leibniz has contributed to establishing this atmosphere is not in doubt, but it is not in doubt in the domain of formal language, and that's why it is possible to give the name "Romantic" to the mathematical efforts to return to the origin undertaken by the logicians and axiomaticians of the last century who only continued the enterprises of the *calculus ratiocinator* while remaining faithful to the great recapitulation of their time. In short, to say origin, why wouldn't he have written *origine radicali*? *Origo* is indeed birth, provenance, source, cause, principle. It is also author, and why not Author? When Cato gave his work on the origins of Rome, he called them *Libri Originum*. *Originatio*, for its part, is a technical term; since Quintilian and his *Institutio Oratoria*, it has meant etymology. The thing is not so paradoxical as soon as one notices the associated adjective, which, in fact, designates root, the originary root of words. *On the root, on the etymology of things*, as though things were words, as though words were the things themselves.

Several consequences follow from this. First, the fact that a state of the world is, apart from the expression, something like a propositional statement. This is because a state of things, momentary, taken from among the sequence of states (*status*), is a concept from statics, one describable by a simple equation: the sequence of states, then, is the series of these equations. Apart from the expression, it suffices to choose, *salva veritate* [to save the truth or with the truth preserved], any mode whatsoever in the cycle of the continued representation from the world to the machine, from the machine to stereometrics, from the latter to its projection, from the plane figure to its points, from the latter to numbers, then to signs, to words . . . ; hence the return to logico-grammatical knowledge. By the way, the total cycle of faithful expression is *also* an encyclopedic cycle; conversely, the encyclopedia is a cycle of representation, as though each cell or discipline was a point of view on the thing itself, on the state of things. The sciences translate each other and leave the truth invariant; they form a geometral.[12] And therefore, the simplest approach is to adopt the simplest knowledge, from which logicism results.

Second, the fact that a series has never been able to be conceived in any other way than as a succession of numbers, signs, letters, words, characters. To say the world is to form a sequence of equations, a table; it is also to produce a string of words, a string of sentences, literally, a text. The *characteristic* model of the successive states of the world is therefore the endlessly recopied sequence of exemplars of a same book, a same printed book, the impression (including the impression the outside seems to make on our soul or wax tablet) being only one variety of expression. This book is quite precisely that of Euclid's *Elements,* the only book we are demonstrably sure constitutes a coherent knowledge and a coherent world starting from the principle of identity, at least virtually and de jure. Elements, which is to say, *stoicheía,* what is in a row, what is part of a line, characters, letters, words, principles, and, in geometry, points, lines, elements, then foundations. It is normal for the metaphor to have led to *stoicheía* and for the book of the *Elements* to be supposed to have been produced from all eternity. This is because the simple and what will be the monad cannot start or finish naturally. There is no root of the elements, no root of the roots, or element of the elements; the *stoicheía* are the very roots: hence repetition, copying and recopying, series, iterative sequence, and so on. The world is the complex of replication, multiplication as such. From the elementary etymology, words are derived: they compose variant families *salva originatione* [to save the origination or with the origination preserved]. Roots are primitive; elements are like primitive terms (*terminus*, limit); the world is derived. As derived, like the words-series and the sentences that are series of series and the texts that are series of series of series ... the world is a nonsubstantial combinatorial aggregate, like every language, like the multiple set of languages derived from a primitive language, for which the essential thing would be to give the alphabet. Monads, elements, simples, and primitive terms are indeed characters; every science, every well-formed discourse, and every text is a monadology, which is to say, a characteristic. The metaphorical model of the Euclidean book is a faithful expression. Leibniz often returns to it: the dream of the world is a book written at random "by throwing the printing press characters pell-mell"; the knowledge of the world, the set of human knowledge, has as its *horizon* the number of possible combinations of the letters of the alphabet. The characteristic is universal: this means that it founds knowledge and world constitution, the activity of the subject and the status of the object; it is a technique, which is to say, a science, algebra, combinatorics, logic, grammar; but also an art, in the Gutenberg mode. The general theory of expression and the gnoseology of impression are also indexed on the technological model of printing. Moreover, this can be verified from Rabelais to Hume. Typography functions in Leibniz's system the way the wax tablet does in Aristotle's: here, the palimpsest is printed.

Third, the fact that the nature of things is not sought, rather the elements of things are sought: *originatio rerum* and not *natura rerum*. At first glance, the difference is slim: the alphabetic parable is, according to Aristotle and even Descartes, a legacy from the atomists of antiquity; the simples here are "the true atoms of nature,"[13] and the participle of *nascor* [to be born] designates something like the substantive of *orior* [to originate]. The status of physics is henceforth settled: the world is written in mathematical terms. The philosophy of nature is physics itself and no longer metaphysics. Here we find a certain modernity beginning the turn that Rousseau and the nineteenth century are going to complete: the question of the origin, shifted away from the question of nature, is substituted for this question so as to have a repetition of metaphysics. Its etymology lost, nature reduces to essence, state of things, set of objects in the world. To designate the first awakening of its constitution, metaphysics, translating the book of Genesis, needs another word, one that would be different in order to repeat the same thing: origin. In Leibniz, the status of the physical world having been settled by the intervention of mathematics, the metaphysics of the origin is expressed as a problem of the emergence of mathematical language (or dynamic language, if the origin of force has to be described), as a problem of the formation of a well-formed language. The phenomenon is well-founded like the sentence that faithfully expresses it. Thus the discourse of the origin of the world is isomorphic with the discourse of the origin of language. Speech is not yet cultural; it comes into being with nature and at the same time as it. This contemporaneous identity occurs in and through combinatorics; nature and language follow the laws of the universal characteristic harmoniously. That is why God, creating, combines and calculates, speaks and does. The distance is zero, de jure for God and de facto for humankind, save the virtual, between word and thing, the same organon presiding at their formation. It will suffice to put man between the two, and not at the point of view where they become equal, in order to reestablish the cultural distance between language and the world it designates. It is a question, incidentally, of the great error of the seventeenth century regarding physics itself: physics was lacking because it laid claim too quickly and as a bloc to its double truth, which is to say, to its horizon and its condition, mathematics. It was a dream in the Leibnizian sense: a combinatorics of notes, a rigorous and coherent one certainly, but whose faithfulness wasn't sought. Experimental verification, abandoned, except de jure, that is, in the imaginary, remained the terrain of dreams to be psychoanalyzed. That said, logico-grammatical knowledge has been entirely at work in the constitution of the world; it therefore serves as the support of the text that describes this constitution.

Arithmetic knowledge is no less at work in the constitution of the world and as a support of such a text: in a way, it is a question of a particular case of the preceding knowledge. Numbers are elements of a given variety. Let's examine the lexicon of the *De rerum:* the arithmetic code immediately reveals itself in it. The world is an *aggregate* of *finite* things, which is to say, a discrete set, finite or infinite; there exists, in the divine understanding, a discrete set of possibles *sejuncta*,[14] separated, distinct from each other. From this point of view, the *De rerum,* like many other opuscules, establishes mathematical relations between these two sets, in one direction, then in the other. The one is originary, the other derived; the one is the primitive set of the roots of the other. *Roots* are on the one side, *products* on the other: production, taken at the root, is a multiplication. Starting from the aggregative multiplicity, the question of the one and the multiple, inherited from Pythagorean arithmeticism, comes to be posed, from the outset, in the opposition *Aggregatum rerum finitarum* [the collection of finite things, 149] and *Unum aliquod dominans* [some One Being who rules, 149], the set and its cardinal number, the herd (*proletarii*) and what dominates it; the aggregated and their master... *Dominans* is interesting: each organic body—and everything is organic—is an endlessly nested aggregate, like the systems of numbers themselves, and equipped with its dominant monad, each nested subset having, for its part, a dominant monad. The world, then, is an aggregate of aggregates, or, to suddenly close the replication, the aggregate of all aggregates: Leibniz, instinctively intuiting the difficulty, everywhere says that the world is poorly founded or nonsubstantial. The *unum dominans* is the dominant monad of dominant monads, hence the comparison with the relation of the soul and the body, and its augmentative *ratione multo altiore* [in a much higher sense, 149]. So there exists something like a scale of sets, in the form of a (harmonic) triangle or of a pyramid (as in the end of *Theodicy*), which infinitely plunges down into the infinitely enveloped detail of things, which ends at a single unity or unit, one that's grasped as paradoxical. These frameworks that have been set forth guide an entire lexicon of quantification: the text moves from the *unum aliquod* to the progress *in infinitum, ad majus meliusque* [to greater and better things, 155]. The aggregate is any set whatsoever, and the dominant unity or unit is *aliquod*. There is some multiple and some single; there is multiplicity, whatever it may be; unity or oneness in general is at stake. Varying on this indefiniteness is called quantifying. Hence the expressions, in great number, from the attack of the reasoning on: reason, which I shall have to come back to, and *full* reason, *in nullo singulorum*, in *none* of the individual things [149], *nec in toto aggregato serieque rerum*, or even in the *entire* collection and series of things [149], *ex quotcumque libris*, no matter how many books back we go [149], virtual infinity, *ab omni tempore*, from all time or always [149], *utcunque regressus fueris*, however far back we might go [149], *pro quantitate essentiae*, in proportion to the amount of essence [150], *pro gradu perfectionis*, in proportion to the degree of perfection [150], *maximo minimove* [the maximum or the minimum, 150], et cetera. The *De rerum* first of all sets forth sets or multiplicities; it gives itself any unity whatsoever, nominally; it seeks its existence and reality. The global scale of the one and the multiple serves it as a base for calculation. The *De rerum* reviews this scale in a general repetition. The series of series, which is to say, the multiplicities, are infinite each in their genus, and any unity whatsoever that was set forth de jure is inaccessible de facto. Said infinite sequences are located by blind thought, the formal thought of the any whatsoever, of the elements, and of calculation. In other words, the table is framed by *totum* and *nullum*, by universal quantifiers, all and nothing. The world, like the understanding, is grasped *ex omni et nullo*; they are drawn out of omnitude and nothingness. Hence the manipulation of concepts like infinite, eternal, complete series, entire reason, abyss, and the final opposition of paradise and the infinite divisibility of the continuum of the things slumbering in the depths without end; the *Confessio philosophi* says this expressly: paradise is the omnitude of new things. The calculation based on the table of infinite totalities locates an existential quantifier: the dominant *one* is given (*datur*).[15] Hence a game space defined between this single and exceptional existence and the universality of the nothing and the all: Leibniz covers and travels this space through a functional calculation by degrees, subject to continuity and equipped with maximal and minimal bounds, literally, a calculation of variations.

The eighth paragraph of the "Discourse on Metaphysics" doesn't proceed any differently when it engenders another type of *unum, dominans* in its genus and its department of Macedonia and Asia, another king, the monadic individual. The substantial ontology and the theology *a contingentia* converge in their form; we agree with God in the same respects. With the same movement and by the same routes, the monad begins to exist, suffer, and act, God to create, and universal mathematics to be constituted. While God calculates, the world is made, a pyramid emerging from the combinatorial abysses of the divine understanding; while substance is unwinding the predicates of its infinite well, Alexander is winning the day against Darius, and later Porus, or Caesar is crossing the Rubicon: the series develop and their terms measure time, the endless small change of sums, integrals, tables, totalities. In every origin, there is calculation; at the origin, there is all the calculation; there is the origin of calculation. Logic, arithmetic, combinatorics, passage from the discrete to the continuous and from countable calculation to the calculation of variations, this is indeed the order of constitution of mathematics. The *dum calculat* [while God calculates] is not only a genesis of the world and history, of existents and their contingence; it is also an ordered genesis of the organon that underlies them: *de matheseos originatione radicali* [on the radical origin of mathematics]. And the *De rerum* indeed has the same structure as the *Initia rerum mathematicarum metaphysica*.

Any sets whatsoever, and then quantified, this is not sufficient to make an arithmetic. They must be equipped with an order structure. What is a series? The *De affectibus* of 1679 defines it: *series est multitudo cum ordinis regula;*[16] a series is a set equipped with an ordering rule; or also: *series seu ordo;* a series is order itself. What is order, in its turn? Here are the opening lines of the *Initia*: "If one sets out that a multiplicity of states of things exists enveloping no opposition, one says that they exist simultaneously. This is why we deny that events from the past year and those from the present year are simultaneous: for they envelop opposite states of the same thing."[17] The series of states of the world, put forward in the *De rerum*, is therefore subject to the principle of contradiction: contemporaneous states are compossible; successive (ordered) states are, at least virtually, incompossible, and all this is so in the order of time. The world as serial order—simultaneity or sequence—is referred to the principle of identity or its opposite. This defines order, globally speaking. Now we come to local order. "If, of two things that are not simultaneous, one envelops the reason of the other, the former takes place first, the latter last. My preceding state envelops the reason for the existence of the following one. And since my preceding state, because of the connection of all things, also envelops the reason of the preceding state of the other things, it results that my preceding state also envelops the reason of the following state of the other things; therefore it is anterior to that state of the other things. Consequently, everything that exists is either contemporaneous with another existent, anterior to it, or posterior to it. Time is the order of existence of things that are not simultaneous. It is therefore the general order of changes, insofar as one doesn't consider the type of change (compare to the *De rerum, sub initio: etsi certis mutandi legibus* [though in accordance with certain laws of change, 149]). Space is the order of coexistence, or the order of existence between things that are simultaneous." Space is the order of things outside order. Thus, local order, chain link by chain link, by immediate proximity, is subject, for its part, to the principle of reason. Conversely, regression along the ordered sequence, from chain link to chain link, only iterates, as many times as you like, this same principle of reason that gives a reason for the successor. In other words, consideration of local order accounts for local order, without possible integration. This is the classic distance between the principle of identity or of contradiction and the principle of reason: this distance is, strictly speaking, more than virtually infinite. It can never be filled. Hence, at the beginning of the text, the argument *a contingentia*, hence at the end of the text, the infinite development of history, which is perfectly symmetrical around divine identity and its actual infinity. World time is as endless as its origin is inaccessible. History has the same power as the proof of the existence of God. The transfinite weight of endless progress, which modernity takes up while expressing it in another way, was discovered in those times: the Aufklärung began in a symmetry with the *Theodicy*. The question is whether the symmetry is a repetition, whether the philosophy of history is not a displaced and distorted but constant way of talking again, without saying so, about natural theology or theurgy. Hegel will follow Leibniz, who envelops the reason of existence of his successor, Hegel, who, in fact, will say that he completes Reason and realizes it, in capitalizing its first letter. They are, for their part, too, in order, or think subject to and expressing that Order, which is perhaps that of command and domination, of the *dominans* in general, as with the causal chain. The principle of reason simply changes status but keeps its denomination; it is completed in a cycle of states already outlined archaically in the *De rerum*. And, to get back to them, space and time are first, as far as the things themselves are concerned, or rather, what is first is their intersection, noncontradictory simultaneity, the *static (status)* state of things. They are not first in the order; they are elementary orders. As an aggregate of spatiotemporal things, the world is in order, whether coexistent or successive. Its structure is simple, the principle of reason, which doesn't envelop absolutely first terms. On balance, the initial elementary sets are themselves orders; they have an ordering law, the principle *ex hypothesi*, which is what I wanted to demonstrate. Let's look at the text's lexicon: *alium ex alio* [one made from another, 149], *praesentis ex praeterito* [present copy of the book from the previous book, 149], *sequens ex praecedente* [the state which follows is copied from the previous state, 149], *regressus in status anteriores* [far back we might go into previous states, 149], *statuum successionem* [a succession of states, 149], *progressus in infinitum*, et cetera. The series in question are well equipped with an ordering law. Any state whatsoever is subject to the principle of identity-contradiction, as simultaneous, coexistent, or spatial; and since two successive states envelop opposite states of a same thing, the same principle of contradiction dominates the occurrence of change, and the principle of reason dominates its reason. The Hegelian terms are already in place. But they are still terms of calculation (whether axiomatic, serial, or analytic), clear, distinct, dominatable. While God calculates, the world is made—space and time—and time is endless like the calculation, without return. Paradise, thereby, is not for right away, and no doubt forever. It must truly take all of time not to attain what is the most highly inaccessible. As a digression or an aside: can the word *prevalence* already be understood? Its prefix designates an antecedent among an order, and its root a quantification. In this characteristic and numeral atomism, is inclination the other (and the same) name for the clinamen?

In the constitution of traditional arithmetic, the theory of proportions has its place, like the processes of quantification and the order structures. Euclid's *Elements,* quite rightly, devotes an entire book to it. The frequency of this form of reasoning in ancient philosophy (Plato, Aristotle) and modern philosophy (Descartes) is known. Therefore, the *De rerum* begins with these words: the dominant unity or oneness is to this world or aggregate what the soul is to me [*moi*] or what my self [*moi-même*] is to my body, but according to a much higher reason. It is indeed a question of an analogy in the Greek sense, taken up again without any changes in Leibniz's mathematics; that is, it is a question of a sequence of relations or proportions, such as $a/b = c/d = d/e$: it is immediately noticeable that if p is the *reason* or ratio common to the three relations, the latter two are strictly equal to it, not the first one. There is a difficulty here.

In the three cases, the terms of the proposition are always of the form monad and aggregate; it relates the simple and the compound, the unitary being and the being by aggregation, the one and the multiple, the substance and the contingent. From which it results that if the world is an aggregate, me [*moi*] and my body are likewise so, and that if God is a monad, my soul and my self [*moi*] are likewise so. The me or self [*moi*] is a mean proportional: it is therefore one and an aggregate depending on the word that is referred to it. More substantial than the body, more compound than the soul; regarding this point, the summary table of the letter to des Bosses of August 19, 1715, puts things in order fairly well. No dominant is dominant enough to always be so on the scale: from master, in a certain order, it becomes aggregative again. Consequently, the analogical sequence cadences the scale of power put into place just now. The world is an aggregate of bodies, and therefore an aggregate of aggregates; God is *monas monadum* [monad of monads]. The self [*moi*] is only a relative unity, hence the critique of the cogito by the multiplicity of thoughts. Hence the question: is God something like the soul of the world? Yes, if the reason or ratio is preserved for the first relation; no, if it is not. But it is not, and God is not the soul of the world. This is Harlequin's law concerning analogy: it is always and everywhere the same thing, and the reason is identical, barring the orders of size and perfection, *ratione multo altiore*. There is always a reason for relations and proportions, but it varies when, following the scale, the order changes. Put differently, there are homogens and homogons, Archimedean and non-Archimedean orders.[18] The proof is that Leibniz later requires different reasons: the order of sufficiency required for an explication varies from the *ex hypothesi* to the full and entire reason, from the accessible to the inaccessible. So access to the infinite stops arithmetic knowledge there: we must move on to another knowledge.

Before getting to this, we must say a word about geometry. Space has been introduced by the notion of aggregate. And the presence of Euclid's *Elements* ensures, at least metaphorically, that it is a question here of an axiomatics or of a geometry of the world and of creation. On the other hand, the theory of proportions is the essential thing of the *more geometrico* in the seventeenth century. There is more: the question of space takes on a lot of importance right in the middle of the text, and twice over.

1. When it is a matter of the terrain on which to construct the most pleasing building possible. Here is the problem. God is infinite, and the world is maximal-optimal. God, in fact, couldn't create an infinite world, under pain of reproducing himself identically or self-creating. Therefore he creates, since he is infinitely good, the best of all possible worlds. The best, since he is good, and only the best possible so as not to bring about the existence of another God. That said, is the world maximum or optimum? Here is the old quarrel of the priority between quality and quantity, morality and geometry. Instead of disputing without concluding, let us calculate. Whether it is a matter of optimization or of maximization, these processes imply a *limit*, a *bound*, a *constraint* (or several). Otherwise they would be impossible to conceive. In order to conceive an *extremum* in general, why it is extremal

must necessarily be conceived. It is extremal by constraints, what Leibniz calls determinations. Let's read the *De rerum:* God constructs the most pleasing building possible on a *terrenum*.[19] Therefore, it seems that this *terrenum,* space, preexists divine act; so creation is no longer *ex nihilo,* since it meets with a principle of limitation exterior to its act. The *terrenum* is nothing other than the *Timaeus*'s *chôra;* God is no longer anything but a demiurge. With teleology and necessity dominating Plato's text, like this text, we would be forced to conclude with notions perfectly opposed to Leibniz's constant and exoteric teaching. We must start over. The *extremum* presupposes a bound. But this limit is nothing other than that without which there would be infinity. But what in fact cannot in any way be infinite, without being subject to contradiction? Three things: space, number, and velocity. A thousand texts repeat this at opportune and inopportune times. The three basic concepts for arithmetic, geometry, and mechanics. Reducible to space and to quantity. Therefore space and quantity are principles of limitation. That is to say, order and measurement. Order, the two orders, space and time, simultaneous things, successive things, hence the quantity of velocity. Order and measurement, which is to say, mathematics. Mathematics, which is to say, something inherent to uncreated logic. *Dum Deus calculat* (number, space, metaphysical mechanics) *limes fit:*[20] to calculate is to practice notions that, of themselves, imply limit, bound, constraint. Therefore, while God calculates, there exist, of themselves, in arithmetic, geometry, and the mechanics of creation, constraints that necessarily make an extremal world. I did not say that number, space, and velocity were attributes of God; I merely said that the act of calculating, in order to create, presupposed them. Hence the solution to the ancient squabble: it is definitely by the maximum that the world is optimal, since precisely the moral qualities—goodness, power, wisdom—can be infinite and have no bounds. So we must indeed, in order to optimize, find them somewhere. Then and only then is the use of *terrenum* coherent and indispensable, and what I shall later call determination by edges rigorous. The *chôra* is, in the same way, a limited, bounded, cut-out space of ground. It is not chance that leads the *Theodicy*'s most famous passage, Section 30, to use, for an analogous problem, the mechanical metaphor of a boat and its headway on a river, its velocity, its inertia, the spatiotemporal references of its motion. The question of the best is easy to solve, on condition of being clear about its conditions, which is to say, about its constraints, and therefore about the concepts that envelop said constraints.

2. Creation presupposes a combinatorics of elements or discrete possibles in the divine understanding. Everyone knows the sorting of the compossibles according to the principle of contradiction and the choice of the final compound according to the principle of the best. It has become clear that the terrain on which to construct the most advantageously was hardly a parable and that it was necessary to the production of a limit without which optimization wouldn't be conceivable. But while such a space is determined, in the full sense, by its edges, it is not only its edges. Under these conditions, at what moment of the process is this space formed? Quite near the origin, as a game space or space of relations. For as soon as the combinatorial act occurs, the calculator forms series, and series of variations, in the sense of the *De arte*. The exhaustive multiplicity of these lines constitutes complete tables, as can be seen teeming in the same opuscule. These tables exhibit the order (they are an order, in the sense defined by the author: multiplicity equipped with a reason) of possible substitutions, the order of exchanges, the complete order of directions or senses of exchange, the East and the West, if you like, and their global circularity. It is a question, precisely, of relative, or better, relational space, which is at issue in the correspondence with Clarke. The proof of this is that in the final analysis the aggregate produced is only a series of series, that is, a table, for its part too, of the general term $a_i b_i$. It is not irrelevant to read it in the direction $b_i a_i$. In other words, the combinatorial act envelops a space, a game space, a space of choices, of directions, of relations, the order of substitutables, the order of simultaneous possibles, that is to say, space as such, filled with things and oriented. No, the assembled notes constitute it, and have done from the origin.

Incidentally, the *Initia rerum mathematicarum metaphysica* deduces space and time from the principle of identity, by definition from simultaneous things, set out at the start. As soon as two contradictory elements, two contradictory propositions, two contradictory states of things cannot be true or set forth *at the same time* and in the same respect, it follows that time is the order of successive things, that is, of things that can envelop contradictory elements, propositions, or states. Two contradictory states cannot be simultaneous. They can exist, but they can only be strictly successive; it is not at all necessary for them to be so. The motive force of reasoning resides in the order of the chain and the modality of the possible. By eliminating these precautions, discourse deteriorates. It is *logically* unavoidable—or there is no longer any speech—for these two contradictory propositions to be unable to occur at the same time; it is an illicit inversion to derive from this the idea that time unfolds regularly by emergence and opposition of contradictions. This is why the passage from Leibniz to Hegel is not as easy as has long been believed. In fact, this idea only becomes truly thinkable when mechanics replaces logic and motion is substituted for time. Then, it is possible to conceive a schema of opposite forces, in simultaneity, suitable to engender any motion. But then the word *contradiction* is slightly ambiguous, due to its traditional logical connotation.

The calculation of creation doesn't stop at a combinatorics concerned with the discrete or the establishment of a relational space. As though this calculation had followed step by step the arithmetization of analysis that, from the seventeenth century on, was allowed by scientific theory, it becomes functional at the opportune moment; series, in fact, can define, by developing them, continuous functions. On this point, the lexicon of the *De rerum* does not lend itself to ambiguity: the elements—essences or possibles—like variables, strive *toward* something, existence strictly speaking, and their compositions, their combined series, like functions, are going to be classified, compared, and chosen lastly *pro gradu*, according to degree. *Pro gradu essentiae,* in proportion to the variable; then in proportion to the *quantity* of perfection, of reality that they envelop globally.[21] We have passed from the discrete to the continuous, by the usual path drawn by contemporary analysis, from quantification to assessment. And just as the global cycle draws its entire loop on the philosophical text, as though the advent of knowledge accompanied the advent of things, so, at the precise moment of this advent, an encyclopedic microcycle is projected on the theory of the determination of the best of all possible worlds. All of knowledge surrounds its birth. The assessment of the maximum is found everywhere. In game theory, there is one way, and one way only, to attain the completion of squares on the board. In space: with one dimension, the straight line is determined univocally by the shortest path, the brachistochrone by the maximal economy of time, the line of the greatest slope by the fastest descent; with two dimensions, the right angle is a case of equality: of the maximum of the smallest (acute) angles and of the minimum of the widest (obtuse) angles; the equilateral triangle[22] is a classic case for the isoperimetric problem; with three dimensions, the sphere has the greatest volume for a given surface area, as can be seen with oil or water. From the discrete to the continuous, from combinatorics to physics, passing through geometry and mechanics, the calculation of variations invades every domain of knowledge and imposes a single law of determination, valid structurally for every discipline and for the world. To my knowledge, the old seventeenth-century proposition, affirmed as dogma and never proved, had never been demonstrated down to such detail, the proposition that from knowledge to being, the consequence is good. But here, *consequence* is an improper word, for, from being to knowledge, the same sequence is preserved. Only the harmony remains.

What about this law? Production is at issue: it is the equilateral triangle that is *produced (prodire)*.[23] Determination is at issue: what is produced is the determined. Hence the preceding models, distributed in all of knowledge. We give ourselves a set of possibles whose entirety is known by God alone, but over these possibles humans have no power. We presuppose that they all strive *pari jure* toward existence.[24] This shows that they are not in any way in order at the outset and that any of them have a chance of attaining existence. And, therefore, all emergence is stochastic. Any possibility can produce itself. There is no precondition, there is no predetermination. The background of being is stochastic and combinatorial. I don't know of a better form to give the presuppositions of all science. That said, what do the operators that are added and superposed onto the initial collective signify: the most, the least, the best organized, the simplest, the best? The traditional interpretation uses two paths; first, it sets in opposition the absolute superlative and the relative superlative, and then takes into account as much as possible of the constraints of the organization as such, of compossibility, of local minima; optimized totality exhibits flaws, patches, gaps, and regional pockets of depression: this is a negative-image view of our world, for we are used to thinking a deteriorating world that has enclaves of increase. Second, the traditional interpretation sets in opposition optimum and maximum, in a discussion we have attempted to close. There is another way to envision the law. It is a question of a principle of determination for a given production. In other words, of a decision: in Leibniz, determination and decision are synonyms, decision, as we know, not being subjective. Since that time, we have relearned this. The principle is indeed something like a superlative. The determining structure is superlative, superposed in a certain way: is it a superstructure? The statement would be a play on words that another play would overturn, since, depending on case and place, the minimum can occur in its turn, the lower limit, what is positioned below. There is no doubt a savage ethics[25] at work in the use of a scale of this type, a hierarchy. This is what fuels the quarrel over the optimal and maximal. Who will be above, the quantifier or the moralist? But maximum and minimum are the quantitative translation of a phenomenon that's easy to conceive without the aid of quantity and without, nonetheless, having recourse to the language of ethics: it suffices to use the lexicon of quality, that is to say, according to Leibniz, of the real. Determination takes place at the limit states, at the extreme states, which is to say, at the periphery, at the exterior, on the edges. And the origin is nothing other than a particular edge. The determining structures for a given production are always at the margin, on the perimeter, as though the word *circum-ference* said more than the word *super-lative,* and not vice versa. This is evident enough in the knowledge of the seventeenth century and the figures of determination cited above; it can always be seen in integral invariants, as can be found in embryology, on the surfaces of stars or the outer sides of black boxes. Trees live by their bark. Here, Leibniz has a sovereign intuition, an intuition of ultrastructure, of a morphogenesis by edges. Yes, the actual series of the universe have no ends or beginnings. At the extreme metempirical limit of these lines and their fabric appears a determining reason, at the edge of nothingness, at the edge of existentiable possibility, which produces them as they are, something rather than nothing, more than nothing, at the edge of nothing. Hence that other intuition, the same one: everything is resolved in a universal doctrine *de continente et contento*, now considered less as an analytic of inherence than as a morphology of adherence. Determination, production, origin, edge—these four terms are substitutable, *salva veritate;* the radical origin is, tautologically, the edge. The terrain, just now, was indispensable in that, precisely, it was bounded, closed, cut-out, and in that a nonfinite terrain couldn't be conceived without contradiction. The world was optimally constituted by the constraint of its edges. The limit, suddenly, is the site of reason and of determination. Determination is what has issued from the term. Production is brought about by its prefix.

In passing, one admires the distribution of the spatial varieties: space of games, of relations, tables of series or combinations, local topology, description of states and of stabilities, ordinary spaces of one, two, or three dimensions, supports of mechanics or hydrodynamics. A "geometric" cycle is completed again when, on the occasion of the problem of evil, which is to say, of a global judgment on the state of things, the text finds itself constrained to pass to perspective, that Arguesian discipline Descartes fittingly called the metaphysics of geometry. The fact that, to appreciate a painting with rectitude, one has to look at it from a suitable distance says everything at the same time. There is an optimal site among all the possible others, and these latter express the local without regard to the whole. There are oblique scenographies, confused jumbles of assembled colors without art or choice, regional pockets of depression: in this case, I am not placed at the true point of view; my one-multiple and site-spectacle relation is adulterated, or rather, it is only the one-multiple relation of one expression among other possible ones that are just as unfaithful. In the optimal site, on the contrary, the limit of all the others and the choice determined from among them, it is the one-all and point-whole relation and delivers the intuitive, clear, and distinct ichnography without confusion or obscurity, order and no longer jumble, combination and not assemblage, in short, the geometral of the world scene. By moving from site to site, I imitate, for knowledge and in my department, the very process of creation; better, knowledge is produced for me the way being or the real are for God: from any whatsoever to the determined, from the multiple to the unitary chosen, from the local to the global, from the confused to the distinguished, from the lateral to the optimal, from the oblique point of view to the center. We must understand, once again, that the fixed point by which the geometral appears is *extremum,* limit and choice with regard to the variable sites, a singularity among the multiple. The fixed point is a center; it is also an edge. Thus "projective" geometry in its entirety is a faithful projection of the constitution of things, in my effort, pain, and project. The ichnography-scenography relation is the one-multiple, distinguished-confused relation; it envelops every concept as expression and harmony. Hence the return to God himself: who turns on all sides and in all ways the general system of phenomena and views all the faces of the world in all ways possible; "the result of each view of the universe, as seen from a certain position, is a substance that expresses the universe in conformity with that view."[26] There is a combinatorial metaphysics for the original production; there is likewise a metaphysical mechanics; there is now a metaphysical geometry. And, since the series of sciences is complete, metaphysics is a projection of the whole of knowledge, of general science. There is first philosophy only on condition of exhaustive knowledge, the way there is first emergence of things only on condition of the exhaustion of the possible.

The cycle of the encyclopedia, completed several times locally at the strong points of the argumentation as if the decisive moments of world production singularly necessitated the whole of rigorous knowledge, continues beyond the exact sciences once nature has been engendered, the earth that is present and has become a stranger to the dawn. A chemistry of liquid fermentation and a mineralogy of rock salts call to mind or suggest that the *Protogaea* and its hypothesis of *oleum per deliquium* [oil produced by deliquescence], both most often forgotten by professional philosophers, are efforts to reconstitute an origin of things, no longer at their metaphysical reason and root, but through an empirical description of their contemporary state. When Leibniz indicates, printed in the monad, vestiges, traces, and marks of its past history, he is not far from the plates and mines, already paleontological, of the *Protogaea*. The director of the Harz mines knew that genesis leaves monuments and that in starting from things themselves, buried in the abyss, it wasn't impossible to climb back up to the sources: the earth too is a palimpsest, like our understanding; it suffices to dig and to decipher the old inscriptions, the impressions, the program. The nascent geology, during the seventeenth century and in its work, is, it too, a discourse *de originatione*. The roots are indeed beneath the earth. But sometimes not so deep. For the text ends with the advice to give abandoned fallow land a good plowing; the soil, too, contains the virtual. This agronomic moment reminds us that Leibniz, a rustic philosopher, is the inventor of the word *physiocracy*. The roots of the future Garden of Eden.

Nothing is lacking in knowledge when exhaustively stated: not the musical theory of seventh chords, nor a "psychology" of affections. Science in its entirety is everywhere in the world in its entirety. The order of science is the order of the world. The encyclopedia is engendered with things the way the things are engendered starting from the root. Characteristic, logico-grammatical knowledge, combinatorics, arithmetic and theory of proportions, geometry and calculus of variations, figures of determination and of the distinguished, mechanics, physics, earth sciences, soil sciences, physiology of emotions... The order of engenderment of the sciences is parallel to the order of engenderment of the things themselves. The history and prehistory of beings is isomorphic to the history and prehistory of the fields of knowledge. The production of knowledge is taken at the root like the production of the world. From the origin of the sciences to the origin of nature, from the progress of the one to the progress of the other, the sequences are parallel and faithful: they express the same thing, which is invariant. The encyclopedic cycle and the metaphysical cycle are two variants of the same order. The *De rerum* is constructed like both, from the upstream (*praeter*) to the never comes to an end (*nec ad terminum perveniri*), in an open series.

Philosophy of Science

Does Leibniz practice the philosophy of science? First of all, how should it be defined? Where is it? What does it do? It is a theory of science, apparently and whatever this theory might be. But a theory is primitively a spectacle, and contemplating a theater presupposes having one's site outside the stage where the drama is engaged. Leibniz uses the word *theater* many times (for nature, for the envelopments and developments of living things . . .), but never for science. This is because he is one of the heroes of an action that cannot become representation without being adulterated, without losing its essence of direct action; the only discourse that isn't feigned, the only judicial act in which the judge must be a party to be able to render a verdict. Yes, Leibniz speaks *from inside* science. He practices it.

In its relation to scientific knowledge, philosophy seeks a site from which it can form a language regarding the encyclopedia, which, well-formed, itself speaks a language that's closed over itself. But, of these sites, there are four possible—and only four—that have been discovered, defined, and practiced by the aforementioned philosophers. Something can be seen *from above, from below, from the front,* or *from the back.* Leibniz has never occupied a single one of these points of view: he obscurely sensed that all four of them were conceivable; he obscurely sensed the adulteration they induce; he obscurely sensed that there was no discourse on science but the discourse of science itself, that the definition of science was objectifiable or thematized only by its own course of study. These four sites define four types or modes of appropriation of science, four clever ways of illicitly acquiring a property, which is to say, of acquiring a sovereign science without passing through science as such.

Quickly: the first of these points of view is the Greek site. Metaphysics is the queen of the sciences, in a position of towering over and dominating. Or: the rigorous sciences are propaedeutics to dialectical ascension; they are initiatory. Philosophy is a thinking that surveys from on high, a set of mother ideas that are generative and constitutive: on the first slopes of the mountain reside a few geometer or arithmetician slaves, or the child the philosopher was, in a world he had to forget. The supremely elevated site lets him judge the false and the true, relevance and opinion. Metaphysics is the toponym of the site. There is a queen, she is normative. She is called science, superlatively.

The second point of view is the Kantian site. Philosophy, become science, extricates the conditions of possibility of the encyclopedic practice. These conditions are layers, underlying formations to be discovered in the act of the subject or elsewhere; the geological, paleontological, and archeological metaphors designate an orientation toward fundament, foundation, origin. The question posed: what does science rest on? The chronology goes from Descartes to Kant, from Kant to Husserl and his epigones. The transcendental (or the historico-intentional) is the toponym of the site. There is a ground, it is constitutive. Philosophy is called science, fundamentally.

The third point of view is the site of the Enlightenment. Philosophy projects in front of itself, in a dynamic of progress, the essence of the true. There is an ever-withdrawing horizon, the site of magnetic fields that polarize the history of science. There is a velocity vector and an acceleration vector, both oriented in the direction of history: this direction is the filter of the true, the false, accident, essence, crisis, and completion. The question posed: what is science hastening toward? The chronology goes from the Aufklärung to Hegel. Teleology is the toponym of the site. There is a telos, it is attractive. Philosophy is the science of points of no return.

The fourth point of view is the site of modernity. The philosopher is a consciousness that is suspicious and lucid, and not easily taken in. He detects behind science the all-powerful evil one who makes science into something other than what it gives itself out to be, who adulterates it, slows it, and appropriates it. Detective epistemology flushes out from behind the mask of knowledge and the language of the expert the representation of class, the ideology in power, the *hic fecit, cui prodest*,[27] the unknown or the unthought, whether impulse-based or dominant. From Marx, Nietzsche, and Freud to our contemporaries, the techniques for reading aim at a palimpsest: active writing is behind activated writing. The question posed: in front of what stage does science, naive, give performances that are not quite its own? Who is the hidden stage manager? Who or what pulls the strings of the deceived puppets who deceive us? The approach is retroactionary: going behind all actual knowledge, slipping behind each and every thing, constituting, in the tradition of philosophy's impregnable discourses, a discourse behind which no discourse can slip. Above, there were no discourses higher, deeper, or more prophetic: here, there aren't any that are more anterior, more archaic. The philosopher sees behind backs, and he has no back. Retroactive is the toponym of the site. There are forces *a tergo,* they are disruptive.

This law of the four cardinal sites exhausts and completes the loop of an adventure, that of the impregnable texts held outside knowledge. The four paths of domination. In these sites of privilege, the philosopher remains, invariably, no matter the point of view, the one who can neither deceive himself nor deceive us, a passable definition of God; he inherits the legacy of priests. The scientist takes his risks and dangerously offers himself to nonknowledge: his business is fallible, and his discourse never surpasses the norms he sets himself. Science comes up short under the law it imposes on itself; it is a game that submits to the rule of the game. Off the field, out of bounds, the theoretician spectator has an easy time escaping the rules, which he calls surpassing; his discourse always exceeds the norms it sets out. The philosopher is a subtle god no one can catch red-handed cheating: he plays outside the game. He grants himself the right to say the very opposite of science, in the name of his privilege: reject mathematics, immobilize the Earth, deny the laws of thermodynamics, et cetera. Talking about science, he doesn't talk science.

This can be refined. Each discipline of the encyclopedic course of study has, in addition, made use of a supplementary site from which to talk about all the other disciplines. As when God is transcendent and immanent, the philosopher is both outside and inside. Each of the aforementioned sites is, in other words, equipped with an alibi, in the word's etymological sense of elsewhere. The Trojan horse. Situated above, but supporting itself on mathematics; situated below, but modeling itself on mechanics, astronomy, and logic; situated in front, but taking its values from biology or history; situated behind, but referring itself to the social sciences. The global distance, generative of philosophical discourse, is accompanied by a local centering amid the cycle of knowledge. The dominant discipline is the court or the alibi of the court. Philosophy remains the science of the sciences, but it is protected by a possible substitute, the region elected as support of judgment and of analysis, a small-scale science of the sciences. Its selection in the encyclopedia and its being separated out would need to be justified; they are generally brought about by a history. How, let us know, can we grasp what calls itself a bird but also just now a mouse?

In every case, the shifting outside is locatable; in every case, it is a question of taking distance from a knowledge that is thereby objectivized, seeing it from the outside to produce a sovereign and unconfined theory of it. Having knowledge without having its knowledge. There are three types of such shifting: absolute exteriority, outside the encyclopedic whole, relative or transdisciplinary exteriority, and total substitution, lastly, when the philosopher starts to talk directly about the object by putting science in brackets. On balance, the question is one of metaphysics (the prefix is thereby clearly defined), or of interpretation by means of a code or superimposed filter, or, lastly, of a dream, in the sense Diderot gives this word. Don't see condemnation here; dreams can be fruitful or premonitory.

Let's do away with the distance. Let's enter into the actual work of science; let's let its discourse speak. Listening attentively, one easily hears its implicit philosophy. Is it, strictly speaking, a method? Yes. A method is acceptable not necessarily when the organon that promotes or justifies it is rigorous, nor even when it holds together all by itself like a systematic or normative monument (hence the derisory yield of most traditionally taught "methods," the yield, which is to say, the relation between the results and the power of the constructed tool), but rather when it is fruitful, here, now, right away. Preferable for what it does or creates, not for what it theorizes. It is a question here not of talking about science—around it, regarding it, on it (that is to say, above), but simply, directly, talking science, a science, some part, some theorem.

Here is the general equation of second-order curves. It depends on five parameters, as we can see. It suffices to differentiate it five times to eliminate the five constants and obtain a fifth-order differential equation having numerical coefficients and suitable for every conic of the plane. Nothing could be simpler and, therein, more beautiful. Let's let this exercise speak; it says entirely pure Leibniz.

1. I start from an equation *determined* by five constants. From an aggregate of signs. I start from *existing* conics, effectively inscribed in the plane by families that are infinite, enveloped, nested, continuously neighboring, expressed by a sentence that could find its place in any *Elements* of mathematical science.
2. I climb back up a finite chain, one having five chain links. It can be conceived with n chain links if the order is left undetermined. In other words, the chain is infinite for something in general: the singular existent has a nonfinite complexity. That is stated in the "Discourse" about the curve of a human figure.
3. In fleeing upstream along the chain, I progressively eliminate the determination, which is to say, the *sufficiency*. For it suffices to set some suitable parameters to determine this or that conic.
4. At the limit of the chain, I conceive the totality of the *possible;* better, I write it clearly and distinctly by means of a set of characteristic signs. This set is infinite for a chain with n chain links.
5. This set of signs is a *series:* in the fifth-order differential equation, there are five groups of differentials of an increasing order. This set is a *combination*. There is an infinite series or infinite combination for a chain with n chain links.
6. The elements of these tables are differentials, distinct and separated *(sejuncta)*, of vanishing entities that *strive toward* something.
7. Only the written equation furnishes the totality of the possible. The proof is that we use this totality to determine if a given differential equation of an order lower than five is indeed the equation of a planar family of conics. From which it results that, in the combinations of five differentials, there are *incompossibles,* and that in the final analysis there is *a single* adequate combination.

We have described the path going upstream; let's now travel the chain downstream.

1. The differential elements are suitable for rectifying, *squaring, cubing*. They supply a foundation for a theory of *measurement* (Gaston Grua, *Jurisprudence universelle et théodicée selon Leibniz* [Presses Universitaires de France, 1953], 338).
2. They are ordered by degrees (*pro gradu*).
3. As integration progresses, from chain link to chain link, I am led to add constants and even arbitrary functions. They increasingly *determine* the being to be constituted. These constants attach, most often, *the conditions to limits,* to edges, maximum and minimum at times.
4. Each differential equation expresses a family: toward upstream, families of families, and so on, ad infinitum: toward downstream, the final integration, attached to the whole equation, expresses the *individual*. Hence the games of relation: unity-multiplicity, individual-family, distinction-possibility, et cetera, couples intended to distribute a classification or to define the harmony.

It can easily be verified that these propositions omit nothing of what constitutes the canonical theory of creation. But they *never surpass* the language proper to the treatment of second-order equations by the infinitesimal organon. Put differently, calculation suffices; it remains to develop it, follow it, listen to what it says. This is what I wanted to demonstrate. Hence two corollaries:

1. The theory of creation is, exactly, a general physics, even more than a mechanics, that is, the application to the world, without displacement or transfer, without shifting outside or surpassing, without deformation, of the expressive characteristic formed by calculation. Harmony, in fact, is the reduction to zero of the shifting outside, that incomprehensible thing that makes things comprehensible. Contemporary science, to my knowledge, has

never known how to lead us beyond this solution, beyond this defeat that founds intelligibility's victories.

2. As an exercise, the reader can practice or listen to as many theorems as may be chosen from the *Mathesis;* elsewhere we have given the example of perspective geometry, here, of the harmonic triangle. He will quickly be convinced, against appearance and the tradition, that there is no theory surveying in flight from on high. The Leibnizian meditation grasps the metalanguage of its mathematics in flight, that necessary rumbling noise that runs among the impregnable calculations and cannot be separated from them. The prefix of the word *metaphysics* here designates no more distance, has—if this can be said—no greater length, than the prefix of the word *metalanguage*. Who doesn't know that this length and this distance are zero in the latter case? Metaphysics, then, is either a physics or a metalanguage.

6
Auguste Comte Self-Translated in the Encyclopedia

We lack an Auguste Comte. For navigating by dead reckoning. The position, calculated in this way on the endless sea, is nevertheless only a retroactive summary, which can block changes of direction or be deceptive regarding site. At least it is a position, in which work is possible and which can be moved, rectified, criticized. We are in need of such a balance sheet today: in a pinch, a bad one is better than an absent one. The crisis of our knowledge has no place: hence we were in despair that the crisis would ever take place; for many, it has not taken place and, for others, has occurred elsewhere. We are lacking an Auguste Comte, and this is why, without citing him, everyone goes around repeating the old Comte, the way one repeats without realizing it those who have not been replaced. The old institutional walls preserve him and make his phantom endlessly reappear.

His encyclopedia of the exact sciences nevertheless died on the first day of its birth. Let's not talk about errors, especially notable in mathematics. His encyclopedia died for two reasons, two instances of praise. First, it *recapitulates,* and the exhaustive knowledge of the author in it is rarely at fault: hence the best comprehensive survey of a present and of its past; and second, it *interdicts* what, for us, its future has become, and the author's sagacity in it is unsurpassable: he dazzlingly perceives what will be—so as to immediately block it. Hence his encyclopedia is the best of the testifying monuments. The synchronic cross section is, moreover, a monumental system. Being attentive to its structures reveals laws worth being written: we shall supply a few in the sections "Classification" and "The Law of Three States,"[1] old philosophemes that have been renewed by mechanics or astronomy. They are summed up in a *circular* figure, closed over itself, like the sectional view of history. At bottom, Comte is to knowledge and its history what Laplace is to the world: he rigorously shows its stability; he traces its genealogy. And now we lack a Laplace, a decisive model of the universe.

Recapitulation

At the end of the eighteenth century and the beginning of the nineteenth, as is readily said, a fever of invention took hold of Europe. It is less said, and nevertheless more true, that at the same time, a fever of inventorying came through. It began, following a Leibnizian dream, with Diderot and d'Alembert's great *Encyclopédie*, which, basing itself on Chancellor Bacon's plan, traced a figurative system of human knowledge. The general mobilization would no longer stop, as though the *ars inventoriendi* [art of inventory] were the basic technique from which the *ars inveniendi* [art of invention] got its force. One after the other, everyone tried to recapitulate, to draw the exhaustive space of knowledge and the complete series of its gradual conquests. Condorcet popularized the idea of Progress; the Enlightenment gave detailed study to the synchronic table of science and the diachrony of its advance. In Kant, balance sheets—under Newton's shadow—take up more space than genesis, which is nevertheless present in his cosmogony and his philosophy of history. In Rousseau, it is the opposite; the genetic component is more powerful than the act of taking inventory and dominates it: sciences, letters, arts, languages, education, sociopolitical contracts, and civil statuses are endlessly taken up again by the light of the origin. The nineteenth century at its beginnings—Romanticism, to give it a common name—will make its enterprise pass into the dissymmetry of these two works; it will make symmetrical, for its part, the universality of the encyclopedic order and the totality of the temporal order. This is, among others, the Hegelian age or the positive age.

Which still weighs on us: what are we to do when the forebears have recapitulated?

What are the conditions for the balance sheet? First, the occupation of the world. The grand voyages, begun in the fifteenth and sixteenth centuries, had come to an end: the discovery of the earth had been completed, and the paths had all been traveled. Humanity seemed to have exhausted all the possible routes; the exploration had closed all the circles. Hence new journeys, scientific missions: one experimented on the pendulum at Cayenne; one took observations at Cape Town and took measurements, by triangulation, of the meridian arcs.[2] The Earth, formerly recognized in a savage manner, became an object of science: the sciences of the earth, which were born at that time. Its global form, its motion, the oscillation of the tides, the disturbances of its gaseous envelope, all subjects of works that defined it as finite. Hence the advent of the French Bureau des Longitudes (the department of the network of circles that embrace the earth), and the metric system, which founded our technologies on its divisions. Arago staying awake at night on Formentera was the new utopian symbol: the world is an island, and the Museum its complete garden, its primal Eden, where its productions are *concentrated*. Recapitulation is also concentration, capital.

With space having been traveled and its circle completed, let's go back up time, in order to make the project symmetrical. An overabundance of examples: archeology was all the rage; Jacques Boucher de Perthes launched prehistory; the developing science of stratigraphy cadenced the ages of humankind and the earth with its vertical probes (journey to the past, journey to the center), and after Buffon and *The Epochs of Nature*, it remained for Lamarck and Darwin to decipher the laws of genesis. This was the century of the recognition of fossils, and not only with Cuvier: look at the mathematicians as they excavated the axiomatic foundations of geometry and re-engendered its corpus; admire how Laplace read Saturn's rings, remnants that served as evidence of a primal origin for his cosmogonic hypothesis; look at the medievalists and the mythologists as they flourished. Freud would soon be able to write and undertake a similar archaic journey. And this happened in very old times; the earth was still damp and soft from the flood: imprints. New utopia:

Napoleon's expedition to Egypt, another journey, one that was not in any way—far from it—a chance event in history. This is the first Romantic journey, both for its date and for its archetypal status. A model. It is a question of gathering the best and most complete encyclopedic collectivity (a dictionary in a boat), of taking it to a privileged point in space, sites that were selected precisely because they were brimming with fossils, and asking it to go back up time. There is indeed a recapitulation, through the gathering of the scientists, and two journeys, one of which—more significant—began in Cairo. Note that the vessel transporting the scientific instruments was lost at sea. There, Geoffrey Saint-Hilaire collected documents for reading evolution, Champollion decoded the fossils of writing, and the nascent Egyptology drew our common genealogy, while Monge, Costaz, and Caffarelli triangulated the Nile Valley. On balance, a map and a history, produced by an encyclopedia. I don't know of a better figure of the enterprises of the time: no thinker of the nineteenth century occupied themselves with anything else, nor did Comte or Hegel. That all this happened under the shadow of power, of a soon-to-be-dead general, and amid the clamors of war is the sign of a marriage, the fossil of an old cohabitation, the announcement of monstrous lovemakings of which modernity is the product.

That was the earth; this is the world. Recapitulation was possible because we finally held the unitary equation, the chapter heading, ever since the triumph of Newton's law in continental Europe. Thanks to which we could conceive a system, of the world and of knowledge. Comte incessantly says, ad nauseam, that Newton's law creates a synthesis between the fall of bodies onto the ground and the trajectories, in the heavens, of the planets and satellites. Mechanics (ballistics), astronomy, barology—one field of knowledge with three regions. Science welcomed attraction or gravitation with an enthusiasm equal to the reservations it had previously held in being wary of it. Coulomb's success and several hypotheses about liquids gave cause to hope that the law was truly universal; hence a few frenzies, including Saint-Simon's, an impassioned one; his secretary remained prudent and circumscribed the jurisdiction of the law to suitable regions, resisting the temptation to extrapolate on the sequence: monotheism-the metaphysical idea of nature.[3] The fact remains that it invaded the world, and soon the universe, since it affected double stars. Under its unitary grip, the idea of system was reborn, although it didn't have to die, Hume and Montesquieu demonstrably being Newtonians. It was the *age of great treatises*, in which the grand *Encyclopedia* seemed to convert itself into smaller currency, region by region. Everything seemed to happen as though, from Diderot and d'Alembert to Comte or Ampère, in the historical segment from the Revolution to the Restoration, and from one exhaustive synopsis to another, the concern for systematizing had slipped into the departments of knowledge. Lagrange, in his *Analytical Mechanics,* rigorously deduced, from the principle of virtual velocities, the set of the disciplines of equilibrium and motion, for solids, liquids, and gases, thereby writing a course on positive mechanics in its genre, the way he had written a course on calculus in his treatise *Theory of Analytical Functions.* From Newton's law, Laplace deduced the ordered whole of *Celestial Mechanics,* a course on positive astronomy in its genre. Here is a worldview, a new eminent model, which was not—far from it—a chance event in history, even if it be the history of concepts.

The System of the World and the preface to the third volume of the *Treatise on Celestial Mechanics* describe the maximal ecological niche for all possible life in the known world: general conditions of existence for humanity or living beings, preservation of individuals and perpetuation of species. A new example of a nonwritten law: that the history of philosophy is constantly a subset of the history of astronomy, that a grand philosophy always coexists with a cosmology, and that the cosmology is the crucial clue to the grand philosophy. No counterexample to this law is known. As with Comte, the alliance of Descartes and Newton is achieved in Laplace, for a recapitulation of the seventeenth century at the same time as of the known worlds: the former sets forth general principles, figures, motions, instruments, geometry, and mechanics; the latter sets forth systematic law and its method: calculus. In the end, gravity is demonstrated in regions of the heavens that seem to escape it: the microsystems of Jupiter and Saturn become reduced models, anomalous sites of the chosen terrains, disparities of proofs. The world is a system, by unicity, deduction, and coherence. But it is a system for another reason: the apparent exceptions, disparities, and residues are, in fact, periodic variations, sometimes lasting a century. Thus the changes cover over the constants, as do the variants for the restorations and the evolutions for the invariants. The solar world is oscillating around positions of equilibrium; it is stable: the great figure of the circle returns, not only for the rotation of the planets or their translations,[4] which are only orbits, but for the global state of n bodies interdetermined by mutual attraction, varying from all sides and at every second, as with a monadology, as well as for the local state of the gaseous envelopes and the fluid lenses of the seas. The world-system is closed, finite, comprehensible to the god of the differential equation table, endlessly predictable because it oscillates, and readable—by this very fact—all the way back to its origins; independent of the universe in the first orders of approximation, it is in a stable and periodic equilibrium, invariant, except for annual or century-long variations. It lastly refers to an invariable plane whose parameters are set, then rectified, by Poinsot, who places the general couple there, the circle's very motor. I do believe the anatomists will import this plane into the map of living things, whose structure endlessly varies around its fixity; the energeticists reexpress this constancy as the invariance of forces: there are no more than transfers from one point of concentration to another. The system of the world indeed expresses all the sciences, in its order, and all the philosophies, and several therapies. The house of humankind is in order, and the taking of inventory has finished. A house now fitted-out for nautical technology, whether a present or future one. There are no longer any voyages but circular ones, on the globe, in space, or in the metaphor of ideas. Philosophical systems imitate the system of the world or decorate a niche that has already been fitted out.

That said, the cartography is, once again, symmetrized by a history, the system by a genesis, and the order by a progress. Cosmogony, in the literal sense, formation of an order, is a science. Laplace's cosmogony continues Kant's: the fact that they are similar and independent confirms the style of analysis. The world is born from the fluid envelope of the solar nebula, another determination by edges. Constants of the universe and apparent anomalies (Saturn's rings) are read together as fossils, once again, and the system is a monument, in both senses of the word; the same holds true for Comte. To be read as witnesses or remainders: the identity of the directions of rotation, the small inclination of the orbital planes with respect to the ecliptic, and the slight eccentricity of the planetary trajectories. Hence the detachment of gaseous packets at the solar equator, where the centrifugal force is maximal and the centripetal force minimal; with regard to this originary cloud of clouds, a law of three states will soon function to engender today's planets, formerly gaseous magma, later liquid masses, more recently consistent solid aggregates, but today still equipped with three regimes, as is fitting, tiered into strata and datable as fossils. Comte extrapolated on Laplace and closed the cosmology of *Celestial Mechanics* into a circle; the friction of the general environment and of the strata stacked on top of each other is not negligible; it operates as a brake: in the very remote term, the velocity weakens as well as the radial vectors; the reunion with the solar globe is, again, predictable. The system collapses into the origin furnace, and the process starts over. The cosmogonic model of the *Vingt-Septième Leçon* is an oscillating one through temporal integration of the oscillation of the cosmology. The order of the progress is symmetrical with the progress of the order, and "revolution" resumes its astronomical sense of rhythmic conservation. Having set out from the sun—as from fetishism—by recommencing circles, positivism returns to the sun—as it does to religion in *The Catechism of Positive Religion;* the nether side and the beyond side of the *consistency* of the sciences are in the same region, said to be vague and cloudy. Whence it results that the map and the history mutually loop into each other and recapitulate each other; world, system, and encyclopedia are cycles. With all things distributed along an oscillating model, how could the past not constitute the horizon? Comte, who employs prediction for the one as well as for the other, admits this. Therefore, the *Cours* is, scientifically, a cemetery of fossils; it is formed with the dead more than the living. This was the age of encyclopedic geniuses; they closed history and philosophy, in order to delude their nephews into believing that they had left them nothing more to do. It is entertaining to see the grandnephews still believe this. The inert power of lazy sophisms.

The Interdictions

In the order of rigor and exactitude, the list of the sciences or enterprises condemned by positivism is highly significant. Comte is distrustful of an abstract theory of numbers and arithmetic considered for its own sake; he dismisses the idea of a mathematical logic when it is presented under the aspect of a general theory of signs or a project of universal language; abstraction pushed too far—formalization—is repugnant to the positive spirit. Thus he recommends that the physicist keep a tight rein on the algebraic spirit, which he considers harmful, while he trusts in geometry and mechanics, which are natural sciences. Mathematical science must remain an instrument: it is forbidden that it take itself as the object of its own practice. This is the first circumscription, which has to do with the nature of the discipline or, as they say, its essence. The second one draws the pomerium of accessible space: only the world—that is, the solar system—is the object of science; the stellar and galactic universe is outside our grasp. The definition and the demarcation here have a spatial nature: the outermost planet shuts a closed, stable, independent, circular, and oscillatory field, which constitutes humanity's dwelling, prepares its conditions for existence, secures its needs, and forms the terrain for the exercise of its means. Mathematics is the tool of a practice; the planetary world represents its limits and encloses its scope.

Comte is skeptical about the works of Herschel and Savary, which seem to him to go beyond our means. This signifies two things: overstepping the solar region and going beyond the borders of the scientific regions. Hence the third condemnation: there cannot be any stellar physics or stellar chemistry; in other words, one does not cross the boundaries of the classification cells in a direction different from that of hierarchy. It is indeed a question of circumscription, since interdisciplinarity has been dismissed, for which astrophysics will precisely be a remarkable paradigm. Conversely, every interdiction thrown onto interdisciplinarity remains of a positivist spirit. The fourth circumscription has to do with hypothesis in physics and the mode of phenomena production: heat, light, and electricity. This circumscription is reductive and electively partitions the region of the quomodo. Lastly, the fifth circumscription reduces the things themselves, conceived in the form of motion and figure, and never in their plurality: hence the exclusion of the so-called calculation of chances.

The table of exclusion expresses marvelously, although in counterrelief, the positive state and ideal: Cartesian, through mechanics and geometry (disciplines of predilection), through metrics in general and the mastery and possession of nature; Cartesian, again, through the well-delineated drawing of secure regions; Cartesian, lastly, through this repugnance for the mixing of types. Laplace, fortunately, had closed the loop of the solar system and shown its stability; the polytechnician spirit kept watch on mathematics within the walls of the new school, where Monge perfected Descartes's analytic geometry. On balance, science, sciences, methods, and objects are arranged in cells—whose boundaries are inviolable: hence the word *circumscription*. Short of this, beyond this, there is no science.

But, in fact, said table constitutes the best of programs for future science. What Comte excluded was the new, new scientific spirit, undergoing development at the time of the *Cours*. Logic was reborn during those very years: Bolzano's *Theory of Science* dates from 1837, and Boole would soon follow. Abstract mathematics, with number theory first in line, had experienced some rapid development around the end of the eighteenth century, outside naturalist imperatives and application concerns. The algebraic spirit dominated in Abel and Galois as much as the arithmetic spirit had reigned in Gauss. Comte had reason to be wary: the two disciplines would devour 150 years of history, to the point of veiling from us the work of the eponymous geniuses of the positive age—Euler, Lagrange, Monge—to the point of presenting the problems they addressed as residues and obstacles, diminished in their shadow. That it took us a long time to free ourselves from this grip, at least in France, and to see mathematics directly is attested by the naivete of the philosophers, who took the advent of non-Euclidean geometries as earthshaking. Formalism, the axiomatic method, the grand thematization of mathematics finally dealing with its own affairs, that is, with itself—in short, abstraction—all this was being born the moment Comte was blocking it. He did not say a word about combinatorics, and modern science is based on it. His dogmatic gesture is only a historical gesture:[5] it assesses the great treatises of the French school and conceals the resource of rigorous science, which, now, is called mathematics. We thought in the field it was excluded from.

Things go no differently with the world. At the very moment when positivism was shutting a second time the system that Laplace had closed, stellar and galactic astronomy was at its start. It would no longer stop taking over the reins from the old celestial mechanics, and our world became the universe. Works of philosophy, increasingly lagging behind several sciences and surprised by Lobachevsky, celebrated Le Verrier; they forgot or ignored Hertzsprung as well as Cantor, and Russell as much as Russell. Comte's interdiction remained, and its tradition obliterated living science. And living science resided precisely in the interdicted zone. The astrophysical revolution, as important as it was formalist, had two results: it opened up new spaces and new times, and it opened up the sciences to each other, causing interdisciplinarity to triumph. The heavens unfold Mendeleev's table before our eyes; it is a furnace where this table is formed. The third circumscription vanishes. And the two others likewise: what would our science of light be if the nineteenth century had not taken seriously both the wave hypothesis and the hypothesis of emission, and instead summarily dismissed them? What would we know about heat without statistical thermodynamics, in which, in fact, molecular agitation is studied for its own sake? What would we know about electricity if we had not set out the electron hypothesis? Lastly, what would our knowledge be without the calculation of probabilities, itself the crossroads of the totality of the disciplines, from number theory to the works about information? On balance, the following are nonpositivist (and it is Auguste Comte who said "non-"): our logic (from existing), our regional scientific languages (from developing at the margins of ordinary language), our mathematics (from being abstract, algebraic, formalized, and axiomatic), our astronomy (from taking the universe as its object and the physical and chemical disciplines, in an original intersection, as its method), our thermodynamics (from utilizing stochastic functions), our optics and our electricity (from having detected photons and electrons), and so on. On balance, all our science is nonpositivist; *it was formed from the interdictions of the* Cours. From which it results that this book, due to its program of bad luck, is a historical witness, irreplaceable and of a high purity: its exclusions had sufficiently cut it off from the future and its references had sufficiently plunged into its present for its dogmas to remain a good instant snapshot. The positive state is less a norm than a synchronous summary. Misfortune came only later: from those who took it at its word and read only the *Cours*'s first two lessons. We lack an Auguste Comte, but the first one weighed too much. The intellectual comfort translated by the *Cours* comes from the fact that it crowned the seventeenth century and blocked the new spirit. Hence the program of bad luck, with regard to living knowledge, of *all* the recent epistemologists in the French language. It is the same program as that of the *Cours*—and they are *all* positivists.

Classification

We lack a classification of the sciences; we don't even know if it is possible. This is why we repeat the classification that has not been replaced, while overloading it, if necessary, with adventitious branches, just as past astronomers added an epicycle, if need be, to the epicycles of an outmoded model. Comte's classification is a dichotomic tree, just like every well-formed table; it is based on combinatorics, something that's inevitable when one wants to occupy a space.

Preliminary questions: Are the operational dichotomies used in the division truly scientific? In general, can one propose a science of classification? If yes, this science ought to be classified; it would have to be both classifying and classified, global and cellular, hence the circle. In Comte, neither combinatorics nor the logic of distinctions in the mode of Porphyry are classified, but he is not sure whether they are, to his eyes, really classifying. Moreover, the dichotomies designate the things themselves, in their order; only, however, the positive disciplines permit observing, knowing, and setting forth laws, disregarding the nature of things; and now these disciplines are jointed to each other according to preconditions having to do with the order of things, the second circle.

Or: the dichotomies are not scientific. In fact, the divisions brute matter–living organism, heavens–earth (high–low, close–distant), and individual–society are so little obvious that the *Cours,* after having created them, contested them. So the classification grows like a savage thought; the arborescence has its roots in what Comte calls fetishism. Here, ethnology confirms: close familiarity with the biological environment, as well observed by Lévi-Strauss, for example, would coincide fairly well with the valorization of physiology as a systematic model and supplier of the base dichotomy; concern for exhaustive observation and comprehensive inventory, combined with the application of a simplified model, are common to both positivist and savage thought;[6] on the one hand, the logic of totemic classifications appears in the forms, not in the contents; on the other, only the abstract sciences are arranged in series, not the concrete sciences; on the one hand, the "primitive" logics are polyvalent and assemble several directions or axes of reference; on the other, Comte simultaneously examined the historical trajectory, the growth of complexity, and the narrowing of the general; lastly, the dichotomies found "in the field" often match up with Auguste Comte's dichotomies: near–distant, resemblance–difference, synchronic–diachronic, static–dynamic, individual–species, and so on. The parallelism needs to be developed; it is fairly fruitful.

That said, can we go to the end of the analogy and set forth a savage mind at secret work behind the positivist enterprise? I do not know, although there exist texts in which the author says more or less this very thing. And that would explain fairly well the lasting success of the classification. So the circle from just now is transposed to history, which, in the third state, is freed from archaic grips, but remains continually mobilized by them. However, the reason I am in doubt is the extent of positive reason operating in the enterprise of ethnologists when they theorize about knowledge reaped on the scene. And soon a certain hesitation begins to vibrate: there is fetishistic spontaneity in the practice of positivism and spontaneous positivism in the practice of someone who classifies savage knowledge . . . I don't know if it is appropriate to place Lévi-Strauss behind Comte or Comte behind Lévi-Strauss; I don't even know if a long reflection or a big book would decide this, since I have never truly been able to decide which we should laugh at first, the spontaneous philosophy of scientists or the spontaneous science of philosophers. Slipping behind the back of knowledge is a long-sought gesture, even a laudable intention, but to do this, knowledge is made to function, and the spiral recommences. It is always possible to draw a supplementary loop. This feedback epistemology seems to rest on a principle of uncertainty or indetermination that dominates the pencil of circles of the known and the unknown. During this time, science continues under its own momentum.

It is not certain that Comte was unaware of these circular traps. It seems instead that the line he drew supported them: this is why positivism is a system. So let's go back to the first case in order to observe a second meaning of the phrase "classification of the sciences," rarely highlighted: each region, of itself, engages in the activity of putting its own elements *in order;* it ends up with—or ought to end up with—a table, which continually resembles, in one way or another, the global fresco. So, the science of classification, in the first sense, is the diagram of the classifications, in the second sense. There may be a circle; there may be repetition, but they are as coherent as a series of models.

— The *Quatrième Leçon* classifies *functions,* simple or compound. The elementary ones—here is the "mathematheme"—are arranged according to five dichotomies of the direct-inverse type, such as sum-difference and product-quotient; the others are conceived according to a tree of distinctions, partly inherited from L. Euler, in which one finds abstract-concrete, direct-indirect, et cetera. This suffices to establish the fidelity of the image: it is indeed a question of a reduced model. In passing, Comte points out number tables in general.

— The *Cinquième Leçon* classifies algebraic *equations* according to the method called, here as well, natural. It is a question, of course, of the old arranging into series according to degrees or number of roots: the sequence is of increasing complexity, a thing that's observable by means of the criterion, but also by means of the difficulty of solving them beyond the third degree, after Cardano, or else by means of the power of the radicals revealed in the expression of the roots. And again, the analogy appears.

— The *Septième Leçon* classifies *infinitesimal calculus*. Horizontally, on the table constituted by this lesson, the law of classification is one of continued dichotomies (and differential-integral belongs to the direct-inverse type); there is symmetry between the first two dichotomies, so that, on both sides of the axis of symmetry, the divisions repeat themselves. Vertically, the law of increasing complexity is found, since differentiating is as easy as forming an equation, while integrating is as difficult as solving it. In passing, the table of fundamental differentials and elementary quadratures is noted. The analogy is all the more striking because, according to Comte, differential calculus is considered finite, limited, and perfect, like the sciences at the top of the general table, such as mechanics and astronomy, and because integral calculus is deemed inexhaustible, imperfect, and open, like the sciences at the bottom of the table. Infinitesimal calculus functions as a reduced-scale encyclopedia; the seventh lesson repeats the second one, which is to say, the *Cours* in its totality.

— The classification of curves in geometry reflects the bad state the analysis finds itself in; of course, algebraic curves follow the classification of equations by degrees, but transcendental curves find themselves in disorder. Strictly speaking, the integration of differential equations—classifiable, in their turn, according to their order—makes families of curves appear, and Comte does not indicate whether Monge knew how to write a fifth-order equation suitable to every possible conic section of a plane. Thus the *Quatorzième Leçon* prefers to make do with the classification of *surfaces*, in the manner of the very same Monge. The lesson gives this attempt as a model, just like the taxonomies or systematics of the life sciences, so that the translation is no longer the affair of the reader, but instead that of the author himself. It gives this attempt, moreover, to be admired as "the most important perfecting geometric science has received since Descartes and Leibniz," which retroactively imposes the idea that the most important thing in Descartes and Leibniz is the classification of equations and curves, on the one side, and the putting into order of infinitesimal calculus through operational symbolics, on the other; and the idea, more general, that every discipline must end up at a table of the same type. Comte first remarks that the principle of classification by form and degree of equations fails starting from the third degree, and that Newton, for example, cites seventy-four different curves in the discussion of the two-variable cubic equation. On the other hand, cylindrical surfaces can be of any degree according to the nature of their base, just like conics, and so on. So an analytical relation expressing their original mode of generation must be discovered. Monge gives this relation by means of a property that's common to their tangent plane at any point. A similar partial differential equation properly states said characteristic. If you like, this equation may be understood as the *name* of the genus or species. Let's integrate this equation: the finite equation exhibits an arbitrary function corresponding to the fact that there is some indetermination in the generation, that is, the base; fixing the function is expressing the base, shifting from the genus (the arbitrary function resulting from integration) to the species (the base determined by fixation of the function). Let's climb back up to a second-order differential equation: in the integration, two arbitrary functions appear: we are at the family. Example: developable surfaces can be cylindrical or conical, and these can have a base that's circular, elliptical, and so on. Family, genus, species, individual. The reader shares the admiration for Comte, less for the epistemological importance of the thing than for the elegance and simplicity of the process. At bottom, Comte and Monge substitute the order of the differential equation for the degree of the finite equation; they observe the scales of indetermination and determination in the process of integration: hence a natural (generation) and rational (fixation of the arbitrary) classification, of increasing complexity. But one must have had the daring to address the tangent plane, which is to say, a refined description of the surface. Hence two profound remarks about Leibniz and infinitesimal calculus result: first, that everything turns around a determination by edges (contingence, extrema, limits, and continuity); second, that the integration techniques are not as far removed as is said from a logic in the mode of Aristotle or of Porphyry, or of a combinatorics, since they suggest a classification of the given by an arborescence of the same style. Leibniz powerfully intuited the first remark and achieved the union of the second one.

— Mechanics is divided into statics and dynamics. Everyone knows how the division, which is Cartesian, like figure and motion, and in any case traditional, rebounds on the entire positive system through the motto Order and Progress. A reduced model, mechanics is also such a model from being the supplier of the section that is transverse to all science, from geometry to sociology, grasped according to the equilibrium or relation of forces. Thus d'Alembert's principle is projected into physiology, social science, and so on, as into astronomy. But mechanics is also the elective model, and it is here that the author employs the best of his genius: the exposition is clear, mastered, and definitive (provisionally); diagnostic and prognostic are far from lacking. Let's move on to the object: the fact that mechanics is divided into the mechanics of fluids—namely, gases and liquids—and the mechanics of solids will soon give us a brilliant physicalist model of the law of three states, including the hesitation over whether there are two or three states: this positive cell is like the ark of a covenant (taken up again everywhere and sometimes difficult) between classification as order of progress and historical law as progress of the order. And its methodical image will be projected in the world order, the solar system. Add to this the big dichotomy translation-rotation, which, by itself, allows one to have a precise figuration of the play of all the chiasms between order and progress, and which allows one to establish the great form of the circle, from which we started out. In these sites, Poinsot's work appears, a perfect model of this logical play: the theory of couples summarizes everything. Victorious over Lagrange and Laplace, Poinsot established the invariable plane for any set of bodies moving in an indeterminate manner, and thereby established the stable reference plane for the solar world, a plane housing the principal couple of all these motions. We shall have to go back over, with suitable demonstrations, a series of discoveries that form the womb of Romantic philosophies, Comte's in particular. Nothing could be more important the day after the Revolution than this theory of revolution.

Therefore, mechanics classifies the things themselves (into their various states, that is, gaseous, liquid, solid) and their spatial tracks (figures of equilibrium and orbits of motion, whether it is a motion of translation or rotation). Mechanics is to these things what positivist classification is to the sciences themselves, seen according to their states and divided according to rest and trajectory. Up to now, we had observed models that were slightly poorer than the figure of the whole; the analogy can now disappear behind the forest of a higher richness.

In the vernacular sense, mechanics knows how to classify *machines*, as the *Dix-Huitième Leçon* does, in the wake of Monge. The translation-rotation distinction divides mechanics once again, and the ten series of recognized apparatuses are distributed according to the combinatory method. The reduced model finally takes on its ordinary sense: it functions, it can be built.

— Astronomy writes its results on complete registers. They are distributed by Comte, in the *Vingt-Troisième Leçon*, according to the law of three tables: there were the Prutenic Tables, then the Alfonsine or Toledan Tables, both of them theologico-metaphysical due to the prejudice of the circle and of the epicycles, and thrown in the face of God by Alfonso X, responsible for such a complicated creation; there are the Rudolphine Tables, finally positive, since calculated based on Kepler's first two laws, therefore on the ellipse. In addition, the heavenly bodies must be classified, and the *Vingtième Leçon* comments for a long time on the question by comparing the problem of naming to chemical nomenclature. "The classification that results from the fundamental division of the circle is certainly as perfect as possible," the lesson concludes, "just like the corresponding nomenclature: all the rest is of little importance." This is indeed what we have been saying since the beginning of our remarks. Anyway, the stability of the solar system allows us to live in a world as closed, circular, and perfect as the philosophy that talks about them and the classification that puts them in order. The circle, having transitioned from a metaphysical prejudice to a positive regime, nevertheless retains its form, unchanged.

Each region of the encyclopedia is concentrated in a site where its elements are in order. All local classification is subject to laws that repeat along the chain: even though these laws vary from cell to cell, they let the invariant appear. The chain is subject to this invariant itself. From the local to the global, the sequence is good and closes in a circle from the global to the local. Positivism is indeed a system, as can easily be proved.

This can be said in Comte's language. Let there be a global phenomenon, "natural," whether it be geometry, mechanics, astronomy, or physics. Infinitesimal calculus, analysis, which is to say, the instrument suitable for working the phenomenon, provides the opportunity to explore a suitably cut out parcel of it, a localized region, a running point, and the like—in any case, a differential of the phenomenon. This is how all the eponymous geniuses of the *Cours* proceeded: Newton, Lagrange, Laplace, Fourier, Coulomb, and a thousand more. The positive law of the global phenomenon says integrally what local exploration says in differential language, and both expressions indeed refer to one another, operationally. The classification is, as much as you might like, a trajectory legalized point by point, an order of the world, unified site by site, a diffusion studied element by element. Consequently, positivist epistemology, thematizing the sciences the way the sciences thematize phenomena, taking theories as facts (the big logical or general facts), is nothing other than a *natural science of the sciences,* a natural science of facts-theories. One can say, ad libitum, a mechanics of the sciences, or even an astronomy of the sciences, but one will prefer to say a *physics of the sciences.* This result was known, but it was interesting to demonstrate it. Hence the status of "logic" in the French university ever since the *Cours:* philosophers observe the fact-science, experiment on it (if they can); they legislate in the end, which is to say, they judge. Since they observe poorly a shifting set, and since they experiment little, to keep their hands clean, they endlessly repeat and judge by their robe. The fact remains that the status of epistemology is still that of a physics—or, demoted, of a jurisdiction.

The Law of Three States

The law of three states regulates the chronic, sociopolitical, and cultural sequence of the theological regime, the metaphysical regime, and the positive regime. Auguste Comte presents this law as an unassailable directive principle, and his epigones have continually read it literally, for lack of critical reading. It is not only a direct discovery, brought about by observations or experiments on the general fact of history; it is also, and above all, translated from elsewhere and from every region, and translated elsewhere and everywhere. And already, by the author, from phylogenesis to ontogenesis.

The fact that highly primitive residues are detected here should not be surprising to anyone educated in the insistency of triadic forms in Indo-European culture, whether it be a question of gods, symbols, concepts, classes, or history. The *Cours* can be read, *a scientia condita* [from the founding of knowledge], the way Dumézil knows to read Livy. The prehistory of positive knowledge is structured as three episodes: its *genealogy* is cadenced like the genealogy of certain gods, certain kings, and certain groups. But Comte's schema, which locates three regimes (*rex*), is entirely ordered from the point of view of the first function, that is, of Jupiter, to choose a symbol from Dumézil. Hence the inevitable end of philosophy in positive religion and the bracketing of the function of production in the last stage, which is nevertheless somewhat Quirinal, since it is the stage of the utilization and transformation of the world, and of the appearance of a new social group adapted to this role. We shouldn't be surprised at the fact that the classic triad can be entirely subordinated to any one of its elements. The ternary schema of the Hegelian method, conceived in roughly the same era, is entirely subordinated to the second function. Mars dominates the struggle of the master and slave, of the person who rules because he is recognized and the person who works; he establishes the historical relation itself, violence, war, and combat. The speed with which the dialectic was culturally imposed and its almost immediate and endlessly repeated triumph, given its continued failure as a method for the sciences in the strict sense, are explicable through the recuperation of a perennial form, dormant but living, of our heritage. The same goes for the law of three states, that long historical story produced by the imagination, neither more nor less imaginary than the Hegelian cycles. It is possible to continue: can it be claimed that the reversal of Marx with respect to Hegel partly consists in engendering Quirinus through Mars, or, rather, in transferring the attributes of the latter to the former, and ultimately giving the third function— the sole representative of work, production, and reality—the armed power of the second function and the sovereignty of the first? And doing this by mobilizing again the dialectical triad? Everything would happen, then, as though at its birth modernity had automatically recapitulated in every possible way the archaic figures of its culture, or better still, global knowledge and exhaustive facts in a general repetition of the primitive forms. A double, triple recapitulation of the totality of things by the totality of history, under the integrally recomposed shadow of the origins. Hence the fascination that this doctrinal set exercises on us, the cycle it forms, and whose edges we cannot or dare not cross. There has been a systematics of systems—well formed, coherent, and closed—since the formation of modernity.

But, once again, the spiral appears, drawn recently for classification and its savage residues. Yes, the primitive triad seems well repeated three times, by privileged reference to one of its three elements, a double victory for Dumézil, who closes this group of systems. But, second, Dumézil expressly admits that the Indians translate into the theological region the aforementioned ternary form the Indo-Iranians project into a metaphysics, with the Romans putting it on its feet in the positive stage of history. Here, indeed, is the law of three states, which could regain strength, anew, for the preceding analysis, Comte being the high priest, Hegel his metaphysician, and so on. Consequently, I no longer know whether Dumézil is behind Comte or Comte behind Dumézil; I no longer know where to start, with the spontaneous religion of the historians or methodologists of the sciences, or with the spontaneous positive methodology of the historians of religion. In the hall of facing mirrors, each man refers to the other as a possible predecessor. Thus one can read the nineteenth century, and sometimes modernity, as a general repetition or interpret our means of reading by means of codes indicated in the object of our reading. Overdetermination of a cyclic group; indetermination of method.

Let's leave aside the residues of the origin and the prison it represents. We come to another cycle, the encyclopedia. The word *state* (*status* in Latin) first designates a *static* phenomenon. A set of any objects whatsoever is in equilibrium and at rest, in a given situation, at a given moment. The *Cours* describes, after Laplace, the state of the heavens and the world as order; it reports, as a summary, the state of the question, in any science whatsoever. A state of things is a balance, a firm foundation. It doesn't fail to stand up, as they say, as the word says. Anyone can describe it, since it is stable. The physical and sociopolitical significations are derived with respect to this meaning: statics lays down the law. The state of nature was not exactly a "state" in the sense of a government. Thus it becomes a fixed point, or the point fixed at this instant, at the instant of equilibrium. To say the law of different successive states amounts to making the fixed point a running point. Hence the passage from the old statics to the subsequent mechanics. Notice how subtly the *Seizième Leçon* carries out this passage, precisely in three states of statics itself: Archimedes and Stevin invented statics and promoted it; then Galileo absorbed it into dynamics; lastly came Varignon, d'Alembert, and Lagrange, through whom statics lastly founded all of mechanics by means of the principle of virtual velocities. The science of states is the first in chronology and the principle of systems. This is the case for positivism. And Laplace demonstrated the stability of the solar system.

A running point, along the trajectory of the moving thing, is therefore, once again, a fixed point, stable, in equilibrium along the orbit at a given instant. It is definitely a state (*status*) in a series of states. So Comte's law, in the principle of his system, is the dynamics of a statics or the statics of a dynamics: this law is isomorphic to many other laws stated in the *Cours,* one principle among others that are the same. In rereading the *Seizième Leçon* and the *Dix-Septième Leçon,* anyone can immediately intuit the quite simple and evident fact that the law of three states is d'Alembert's principle generalized. Hermann, Euler, and especially Lagrange extend the principle to all of analytical mechanics; Comte, here at least, extends it to the philosophy of history. Therefore given "any *system* whatsoever of bodies acted on by any forces whatsoever" (the running point, instantaneously fixed along the trajectory, is a particular case), its state, in the statics sense, is implicitly described, at a given moment, by a differential formula stemming from d'Alembert's principle (of which the Newtonian equality of action and reaction is a particular case), modified by Lagrange and others. Making the formula explicit, a *system* of differential equations arrives whose integration entirely determines the various circumstances that are relative to the motion of the system (of bodies). This is precisely the table of equations that forms the understanding of Laplace's ordering god and allows *predicting* everything. The integration of this system, stated in the *Dix-Septième Leçon,* does not happen without making arbitrary constants or functions appear, which can be fixed if one knows the situations at the limits, that is, the *initial state* of the system (hence the cosmogony of the same Laplace) and its *terminal state* (hence Auguste Comte's oscillating model). Then, and then only, is the general motion, a succession of states, entirely determined—for the god of the former or the Jupiter of the latter. The laws of the world are isomorphic to the laws of history, and mechanics supplies them, in the *Première Leçon,* in which the latter laws are at issue, and from the *Dix-Neuvième Leçon* to the *Vingt-Septième Leçon,* in which the former ones are at issue. For the law that determines motions is indeed the law of three states—initial, running, terminal—which is what was to be demonstrated. But the base formula is indeed d'Alembert's principle. And the law of three states is indeed the principle, generalized. The matter is as clear as daylight.

When Comte declares, in season and out of season, that statics founds dynamics, when he repeats, by another name, the principle in physiology, he repeats in another language, then in two, then in three, something he had already translated in his very first lesson, where the words betray him: point of departure, transition, fixed and definitive state. In other words, the law of three states is the unspecific repetition of a form said everywhere in the system of order (statics) and of progress (dynamics). The system is a system from incessantly translating the law in all places. What places? That of "systems of equations," of "systems of bodies," of the "system of the world." From which comes that of knowledge and of history. Our results in no way differ from those we obtained regarding classification. Mechanics gives a model of a law that, itself, is a model.

The law of three states is a rule of natural formation and good "logical" formation. The word *formation* has a precise sense in each cell of the classification, hence its success with the subsequent epistemologists, whatever their elective region. The positive state, a norm and an end, is well formed, in the same way as logico-mathematical language, after long transformations that can be understood in the language of physiology, physics, the theory of the earth, astronomy, or mechanics. But the translation of the law in d'Alembert's principle contains enough generality to describe *any* motion whatsoever of a *system* of *any* bodies whatsoever. Let's now define what is undefined here.

Comte gives a particular care to distinguishing motions of translation and motions of rotation. This dichotomy, he adds, suffices to determine any motion of a system. In fact, the dichotomy runs all along the expositions on mechanics and astronomy. So, if our translation [*traduction*] is faithful, the positivist system, in its general assertions, will have to include a global translation [*traduction*] of these two motions, which require three points in order to be defined. We shall give such a translation [*traduction*] later, when we celebrate, with the pomp it deserves, Poinsot's victory over all the *Cours*'s eponyms. That said, it remains to give some specificity to the undefined bodies. What does mechanics apply to? What does statics or dynamics concern? Look at Archimedes, Stevin, Pascal, Daniel Bernoulli, Euler, or Lagrange; they all distinguish, as did Comte after them, a hydrostatics, a hydrodynamics, a fluid mechanics in general from ordinary mechanics—that is, the mechanics of solids. So the *Cours* must be read, for a moment, in the reverse direction. The *Trentième Leçon* makes it clear, with regard to thermology, that there are *three states of bodies:* gaseous, liquid, and solid. Hence "the illustrious Black's great fundamental law," according to the intolerable redundancy of adjectives of the august style. It is a question of absorptions and emissions of heat, according to the direction by which the chain of states is taken. In passing, here is the fault line, indicated in a footnote: thermodynamics takes over the reins from seventeenth-century mechanics and will govern modernity, the child of fire starting from the Industrial Revolution—blast furnaces and steam engines, machines for changing states. Comte celebrates Black and Fourier, and is callously missing Carnot, Joule, and Mayer, even though he could not have known Clausius, despite a few brief intuitions in which he glimpses the other side of the fault line. The fact remains that Black states a rule of formation and transformation that is, in all exactness, *the law of three states of bodies that are now specified as being gaseous, liquid, or solid.* The classification of mechanics according to the nature of the objects it considers or makes move is consequently dogmatic and historical, logical and genetic. In other words, the classification here is compatible with the law of three states, a new translation [*traduction*] of a global figure of philosophy. There is, on the one hand, a statics of gases, liquids, and solids, and there is a dynamics of three classes, a dynamics founded, let's repeat, on the statics: statics of a dynamics. On the other hand, the gaseous, liquid, and solid states follow one another in the order, dynamics (via heat) of a statics (of states). All our results are once again present. Now open up Laplace and the corresponding lessons; you will find in them a statics and a dynamics of atmospheres, of seas and tides, and then of heavenly solids; you will find in them the law of increasing densities toward the center of heavenly bodies, which regulates the order of states and causes a body in space, at a given moment, to have a solidified central core surrounded with fluids, liquids, and gases, remainders or fossil traces of a primitive state. The heavenly body is in a historical state, just like any body.

In the segment we are traveling, from the *Trentième Leçon* to the *Seizième Leçon*, it is understood that one must read more slowly. The sequence of states is always the same. The physico-chemical law of matter, which is isomorphic with the law of history, is identically the law of the world. This is so in two ways: cosmology and cosmogony. For celestial mechanics, as we have just seen, earth, water, and air are in *order*, in strata that are evidence of a *progress*, according to the rule that distance imitates time, the most distant from the center being the oldest. Astronomy applies the formulas of statics and of dynamics to this set of states, a synchronic cross section of the world. Who will tell, in passing, the residues of primitivity of this perfectly scientific view, in which three of the elements are put into order by the fourth? For cosmogony, here is another primitivity, positively chronological. The solar world is stable in its whole, and rotation has won out over translation: the orbits are closed in the idealized model; variations occur only around positions of equilibrium. Once again, statics wins out over dynamics; therefore rotation wins out over translation, and order (cosmos) over progress. The cosmogonic project implies the idea of making *the global schematic circle go backward along time's straight line,* that is to say, *the classification go backward along the law of states,* or, if you like, again, making the order go back up the progress, toward the upstream. Already, the *Vingt-Huitième Leçon* distinguished physics (mechanist) from chemistry, insofar as physics studies bodies while leaving their molecular composition unchanged, whereas the actions of chemistry highlight changes of state. Disregarding its own interdictions, the *Vingt-Septième Leçon,* which repeats the word *formation* at will, gives something like a cosmogony of the astrophysical kind. This is the Kant-Laplace hypothesis on the origin of the system of planets, founded on the theory of *primitive fluidity.* Here, the sun is no longer the fixed point; it was already no longer so in cosmology, having been drowned in Laplace-Poinsot's invariable plane; it is originary as a *source of heat:* this is the moment when thermodynamics curtly takes over the reins. The solar mass rotates, and at the equator, gaseous packets become detached, which also rotate. The primitive motion is, once again, one of rotation, but in the furnace of origins, the primitive state is gaseous, nebular. Hence the rule of formation of the world by cooling and condensation, by liquefaction of gases and solidification of liquids. The law of three states indeed moves to cosmogony, and the current world, in its simultaneous triple state, remains a fossil witness. Let's now notice that the dominant word used by Comte to characterize the positive regime—*consistency*—incessantly returns (in the *Troisième Leçon* and again in the *Trente et Unième Leçon,* the *Trente-Troisième Leçon,* the *Trente-Quatrième Leçon,* etc.) in order to express the solidity, rigor, or rigidity of the contemporary sciences, in contrast with the cloudy and vague themes of the previous regimes. And consistency is, once again, *status.* The demonstration is indeed closed over itself, like the world it talks about. And Comte will close the cosmogony into a cycle by regular returns to the solar furnace and recommencing repetitions of the origin. The history of the world oscillates like Laplace's system. Positive philosophy oscillates around invariants;

it endlessly translates the same themes. It is a cycle of translations [*traductions*], a repetitive encyclopedia.

This law of the three states of matter is surprising in that it groups into a single crossroads positive physical experimentation and its exact expression, a powerful archaic constellation, the element fire becoming the orderer of the three others—air, water, and earth—and lastly a speech found again in several regions of knowledge: physics, astronomy, and mechanics. Its rational generality borders on its metaphorical primitivity, hence a secret—and, for this reason, poorly perceived—force of expansion. One day we shall have to read Bergson as a good reader of positivism, as a well-informed critic of the bounds of consistency, of the solid, that is to say, of Comte-style perfect knowledge, seeking to go back up the chain of states all the way to fluidity. In Bergson, the *Cours*'s hidden metaphors are deliberate and fully utilized, as well as really heuristic. Bachelard will be the final representative of this tradition, perceptible in his work in multiple ways.

The Figure of the Circle

The law of three states is projected in still other sites. The *Vingt-Deuxième Leçon:* Longomontanus marks an intermediate stage in the progression of knowledge about the earth. He no longer believes in rest and doesn't yet believe in the double motion of translation and rotation, but only in the motion of rotation. The earth rotates but does not move. The same goes for the models of the solar system: Tycho Brahe forms a transition and synthesis, to Comte's eyes, between the Ptolemaic and the Copernican systems. For Tycho, the planets gravitate around the sun (i.e., heliocentrism), and the sun gravitates around the earth (i.e., geocentrism). The famous Newtonian likening of falling bodies and heavenly orbits is articulated by the *Vingt-Quatrième Leçon* as a universal similarity with three stages: planets tend toward the sun, satellites toward the planets, and projectiles toward the ground; in each case, the curve is the same, a conic section. Let's move on to alterations and the *Vingt-Sixième Leçon:* Hipparchus discovers the precession of the equinoxes, Bradley the nutation of the terrestrial axis, and Laplace lastly brings the century-long inequalities back to equilibrium; the history of exceptions ends in their rule, the series of paradoxes ends in Newton's law. All this progress by stages conceals an order, thought in terms of invariant, equilibrium, and closure. The history of mechanics leads to the closed system of Lagrange, the history of astronomy leads to the closed system of Laplace, and the history of philosophy leads to the system of Comte. In other words, translation is a rotation, and the comets themselves have elliptical trajectories; all alteration returns with time to stability; the three states form a cycle via exchange of heat; dynamics is founded on statics and virtual velocities; the known world refers to Poinsot's invariable plane, and cosmogony, doubtlessly open in Laplace, returns to oscillation in the *Cours*. This is the great figure of the circle, which dominates our exposition. When one tries to take a totality back to its origins, the encyclopedia back to the beginnings of knowledge, the closed world back to its birth, motions back to their genesis—in short, when one wants to reverse the global schematic circle along the straight line of time—one concludes that this presumed straight line is, in its turn, only a closed curve. The translation-rotation distinction is suddenly pertinent and crude; every orbit is closed on itself. The encyclopedia is a dogmatic and historical cycle: hence the figures drawn regarding the classification, hence our references to a recapitulation that forms the era's horizon, including for Napoleon, hence the program of interdictions that delimit the future of the positive state—definitive and fixed. Comte's system is structurally suited to the system of the world and synchronically suited to the zeitgeist. Its dogmas are suited to its cosmology (to statics), and its history to its cosmogony (dynamics founded on statics). Each planet is subject to the law of the whole and to the age of its formation; each region, each cell, of knowledge or the system, repeats in its language and its department the discourse of the globality. Hegel: the encyclopedia is a circle of circles, a cosmological word. Position is no longer calculated by dead reckoning, but rather astronomically. In addition, the law of three states, in Black's sense, is that of a reversible transformation. If it indeed serves as the model for Comte's law, then the historical schema of positivism must be circular. Which is what I wanted to demonstrate.

But let's ourselves return to the dawn of knowledge and of time. Already during the fetishistic state, the couple absolute need–absolute impossibility is at the natural origin of the history of religions and the history of the sciences. Hence a few circular drawings possessing generative power: attempting to solve unsolvable problems with urgency, observing in order to obtain a theory and having a theory in order to be able to observe, et cetera. Something like an initial presumption institutes the spontaneous synthesis of these opposites and launches the process. Hence the theory of the twofold seed. We have found these closed figures everywhere throughout the lessons on mathematics, as soon as the question of the beginning had to be dealt with. The birth of geometry, for example: it was impossible to measure inaccessible distances, heights, and intervals. The pressing need is blocked by an obstacle without recourse. Comte does not cheat: the obstacle is never inferior to the power it opposes. They are equal. So the need must *turn* it or turn around it. From this a *circuitous route* is born, a *ruse,* an *indirect* course. So mathematics as a whole *arises* from a circle, *is* a circle. Derived from observation, like natural science, mathematics makes observation possible, as an instrument. From the couple impossible–necessary results mathematical determination, which groups the set of reason's ruses required to indirectly reach an inaccessible goal. As many examples as you want of this schema can be found in the first fourteen lessons. As a cycle, mathematics is a reduced-scale encyclopedia, and our results are invariant. That said, what is a couple? How are we to represent the couple of two opposite forces? The answer to this question seems to us to be decisive. A couple is a figure of statics that does not apply two equal and opposite forces to the same point, but rather to the two extremities of the same segment. *It is a figure of equilibrium and of rotation.* Poinsot, who invented this, showed that the set of the solar system, or any system of n bodies, is referred to an invariable equatorial plane, such that the set of the system's couples is summed up on it into a general couple. This suffices. At the dawn of time, two equal and opposite forces were in equilibrium in human nature, forces that were so general they expressed the absoluteness of its needs and the totality of the problems human nature had to solve. These forces had to launch the broadest circle, inside of which all the particular couples and regional circles had to, with time, draw the local motions of history and of the system we now know. The secret of Comte's philosophy and, perhaps, of contemporary systems resides in this invention, which is of a brilliant simplicity. Maybe one day we will find out that while Newton has been imitated, followed, and translated ten times, Poinsot, during the Romantic era, had been just as frequently. To see this, one need only, unlike philosophers, take the word *couple* in its precise, nonvernacular sense. Generating a motion from a couple of opposite forces applied at the same point is truly the absurdity of perpetual motion.

We lack the space and time to unfold, amply and in the same style, the dichotomy and diagonalization techniques used in the *Cours*. We may have the time to return to them elsewhere. To conclude, let it suffice to say how the global system, in its circularity, electively follows a diametrical line, how its sphericity refers to an equatorial plane. Is the philosophy of the sciences projected onto the philosophy of history, or vice versa? Order onto progress, or vice versa? These questions have no meaning. The system holds them together and traces a median route, from the origin of knowledge and time to the end of history and the closure of science. Thus Comte, when all is said and done, is the guardian of the dead.

It must never be forgotten that he was originally from the south of France. An heir to the troubadours. Like them, he never loved anyone but the distant princess, and not just the deceased Clotilde. The couple. When he had to choose between the dead and the living, he immediately opted for the funerary monument. Thus the inventor of modern history of science—and, as a corollary, of French university ideology—was, at least in the exact sciences, merely a collector of tombs: the great dead of the *Catechism* and the vast crowd of shades who, according to its formula, principally make up humanity.

We lack an Auguste Comte, a new calculator of position. May he, should he appear someday, forget the troubadours of the sun a little in order to start loving living princesses.

Part III

Painting

7

Ambrosia and Gold

Descartes had taught seventeenth-century mathematicians the division of the Euclidean plane into quadrants, according to two coordinated lines that meet at a center or middle that can be called the origin. Straight lines and point of reference. A clear and distinct—measured—language of events that are twice extended is possible if this reference is assigned. Geometry gives us things to see, a domain of intuition. Algebra gives us things to speak or write; it is the terrain of discourse. These two varieties have a common vicinity, the interchange by which they flow from one to the other, the reference point, the placeless place, but the place of places, the zero of measurement and of logos but the origin and possibility of speech and writing about the phenomena of place. The punctual hole[1] by which words diffuse into space and by which the things of space, endlessly, are going to be said or written. Representation becomes discursive by the fixed point; by it, discourse is representable. In it, the seventeenth century resolves and condenses.

With her hand, delicately, with her lowered gaze, the woman weighing gold designates it, and Vermeer's plane is divided into four parts. We can talk about the painting starting from this center and origin, then plot the horizon and the vertical ordinates. With its gaze toward the infinite, the sun, through the high window, indicates the point; the light descends onto it, symmetrical with the woman's present but absent gaze. These gazes form two bisectors of the quadrants, diagonals of the evident. The infinite and the finite along this fanned-out trajectory.

Descartes had mused over simple machines that distribute forces around a real point. Winches, pulleys, and levers: Pascal, Huygens, and Roberval taught the balance and the balance wheel to their century so well that space, time, and the counting of time, nature and society were all conceptualized using them as models. Or the century had refined simple machines so effectively that it ended up discovering the practical effectiveness of a stopped, anchored, fixed point around which the designated force multiplies its mastery. It remained to mechanize this fixed point, to mathematize it, to speak or write it in a universal language: then its sway invaded cultural space. Geometry discusses its varieties by the center; astronomy and politics define theirs by the sun, and all forms of representation organize themselves around this reference.

The gold-weigher's hand, a solid and light hand, holds and designates the real point around which the balance is in peace. Her gaze, veiled under her eyelids, indicates where one must look.

It is no longer an abstract point, since it belongs to the beam and to the balance, since it allows for lifting weights and weighing obstacles. It is an element of concrete extension, a fragment of metal in which the forces are level. And yet it is only abstract; the point is an abstraction of space. It belongs to space, and it is its negation. Hand and power are effective by its means, yet do not attain it. Scarcely the tip of a stylus. The dry tip of a compass. It is the nonreal practice of the real. A spatial element absent from space. Absent, and all presence is represented through it. Passes through there, through a vanished there. A spatial element suspended, not touched, by the hand, looked at, not seen, across the eyelids. Absent, present, a fount of representation; concrete, abstract, source of force and equilibrium; seen, not seen, theoretical; without content, deprived of meaning, practical. That in relation to which all content and all form take on meaning. Meaning, direction, position, site, difference. Orientation. Orient, Occident. Without form, formal. First formality, posited, deposited by the dry stylus, which is erased. Luminous hole in the center, origin of all formality, language, or writing. Representation, present at the limits adhering to absence, refers to it. Relation or logos. The nonpresence of discourse. In the middle of the painting.

To calculate is to measure in relation to it, zero. To represent is to equip space with a network for which it is the absent pole. To work is to distribute forces around the null support. To write is to defy Zeno with a signaletic continuum of unassignables like it. To speak is in the hollow of this indicative. Index.

The last finger is parallel to the beam. The pinkie [*l'auriculaire*], listening. The birth of language. Reason, language, relations.

The balance that's level due to the peace of the fixed point. The ruler beam and the three verticals. The geometric center of the painting, the static pole of equal equilibrium. Exact middle, point of reference, Cartesian space. There are four quadrants on the wall in the background, and, in fact, in the upper right, there is a second painting. One works without difficulty only on the first of the quadrants; all the rest ensue by combinations of signs. In a way, in geometry, the painting of the painting is also found. The window, mirror, and curtain, on the left wall, drawn in squares, iterate the points of reference. As does the floor with its quadrangular tiles. Paving space. Space is a global pavement, locally paved. The trihedral room, a trihedral repeated by the rustic table, is relief in front of the intaglio recession, all of it orthonormal. Therefore, Descartes everywhere: horizon, verticals, normals, and the referent central point iterated wherever objects made by the hand of man lie. The relation of the hand to this point is the subject of the painting. The light and the gaze, along the diagonals of the first two quadrants, descend toward the point, their intersection. What is presented, if not the site where the ray of sunlight and the direction of the gaze meet? This punctual site, through the segments of the balance, gives the law of the network of straight lines. This law organizes the space of the painting. And the painting, everywhere, repeats the point, on the floor, the table, and the mirror. Here is the fundamental theorem of all representation: given a set, it produces a subset—here, the point, the empty subset—which produces a law that reproduces the set; and the set, through this law, reproduces subsets, and so on. It is a circuit, an autochthonous, local, and original circuit of functioning and production, in the very site of the represented. The fact that its loop comes full circle or feeds back on itself, production and reproduction, clarifies the iterative prefix in the word *representation*.

There isn't yet a painting. Only a point and points, straight lines, trihedrals, forms, a reference system, and a rule. The Cartesian syntax of space, a geometry. But Descartes's geometry is indeed ruled by this same theorem: the Euclidean variety that is a plane produces a subset of lines and points, which produces a law that reproduces the variety. Thus Cartesian space is one of representation. A statics syntax gives some reality to these forms: hand, balance, fulcrum point, horizontal equilibrium, and perpendicular pans. The space of representation is that of the fall of heavy objects and simple machines. The horizon and the verticals, that is, the reference system in its entirety, are suitable for mechanics; extension is suitable for motion. A syntax of optical paths completes the first two syntaxes: the equality of the angles along the path of the diagonals corresponds to the equality of the weights, which corresponds to the equality of the spatial divisions. The point is middle, center of gravity, site of light incidence. Three series that are faithful to each other, for which we don't seek which one would be the determining series. Thus knowledge that is reducible to the syntax of reference (all the knowledge that was representable during the seventeenth century) is presented here.

The set of this knowledge (forms and theories, directly faithful to practices), all the abstract discourse of philosophies that accompanies it, is brought about by it or promotes it, and the contemporary cultural syntaxes together are describable by an installation of the punctual reference. And again, the point of reference is a subset that carries a law to be reinjected into the set. It is, in this way, that the entire seventeenth century was one of closure and of representation. But all this, demonstrated in places or endlessly verified, as in Vermeer's painting, is only syntax, only organizes forms, theories, knowledges, or philosophies; is only syntax because, in the self-productive functioning of the circuit, the subset considered is only the point, the *empty* subset. This is the theorem of representation in general. It doesn't say anything about what is presented, about what is represented here and now. The content, as we say, is absent or wholly indeterminate. So there isn't yet a painting; there are only formalities. Formalities, however, in which a rule was read, one that must be followed. To no longer have to talk about extension and geometry, figure, motion, equilibrium and mechanics, light, optical paths, and gaze, but to be able to welcome, inside these vacuities, the compact populating of meaning, it suffices to *fill* this empty subset. So let there be the rule: if this rule concerns the point, it is a matter of syntax; if it concerns a nonempty subset, it is a matter of a semantics. Let's verify this rule.

None of this is very new. The abstract remains the theory of absent varieties. Nothing is as absent as a point. Theoretical discourse considers an object to be a point. So it talks about something that is present and designated as a sign rather than a thing. Theoretical discourse comes to the concrete, to practice, when it considers a point as an object. The old mechanics was, in fact, called abstract when it was reduced to statics, to the kinematics of the point. Reduction is nothing else: putting to the point. The passage from the object to the sign via punctuation. Punctuality, the first formality, punctuation, the first formalization. But this mechanics is called concrete when it substitutes an entire material system for the point. Likewise, optics—merely geometry when the sources were punctual and the events without any assignable size— becomes physics, properly speaking, when the foci are in inflation and so on. The same holds true here for the history of atomism: it is pure combinatorics, reasoned analytics, formal mathematicism, as long as the atom is only simplicity, ultimate term, element; on the contrary, it becomes concrete practice as soon as a system is introduced. The real invades the formalities when it swells the point. Physics progresses when an entire discipline, constructed with a view to a system, is applied to the corpuscle. Leibniz had perceived this and called the monadology a metaphysics as long as monads were merely points or atoms, and then filled them with a world so that finally they could be in the world. Hence his encounter, in the correspondence with Father Des Bosses, with the idea, so incomprehensible and now so clear, of *puncta inflata*. What must be practiced is the inflation of the point.

The balance for weighing gold determines the center, the middle, the fulcrum point, seen, looked at, the bearer of the laws of all of space. In addition, it determines, by the axis and the beam, a division of the painting-plane into four quadrants, like an escutcheon. Each of the quadrants is a nonempty subset (the center is an empty part). In the upper left, the only totally visible full part of the wall in the background is bare, unpainted or painted in a shading of light. In the upper right, the second part of the wall is a picture: the quarter of the painting is a painting, the escutcheon's *mise en abyme*. The *mise en abyme* is the end of days, the Last Judgment. Christ in glory at the top center, lifting his arms vertically, an inverted balance of the inverted world, dividing the chosen from the damned. Christ in the center, above the head, above the earth, in a cloud populated, on both sides, with those known as the Church Triumphant. The painting of the painting is divided into four quadrants by Christ in the middle, the high and the low, heaven and earth, the right and the left, the condemned and the saved. The weigher, with her shoulders aligned to the beam and her head aligned to the axis, masks the axis and leaves the beam free. The Last Judgment, the weighing of souls, the last weighing, irremediable, without further appeal, the bottom. The end of ends, the bottom of the bottom, closure. The painting of the painting, the weighing of weighings, stands out like a balance: the Son of God on the fixed point, the triumphant ones on the beam, with those summoned naked to the legal proceedings populating the pans separated by the woman. It is no longer a question of a law or of a mechanics, of center, of middle, of horizon lines, which is to say, of forms; rather, it is a question of figures, of bodies, of content and of supplication, reality, fate, *lesson*. The full subset definitely has the density of a meaning.

Hence the repetition of the theorem. The set, the painting, produces a subset: the painting of the painting, the *mise en abyme* of the escutcheon, which produces a law: the weighing (of souls, invisible, at the end of days, in another space), which reproduces the set:

the weighing (of gold, visible, on the table, here, now). A formal or abstract theorem, when applied to the point, to the empty part, passing from syntax to the signified as soon as the point inflates, as soon as it is a matter of the full part. Henceforth we shall call this subset canonical. Every work of the seventeenth century includes at least one such subset. Or rather, a work belongs to this period if and only if there exists in it, when considered as a set, at least one canonical subset. It could, of course, happen that there might exist only one; it could on the contrary happen that there might exist so many that the entire work would only be a set of canonical parts. Hence the two examples chosen: Vermeer's *Woman Holding a Balance* and Poussin's *The Feeding of the Child Jupiter*, the one minimal and the other maximal. The work can be one of science or of philosophy, of the fine arts, as they say, or of literature. This modality is of no importance: the theorem, the cycle, and the division are invariant across every modality. These three things define the seventeenth century.

Balance of justice, balance of accuracy [*justesse*], suspended balance, threat, order, promise, over the head of the one who holds a balance in her hand. Whatever you bind on earth, I shall bind in heaven; whatever you loose on earth, I shall loose in heaven. A grave head in the other world, a dreaming head bent under the weight of things on the scapular balance. The machine in the hand, like a master and possessor, and the head in the clouds, like a slave and someone possessed. Technology in the hand, culture in the head. And the curves of the body to bind the two together, to nest one in the other. Head of gravity, belly of gravidity. With science precise amid the objects (precious as souls or false as sinners) in disorder on the open table, out of the open tomb coffers (the heavens are open), the lustrous pearls separated from the chaotic fabric of a blackish blue, exactitude at the horizon, the refusal of images by the turned mirror, science here below populated with images, and ideology, as they say, which drowns you up to the shoulders and breasts, a flood from above coming to hand level, an ideology that's precise as knowledge and partitioned like a balance sheet and rigorous—the two balances are fed by each other, like the head by the hand and the hand by the head, the balance of weights, number, and measurements, and the balance of happiness, fates, and the infernal.

She is pregnant. The space is pregnant with itself, and the painting is with child itself. Due to this implication, the painting is self-regulated, like a cause of itself. The pure development of an envelopment, the pure envelopment of a development. A Vauclusian spring [*source*] or resource. The painting fabricates a self-motor, perpetual motion. That is called creating—making the autonomous, the autonomous beauty separated from our gestures, the foreignness of art that's independent of us. Perfect, it functions all by itself. The painting in the picture: the quadrant carrying the law of the painting, but the painting carrying the law of the quadrant. And this is so as much as you like: the part in the whole, the *mise en abyme* in the escutcheon, empty part or full part, the local in the global . . . science in dream, culture in knowledge, the son of man in the womb of the woman and over the head of the woman. Self-regulation to the point of equality, perpetual motion on the serenity of the beam of justice: full, level. This beam has deposed potentates from their elevated seats and pulled upward those whose pan was on the ground; it has lavished the hungry with goods, and it has sent away empty and hungry those who had possessed gold.

Why did the laws of art seem so absurd? Because, here at least, they evade that fundamental law of space and bodies, of numbers and weights, the impossibility of perpetual motion. Something the balance says exactly. Something that can be shown, precisely and rigorously, on the balance. Imagine a metaphor, a transport into another space, where one balance would feed another, and this other would feed the first in return and reciprocally; autonomy occurs. The painting functions all by itself. The hand no longer weighs on the beam; it leaves the weights to their own demands. Vermeer's hand has withdrawn forever. Extension resurges of itself. The space is a resurgence of itself. The part frees itself from the whole, and the set from the subset. The son of man is in the woman; He is above her head.

The painting is its own father and its own son. The only creation is autogenesis. The work is from here, from there, from the past, or from now. But it functions in perpetuity. The balance has the form of an inverted genealogical tree. The son is the father of the father. Of his gaze and of his hand, the mother.

Something, first, like a circle. In the center, which seems to be the center, but which is not that of a circle, a woman is feeding Zeus, a standing child, from a horn of plenty. A second woman, to their left, is holding a honeycomb. A man is milking the goat Amalthea, to their right. Above are two naked women, lying. Slightly displaced from the mass in a circle is another shepherd, standing. They are all looking at Jupiter. In the center, the true, a spring.

The partition is written by the composer, clear and distinct. The escutcheon is divided in four by saltire diagonals. First theorem: *there exists a canonical subset, a nucleus.* Which? If I choose one randomly, the first mentioned, for example—I derive from it a simple law, which is the gift of drink. The law is easily reinjected into the set, and this is the subject of the painting. This seems tautological and yet is not. For the circuit is repetitive for every other part. The woman to the right is giving honey to drink, and this is the same law. The naked women from above have tilted the urns: one urn standing, the other lying on its side, retaining and pouring. And the shepherd on the left is going to give milk to drink. Honey, water, milk, modalities of drink. Men, women, standing, crouching, lying, varieties of givers. Hence the repetitive list of objects: the horn of plenty, the honeycomb, the two urns, the breasts corresponding to the urns, and Amalthea's teats, all of them objects that are variable around the functional invariant of the gift of drink. A cyclic group, drawn in a circle, of subsets that respectively state the same law to be reinjected into the set. In the center of the circle, at the intersection of the diagonals, is a spring, and the empty part again repeats a similar law. Hence the new theorem: *every subset is canonical.* I have changed quantifiers because of duality. The first quantifier is merely existential; the second one is universal. Every part carries the law that reproduces the whole, which produces the parts, and so on, including the empty subset. Let's verify this: in the background, the decor in fact repeats it; a vine, hence the grape, a new horn, a new comb, or a new urn, hence wine; an olive tree, hence the olive, a new breast and a new teat, hence olive oil. I have only varied on the same sites. So the man on the left is outside the cycle: at his feet, a satchel, on the ground, is that neutral element that formally states the law. Put there, whatever its content might be. What is the satchel? An urn, a breast, a teat, a comb, a fruit, a horn, any container whatsoever, swollen with something that could be water, milk, wine, honey, oil, or a combination of them, which will be opened, one day, to drink. The satchel is the formality for which the other objects are a concrete model, a variant. And therefore, its possessor is outside the circle and has let it fall. First result: exhaustion. There are no other parts, and therefore every subset is a canonical nucleus. Second result, the written law. For, beyond the concrete variations, across definite drinks and specific producers, I am informed of the abstract. The abstract is now any object whatsoever, indefinite. The recapitulation is such that the lists are closed and their order law-abiding. The theorem organizing the representation has encountered completion. This theorem is so perfect, I do believe, that the work loses those shaky lines that make the work fragile, even though autonomous, and the beauty is lost, as in the academic. Death by pandemic.

In the seventeenth century, there was already a mature theory of representation. We state it differently, granted, but we must be faithful to the old one. Of something represented, it separated the scenographies, profiles, perspective views, or the oblique projections of a situated site, from the ichnography, the flat plan, seen, if you like, from the point of view of infinity. A theory that's valid in geometry, in architecture, for perception, canonized even in theology, it traverses knowledge, the culture of the time. It explains the utopias because it describes the topos (space or world). The ichnography or the geometral was something—fairly inaccessible, virtual like the infinite or absent in a way—like the sum or integration of scenographies. These latter varied, but the former remained fixed. The essence or in-itself of the object, accompanied by their problems. Poussin's painting attempts a completeness, the plan, the geometral, the ichnography. The creator wants to distance himself to the infinite: to play at God in order to give Zeus the milk of the breast. I am the father of this god; here are his mothers. Each nucleus or each subset, in the above sense, is a scenography. As though the oil, or the wine, and the honey, and the milk were only singular views of the geometral drink; as though the urn, the breast, and the comb were only profiles by which drink is given. Hence the semaphorism of the bodies: seated, crouching, lying, standing—positions and situations. And the passerby, stopped by the scene, satchel on the ground and his eye riveted on Jupiter, is something like the et cetera of the rubric of profiles placed in a circle, a cylindrical projection, as though to stop the infinite flight of possibilities, and these profiles figure, discrete, on a background in which they are repeated as though to block, from behind, this irrepressible fount of the center, in front. The et cetera is formal, like the indefiniteness of the content. But the scenography is always more or less the geometral, at will, the particular that the scenography delivers. So there are, indeed, as many nuclei as groups. Everything can be engendered starting from each of them. Our results are stable by translation into the language of time. The scene produces the plan, which produces the scene, and so on. And the fixed point, in the center of the circle, is a spring that never stops. There is perpetual motion around a stability. Essence and attributes.

See now that the representation is, all the same, *analytic*. A partition into subsets or a circle of scenographies, division. From the comb, honey, from the breasts, mother's milk, from the urns and the spring, cool water, from the grapevine and the olive tree, wine, olive oil, and from Amalthea, goat's milk. And from the satchel, perhaps, something no one will ever know, should he or she be mortal. But what drink is the nymph feeding Zeus? Nectar, ambrosia, hydromel, what have you, but most certainly the drink of immortality, whose composition is a mixture of every element of every subset. Poussin composes a partition and a plan; he prepares a composition of a higher alchemy. The horn of plenty, as is natural, contains everything and the entire painting: the painting is analytical of it.

The satchel, above, was a neutral element; the horn is indeed the maximal element. There is, in the cycle of representations, a dominant scenography, the optimal synthesis of the serial others, and serial by divisions, the scenography in which Jupiter drinks before thundering, since Leibniz said that a set of monads included a dominant monad. Theorem: *the painting's composition is the analysis of the drink's composition.* The immortality stemming from the horn is the entirety of the ingredients, just as the ichnography is the integration of the scenographic groups. *Perspective geometry, the projective one, is analytical.* It contributes to chemistry. And this is why the maximal object is a horn of plenty, the mythical krater in which mixture is made, the spring from which perennity endlessly flows; it is cone-shaped. The circle in which the god drinks is the cycle of the painting itself. If the god is present, it is a cone. If the god is not there, it is a cylinder. This is not visible in the sectional circle. The representation, cylinder of all the cones, infinite of all the finites, is that horn of plenty without end and without exhaustion by the inexhaustible analysis of all the sites. One would have to have drunk the drink of immortality to be able to reach its bound. It has no bound; this is the business of Jupiter: and in its presence, he is always a child. Adults and age are possible only for the profiles; the limited sites or finite singular scenographies are the business of mortals, those who only drink milk at the breast of their mother, honey from the comb of bees, wine from the old grapevine—liquids from here, from which time flows.

A partition into subsets, a geometral that is divine, presented, and given-childbirth-to of singular sites that are adult and finite, analysis and composition, mixture. Let's return, in a cycle, to the first language. Let there be a set of elements—by which I mean the parts themselves. They are stable, generic, invariably formed by a couple: urn-lying naked woman, naked nymph and lying urn, Melissa standing and wax honeycomb, dispenser of ambrosia-horn of plenty, milker-Amalthea, observer-satchel, vine-grape, olive tree-olive. Curetes on Mount Ida or Dicte. Producers and products, like spring and water. Like painter and painting. The operator and what it gives. A set equipped with this operation: giving. Producing and giving drink. An exhaustive list without omission or repetition.

Either the set of productive Curetes or the set of produced objects. The representation painting is a graph: a set of couples, a subset of the Cartesian product. The cycle drawn in form is a graph. There is no longer any scenography or Cartesian analysis, nor combinatorial composition; there is no longer any ichnography. The simplest term suffices, the root, from which all the others can be derived. Poussin draws the graph.

To give is, in its essence, to produce immortality. To compose the drink of immortality. The inextinguishable liquid time of gifts that never stop—exchange. To give drink, the Callirhoe Spring of time and of good times, irrepressible and rare.[2] A feast of the gods where the stranger arrives, coming from elsewhere, from the bottom of the mountain, with empty satchel and famished. So as to soon steal the beverage, and the gods will be thirsty, with their faces turned to death and the spring dried up. A cyclic banquet and round table, from which the messenger-traveler is excluded. Continuous gifts and diverting that ruptures. Exchange in a circle and the thief outside, on the roads and in the hedges. The exchange of liquids and the unanimous changing of beings, a chronic circulation of blood in the community.[3] A cycle of metamorphoses, in which the wine, milk, spring water, and honey become nectar and perennial life, a cycle of transubstantiations, the last supper, in which the shepherds become gods. A cycle of transformations, as was said of Philemon and Baucis, each of them is like a tree, which bears fruit, from which a beverage is derived, which gives immortality. Because the immortal, in return, in exchange, changes Amalthea's horn into a horn of plenty, eternally producing. Each of them is, in its kind, a bottomless horn of plenty and of gift. Each of them is a spring. Of milk, of wine, of honey. Each of them is a fount—a fount of gift. Through the operation of giving, of giving drink, each of them is a tree, horn, or spring. Time and eternity flow from everything.

Poussin's painting is a set of generic elements, perfectly defined, for which a list can be drawn up. It is also a set of couples. Then a graph. And so on. On it, operations and applications are defined. The entire language of theory, from the simplest algebra of sets to the more complicated algebra of structures, can be mobilized here. The word *structure* is not a magic word; it designates a moment in a method. This method can be more specifically named as soon as a neutral element, a maximal element, and so on are recognized in it. Hence all the results simultaneously: whether it concerns a cyclic group, an invariant across variations, the canonicity of each subset, the ichnography that's stable across the scenographies, the analyticity of the composition, or the encounter of a perspective and a partition, the notion of algebraic structure aids in expressing all this at a stroke. Let's now reverse the discourse and deduce the totality of its results from simple axioms. This is a superfluous rhetoric one can easily practice. It suffices to take the place of the observer, outside the cycle, satchel on the ground. It is this traveler—arriving by chance or encounter—Hermes himself, who doubtless had the idea of the method.

Zeus's immortality was born of all the agriculture and the first fruits, all the streaming liquids of mother earth, all the drink that the breast of my mother the earth endlessly gives, her breast, her teats, her fruits, her combs, her urns, and her abundance, all that flows from her bunches and which she gives as drink to the child—to the god child of the agrarian religions, to the god of what theorists who aren't afraid of using an imbecilic pleonasm call the agrarian religions, as though there were other religions than agrarian ones and other gods than of a product—Zeus's immortality was born of the perennial mortal fecundity of fruits. The ambrosia river, the honey and wine tributaries. Zeus born of Rhea, the flowing one, and of Cronus, the time that mortally flows, and, through them, of Gaia, the earth. Of the hard earth from which time flows. Of the earth of fruits that give endless time as drink. The god child, fruit of fruits and product of products. Fruit of trees, consequence of springs, product of fruits that flow from the flowing horn. A single personage, alone without couple, a singleton, without producer and without product, fruitless tree or treeless fruit. Sterile eternity—but fruit of every tree, and in return, in exchange and by a cycle, tree of every fruit. Fabulous and fecund eternity. The last product, said to produce the whole of the producers. The self-feeding theorem is found again, intact, in the cycle of the myth. Invariant across the syntaxes and the semantics. *The Feeding of the Child Jupiter* or *The Feedback of God*.

The sterile immortality of the work, a product of a tree struck by lightning, a work that would never be talked about if, fecund, it didn't give to anyone who sees it another bottomless horn of plenty, from which its own partition comes, from which surges its geometral with its perspectives, from which flows—endless—the analysis or—unknown—the composition, from which the structure is calculated, from which comes the horn of plenty. Uninterrupted motion, the time of the work, cyclic and linear, which the work promotes of itself, as cause of itself. The place of a discourse that draws a place where a discourse is woven.

What is called ideology is never anything but a discourse that draws a place where the one who is eager to hold this discourse places himself. We must make a list of the cultures that have refused this habitation of space. I say "we must" as a challenge. You will find little philosophy that doesn't have a fixed point. Those who walk, walk without going back around to where they were.

From which it results that mathematics, an infinite, objective, and rigorous discourse, could not exist without Zeno, who preceded it and never knew where his feet were.

It appears impossible to talk about a space that, by essence, is muteness. Beneath my pen is a blank page. It seems, in fact, stupid to bet a penny on its implications. And yet, I do risk it. I draw a point, a stigmatic pointiness in an arbitrary place.[4] And then another, anywhere. Same or other, I don't know. I don't say anything; I mark. And I fold the sheet of paper so that the drawings correspond. The fold is the axis of symmetry, application, and coordinates. There you have it. I have invented Cartesian geometry. The infinite possibility of talking, via algebra, about every variety of space. Descartes musing over the implication of the blankness. Over the fold [*pli*] or application, over the absent same-other point. If this is possible, the rest is possible *a fortiori*. The rest is literature. So laugh at the proofs that forbid walking. Prefer the emptiness that makes speech, rather than the speech that makes emptiness. Study mathematics and drink new wine. From the horn, directly.

Note.—The Washington Poussin we are dealing with here is no doubt the original of the Californian one, reputed to be fake. According to Denis Mahon, it was painted around 1637. Doris Wild suggests 1639 instead.

8

La Tour Translates Pascal

We are so accustomed to nothing having meaning or reason anymore, that we are hardly surprised when the things we encounter are devoid of them. La Tour's work is meaningless. Absurd, false, vain, ridiculous. His high perfection of technique stifles the demand for meaning a second time. It flatters us—us, who are submerged, filled, overflowing with means. We praise pure painting, the way our ancestors praised pure poetry, without seeing the evident fact that these words, a hundred years late, like most of our words, are stripped of all signification. Listen to our language: either the sophistication will soon burst like a bubble, or it will progress to the point of praising gurgling or blitiri. Our sleepy senility finds itself at ease in the absurd. This benefits many.

Absurd, false, vain La Tour. This simply means that it is impossible, at the Orangerie, to answer simple questions. Who? Where? Who is here? Where is he? The questioning revolves around itself. At what date, at what moment in time, and what time? Everywhere the locating has been skipped. The reference has been done away with. Lost, without place, without bearings, without weight, suspended, without base. Not elsewhere, but nowhere. Not in the past, nor tomorrow, never. Not an other, but nobody. Who is this woman? A noblewoman, a middle-class woman, a peasant, a harlot, a mystic saint from the calendar or from hagiography? Where is she? In what inside, outside of where? Dressed, disguised? Posing, quite simply, like a model in a studio, with her satin apron, well ironed for the circumstance and put on for the pose? Theater without scenery, small theater. Posed there, without reason. Without reason, which is to say, without relation. Devoid of name, title, role, site, entourage, and coordinates. Her tear is beautiful, as are her pearls and the interlacing of her blouse. And what of it, since everything and nothing can be said about the beautiful? What is at issue? What, who is at issue, since nature is absent and social or worldly location has disappeared, since objects have been done away with, since locating has been rendered ineffective, since society and the milieu have dissolved and human locating has been stolen, since place has been removed, since spatial locating has been erased? There is nobody, and this phantom, stripped of all relation, is nowhere. Was and will be nowhere. Since the morning of the tenth of May, which is to say, three centuries, we have known where utopia is. Scattered in space or gathered in a few imaginary rooms.

La Tour of solitude, the tower [*tour*] of solitude. Who has ever experienced solitude if he has a place, a milieu, a name, and a belongingness? If he wears clothes like signs, signs of integration and recognition? If he knows the precise points to fix his gaze on?

Pascal

Are we entering utopia or the waiting rooms of human nature? It is possible that this is the same thing; it is more or less certain we will never demonstrate it. Blank solitude, impregnable to things and a world that does not concern it in any way—or that inhabit this solitude only to divert it, to deliver it up to noises that act as forgetfulness for it. We shall never prove this, for it is undecidable. But in the seventeenth century, a few people did decide it. The misfortune of men and the solitude in the stove-warmed room. Erase everything, uproot everything, abolish the world, the surrounding people, the objects, the very body. Hats and cloaks pass by in the street, devoid of meaning, as in a theater of illusions; here they are, next to Jerome, penitent and decrepit. The cardinal's hat, all the posturings of the social institution. "All of humanity's misfortune," Pascal said, "comes from not knowing how to stay at rest in a room" [L136-B39].[1] Inside, for outside is agitation, excesses, empty games, deceit, and chance: cards and dice, brawls between the blind over nothing, and naivete that poses and gets cheated by the clever. In a room, Magdalene. The sinner in solitude. The mirror, the candle, and death. Not Utopia, but alibi.[2] Outside is alibi. Inside is recentering, around the poor candle, along with the death that's recognized, discovered, cried over, betrayed, and hoped for, the recognition of nothingness, the skull refusing to see, with its empty eyes, its image in the dark mirror. Pascal. Georges de La Tour illustrated the *Pensées*, which was quasi-contemporaneous.

Rocks

The old man is standing, a rare posture in La Tour's works.[3] He is figured by lines and angles and constructed through equilibrium and rest, along a reference axis system that aids and protects him. Simple geometry in an orthonormal space: pencils of lines are parallel to the Cartesian axes, with staffs and legs ordered along the vertical axis, which just about emerges from the spinal column, and the belt and ribbons of the hose aligned along the horizontal intersection line; pivoted with respect to the bright plane, half the body is leaning onto the dark plane, as though it was orienting itself along the bisecting trace of the vertical trihedral, as though it was straddling symmetrically around the bisecting plane passing through the vertical intersection line and the staff: the support point of the staff precisely defines its trace on the floor. The figure, exactly, has found its *middle*. A middle that is not possible or defined except by the well-formed reference. In this site, motion has found its rest. The figure is geometric; the construction is static. Organizing lines by intersectings leads to the middle; assessing weights leads to stable support and *firm foundation* [L199-B72]. A foundation defined by the support polygon, the end of the cane, and the two shoes, enormous, bases of imposing columns. Have you ever measured the feet of these indefatigable walkers? Why a static assurance so rigorously constructed? Because the triangle, on the floor, sets a fall back upright; the upper body, prey to old age, is falling. A local trihedral is drawn there: the scapular line forms a fairly open angle with the horizon, repeated by the line of the elbows; the axis of the head and the face forms the same angle with the vertical; the anteroposterior arch reproduces it a third time. Hence a volume in disequilibrium, out of plumb, referred to this trihedral, orthonormal like the first one, transformed from it by this very angle. The position of the figure has found its middle; the posture of the body has lost its center but finds it again at the center of the triangle, at the center of gravity, at the lowest point. Thus the painting is spatially referred, then centered: geometrically, around the bisecting plane; statically in the base polygon.

Hence this lesson that we must, in every case, find a fixed point, a middle for the situation, a center of gravity for support. Otherwise, when misery comes, when misfortune appears, and death is announced, they throw you to the lowest point, like Job on his ash heap, to the point of the lowest descent, to the point of the heaviest suffering, below which falling no longer continues. But the old peasant remains standing: not crushed by the weight, only deviated. He has discovered his staff, the staff of his old age. Hence the Pascalian legend: we burn with desire to find a firm foundation and an ultimate, unchanging base.

The fall came, but the support lifts it back up. And this is why I ought to have put the *Old Woman* first and not the *Old Man*. She, too, is standing; she is in the middle of the trihedral, right in the middle of a more or less identical trihedral, but she is strong, powerful, straight; the fall may come, and pain and old age; she will be there, standing sturdy in order to console the old Job and his shard or mock him, or to take pity on Sebastian, her eyes, nose, and mouth proclaimers of life, facing the light without blinking, facing the source and not turned away from them, like her man, her shadow; she is nonetheless intimidated, sensible, shrewd, confident, exceeded by what she is daring to do and by herself, by that defiance rising up from her entire female body, lending support to herself, constant and unchanging, without support from anything other than herself, her hands open on her hips, her stability collected, gathered over her pelvis, the pelvic basin, the waist, the portico of stability, of stance, of state, of gravity, where the holiday apron is poorly attached, suspended from this beam for the occasion, unfastened, disheveled, like those garments a body full of health denies and rejects, dressed randomly and since one must do so, and not protected by swaddling clothes or announced by attire or adorned with deceitful regalia; her feet are veiled, the right one lifted, no doubt, like the beginnings of walking or an inchoative affirmation, the feet veiled because the solidity is not there, nor the constancy and unchangingness, but rather they climb back up, as indicated by the vector curve of the arms, to the very center of the trunk, on the portico, the framework and the porch of the waist, which is preserved from any endless falling by its belly, from which, in the past, came and from which, soon, will come the newborn, the one who rectifies and redeems the fall, the newborn of the incomprehensible hope for life, a standing woman, a middle, an umbilicus, the tower, the tower [*la tour*] of brass and of Lorraine,[4] self-stable, invariance of herself, the mother of the mother of the mother of Eve, and it is Adam who falls and whose back becomes bowed, who bends with old age, with death, and with the weight of works achieved outside of himself, and who engenders this work and this humanity that is seated, crouching, lying down, fallen, broken, this humanity that seeks, in despair or diversion, a support elsewhere than in itself. The strongly risen woman, risen before the daylight and before any house. Stability centered by the womb.

The helpless and confused father with his exhausted back over the kneading trough, in front of the oven, the mother of the earth, but Eve first of all, the final and first unchanging base. La Tour's parents and our first parents, what did they do in the past? They fell and collapsed. Who remains standing, after them, in this iconography of gravity and defeat? No one, or just about. *The Hurdy-Gurdy Player with a Dog* is already marked. Behind his back, the reference trihedral is still there, of the same design as the one exhibited by the *Old Woman*, the three planes still distinguished. He is standing, referred, again placed in the middle; he is nonetheless dotted with signs of the impending fall. The main sign of collapse is the white rock, as intensely lit as the player's left calf and half his face, the rock having fallen from the wall, the mark of the breech in the spatial locating and in the equilibrium at the highest point. Rocks fall; they move to the lowest point. You will be counting more and more of these rocks soon. The first hurdy-gurdy player is standing; the trihedral is drawn; here is the rock. The three objects to the left might be hunks of bread; the hurdy-gurdy player is a beggar: what if your brother asked you for bread and you gave him a rock instead? Fake charity, trickery in the pity for a blind gaze. The second hurdy-gurdy player is sitting;[5] the trihedral is effaced, erased lines, ten or so rocks. A triple fall whose mark is the growing pile. What collapses: the body, the surrounding space, the wall confidence once leaned on, hope, and wisdom. Human exchange collapses, as well: the poor will no longer be given hunks of bread, but only rocks. All behavior is in alignment with the lowest low point; the rocks roll along the hill, by the line of the greatest descent of weighty bodies. Spinoza or Pascal. The fall is accelerating. Saint Jerome has left the cube where the hurdy-gurdy player was sitting; he is on his knees, squatting, on the ground, naked, his feet twisted; the trihedral is vague or has almost vanished, rocks again.[6] Rocks and the skull, a rock among rocks, rocks and the dead. From bread to rock—from rock to death. All the way to Job's collapse; only a shard subsists in order to scratch his weeping wounds.[7] The reference walls are now destroyed: there will no longer be a background; there will no longer be rocks. A few skulls. Crumbled space, statics fulfilled, like Scripture, the Scripture of weighty bodies, of mortality. Those rocks about which in the past it was written that they would build a Church, the temple devastated, space desecrated, destruction. Of space, not a rock remains. Rather unfortunates like rocks. Magdalene and Sebastian, each of them a rock.

Falling is indeed at stake. The entire seventeenth century described it the same way, in the affective realm of serene reason and the figures of faith. The two first parents, standing, Eve especially, are prelapsarian. Eve stands sturdily on the bare floor of the primal earth. Onto which debris rains down, behind which the scenery crumbles. When the reference falls and comes undone, the body caves in and twists over itself, as though the reference were, in fact, its skeleton. A skeleton leaving behind only rocks and a skull. A site of execution and a site of the skull. Removing spatial reference amounts to losing all geometric site and the sought-after middle. Accumulating rocky debris, throwing declining bodies to the ground, and the withered flesh of Jerome and Job amount to following the Pascalian law of the statics of liquids: you will find a firm foundation and an ultimate unchanging base only in the lowest of all possible sites, where falling is no longer possible, the ground of the humble and humility. Humiliating humanity is literally throwing it to the ground, just as much as showing it the perishing of its flesh and the threshold of death. Every scientific strategy of Pascal's apologetics is found in La Tour's icons: space loses its references, the middle is unfindable, equilibrium is nothing outside the fall. Fall: a figure of statics, the descent of weighty bodies, rocks, a figure of the body, standing, sitting, thrown to the ground like Jerome, Job, and Sebastian, a figure of faith. Pascal, both a genius of statics and a psalmist: "Happy are those who—not immersed, not carried away, but immovably firm—seated in a low and secure base, rising only after the light has come, but after having rested there in peace, hold their hand out to the one who must lift them up in order to make them stand upright and steady in the porches of holy Jerusalem . . ." [L545-B458]. "O holy Zion, where everything is stable and nothing falls. One must sit not under or in, but rather upon, and not standing, but seated: being seated to be humble and being upon to be secure. But we shall stand in the porches of Jerusalem" [L918-B459]. La Tour, painter of space and of statics, of the fall of bodies—in both senses of *fall*—of simple objects and of references, which are figures of faith. Rocks can be children of Abraham.

From which they do not rise before the light . . . Eve looks the source in the face. And that is not nothing: barring exceptions (Joseph or the child-god), only women, in La Tour's work, are judged worthy of carrying the light. Wise virgins or strong women, repentant harlots or midwives, with candle in hand. Collapsed men, slumped, transpierced. Either the source is absent, and that is called daylight, or it enters the painting, in a woman's fist, and that is called nights. And, therefore, Eve saw face to face some absent sun, to which Adam, wearied, turned his back. Magdalene, postlapsarian two times over, looks at the lamp, or its image in the mirror. The man is turned away from the source. *The Hurdy-Gurdy Player* [*Veilleur*], sitting or standing, emitter of music and supplication, listener to music or the noises of the brawl, already no longer sees anything, blind. Face to the light, woman; face in shadow, man; face returned to the source, halfway, the blind man. With the sun forever absent from his gouged-out eyes, ears are left to him to listen to speech and song, wakefulness [*veille*] is left to him to chant hymns and laments.[8] Night is left to him. Nights. The children of the man who one day turned away from the source will no longer see anything; the male children of the blind man will no longer see anything. A few women will see the bare and sole light, the feeble flame of the night. Never the object: no painted objects, no seen objects. Blindly real, or the entirely essential distraction of the clear-sighted: they have eyes so as not to see. He is sitting, blind; but when he is standing, and if he walks tomorrow, it will be thanks to the dog, to the dog lying down—a support that's outside himself, a dog lying down who looks, who looks you in the face until you are afraid. The dog carries the blind man's gaze forward, at ground level. The eyes of blindness have themselves fallen, thrown to the ground. The fall and the gaze, the fall of the gaze. The only clear-sighted eyes, at the level of the stones, are nestled in animality. At the feet of the struck Saint Jerome, turning his back to the light, is a bone skull and its dark orbits—that dark hollow that Magdalene at a mirror is going to touch with her waxy hand and her fingertips, like someone blind. The gaze falls to the ground—humility—where it finds death—the dead head that is turned away from its own image in the mirror. The fallen body; but the part of the body that is knowledge has also fallen: the eye. By which the seventeenth century kills, out of despair, representation, which one too easily calls one's own.

Multiple transitions. The apostles transport the message. What heavy gravity causes James's eyelids to lower more than the weight of the satchel and more than his fatigue slumped on the big walking stick?[9] A motionless traveler, statically fixed in an absent ecstasy, he avoids seeing the light, not like the old man or the hurdy-gurdy player, blind or turned away, but with eyes half closed and an oblique gaze to his left. What does he not want to see, what can he not see face to face, the sun or death, or God himself, whom he formerly accompanied but who has gone absent forever? What heavy gravity stoops Philip's shoulder and breaks his neck? The enormous weight of a lightly drawn cross. Turned away from the source, like the old parent, eyelids lowered like James's, yes, the vanished eyes are going to fall to the ground soon; they are mid-fall; the painting sees via a few crystal buttons. Only Jude is the son of the old mother, standing, his weapon on his back; he dares, he dares the face to face; he gazes formidably. Why? Who is Jude for the Christian tradition? The patron, the protector, the emblem of desperate causes.

All three laden—with the satchel, with the weapon, with the cross. The three inevitable big functions of the soldier, the priest, and the foster father. Chance—that is, history—which preserved three-twelfths of the troop, did not do things too badly. Jerome, the scholar, bent like Philip, has dark orbits.[10] He does not look directly at the light; he seeks it in the mediation of the written. As though luminosity no longer resided anywhere but in knowledge.[11] The source, absent, is hidden between the lines. Not yet blind, like those who listen or sing, but with tired eyes, myopic or presbyopic, his spectacles at mid-distance, instead of Philip's eye-buttons, he is reading—the first handwritten page of the books that will follow, open or closed, always abandoned for a higher practice. Face in the dark, writing and skull in the light—the scripture and the skull that will border each other in the solitude where Magdalene contemplates and in the cell with red patches where Jerome, once again, is flagellating himself. The reader, too, laden with the weight of a knowledge that resembles death. In Port Royal, during those days, one abandoned science, philosophers, scholars, and scientists, Descartes, whose ideas were roughly true, Montaigne, with his foolish project, Copernicus, with his concept of the center of the world, integral calculus, rooted in the tradition of Archimedes, those other princes of another world. The fall has perpetrated its work and followed its path, the slumped bodies and fallen rocks, the lowered gazes and gouged-out eyes, the closed knowledge, excluded, the dead science. The worldly absence and the face-to-face confrontation with death remain. Vanished space, light soon to be dark. Nights.

From which the real authenticity of the *Payment of Dues* comes, through the unproven certainties that are brought by a cultural coherence for which Pascal's work is another figure. Through the history of art, its own techniques, the filiation with Caravaggio, et cetera, I don't know; through what is called, poorly, the history of ideas, I do believe. If it is true that after the stature, the stance of the mother, who can be called the tower [*la tour*], the mother of La Tour or the mother of humans, of their bodies, and their works, a Pascalian statics imposes its rigorous law of mathematics, physics, and faith, if it is true that after Eve, who is standing, collected, gathered all around her belly, everything falls, postlapsarian—the naked men, the objects, the lines of location, the direction of gazes, the eyes themselves as well as the rocks—then the earthquake that makes everything vacillate, that event during which postures lose their foundation and base, that inchoative moment of the fall takes place right here. The painting makes us dizzy; the high winds of the night have jostled the vertical. The oblique candle obliquely demarcates the shadows; its brightness explodes multiply in disorder. The name of the scene has little importance; its toppling effect is the very subject. A thousand Judases wait for you in every neck of the woods, and their proper names matter little. At this moment, original, repeated, common, and exemplary, the beam of the scales loses the horizontal, and justice loses the equilibrium of scales. The level and the straight are lost; the dues are not paid equitably. Once the difference has been opened, equality is no longer to be found, either by the increase of the deviation or by its recovery giving profit. So history begins and its perverse games along with it. It is lapse, according to Scripture [*Écriture*], the fall in the literal sense, which is to say, it is error in the writings [*écritures*], which is to say, theft. The book is open to mark this deviation, in ink and with a quill, this static deviation and this falsification, this deviation that will persist, in history and in the work, everywhere some exchange takes place: loaded dice, denial, players blinded by their helmets; brawls in which the clear-sighted man attacks the blind man, laughter to the right, crying to the left;[12] cheating at cards over louis d'or and thievery in the middle of the street. Money is the sign of injustice, its written sign, engraved on metal, and the origin—through force and law—of writing, marked in books in which everything is false and rigged: those books that, little by little, will close. As long as it is a question of a single person, the law of statics descends along a single vertical line. From the first group on, this law acts by compensations, balancing, dividing, along a horizontal line; this law governs equilibrium and disequilibrium; it becomes a balance. Here, visibly, the beam has trembled; it ravages the bodies. The aligned heads have more or less the same angle as the one measured by the inclination of the candle from the plumb line. The human deviation is always in place. It is to be measured simply, like the angle, by the compared weight of the two piles of coins. Here is the reason for the fall: unequal distribution. Originary error, originary lapse, and originary theft that call for a redemption. The polysemic explanation leaves the naming of the subject free. From statics and balances, Pascal had derived just as many models.

Ropes

"Ropes" is a Pascalian term. "It is unjust that anyone should attach themselves to me, even if they do it with pleasure and voluntarily. I should deceive those in whom I had created this desire, for I am not the end for anyone and do not have what it takes to satisfy them. Am I not ready to die? And so the object of their attachment will die. Therefore . . . I am guilty of making myself loved. And if I attract people to attach themselves to me, I must warn those who would be ready to consent to the lie that they ought not to believe it, no matter what advantage it might bring me; and, likewise, they ought not to attach themselves to me; for they should spend their lives and their cares in pleasing and seeking God" [L396-B471]. Ropes of affection, which must be broken in view of death.

A rope [*corde*] is one of the rare objects that appear frequently in La Tour's works. Attachment and detachment. Around the execution column, it winds, knotted broadly; the tower [*la tour*] has undone its bonds. They had tightly bound the living victim; Sebastian is freed only dead. Irene, the peaceful fiancée, has just released the ties.[13] The standing hurdy-gurdy player is towed by the dog; the gaze travels along the leash. Sitting in order to cry out his lament—the animal has fled, no more guide. First detachment, first solitude. "'This dog is mine,' those poor children said; that is my place in the sun. . . . The image of usurpation . . ." [L64-B295]. The support that's outside of one is not only the staff of the old man or James, the tool of statics and the scaffolding against falling; it is, in general, a bond, a relation, a rope. Holding oneself upright, of course, but above all, holding, holding together, holding another thing. The entire work unties, cuts, detaches. And the string instrument will fall silent during the brawl. On Philip's high shoulder, the cross is held, crossed by a hurried lashing. It is coming undone. The horizontal beam where the arms are opened has fallen to the ground where Joseph is boring into it;[14] what remains is the wood standing over the transpierced young man: the untied thread descends in swirls. Everything is falling, untied. The fall and what you are going to untie on the ground. The rope that flagellates Jerome is parallel, in space, to the strings of the hat. Knots on the one, tassels on the others. Red at the end in both cases. Question: Where is the blood, at the end of what rope? The rope that falls to the rocks, or the one that lashes the flesh? If you wear a biretta, an insignia, you show your strength, the harm you can do, the harm you have done, the blood you can spill, that you have surely spilled. "The ropes that attach the respect of men to each other, in general, are ropes of necessity. Men fight each other, strength to strength, all of them wanting to dominate, none of them able to. The masters, lastly, let imagination play its part. These ropes that therefore attach respect to this or that particular individual are ropes of imagination" [L828-B304]. Leave these ropes behind your back, as masters of error and falsity, or grab them to give discipline to yourself. "Know that you are only a king of concupiscence" [L796-B314]. "Various assemblies of the sensible, of the pious, in which each man rules in his home, not elsewhere" [L58-B332]. Detach yourself from the ropes of necessity, form the image of the ropes of imagination, turn them against yourself. Strip off the hat and the cloak of blood, and let blood flow with your concupiscence.

A man dressed in brocade: this garment is power. "He will have me whipped if I do not salute him" [L89-B315]. The cardinal throws off the habit, and *therefore* whips himself. "Being dapper is not altogether vain, for it shows that a large number of people work for one; it shows by one's hair that one has a valet, perfumer, et cetera ... Being dapper is showing one's power" [L95-B316]. He shows all that, the naif: his band, the thread, the braiding.[15] Between the two profiles of the pure beauty that is loved and the marked face that no one will love anymore. He displays—everything is in front— the fine knot with two pendants over his stomach. All decked out with ribbons, trussed up with the ropes of imagination. Four clever women, behind him, keep an ulterior motive hidden behind them and more than one trick up their sleeves [L90-B337, L91-B336]. His rope displayed like a sash is being cut on his left, while on his right the strings of his purse are being grabbed. Granted, the band, the thread, and the braiding protect, but not always: or they are all the more deceptive for not always being so. The cleverness of the people is sound; they sometimes dress up in finery in order to skirt around the half clever. Gazes that are crossed, absent, quick, parallel, attentive, sly, complicit, turned away—the circular clatter of the reason of effects. Of effects or consequences, of effects or appearances, of effects or items of clothing. There is always somebody, behind, busying with cutting the ropes of imagination. He imagined himself protected by the four lackeys represented by his display; he is robbed, in broad daylight, by four scoundrels. He is cut—understand by this what you like. One more trick and the trickster hides the master card behind the beribboned garment, but the women's gazes, combined, turn around him and again pass behind.[16] The deceiver deceived, this never ends. The side from which he envisions things, and the side he has not seen. The social bond, a rope of imagination or power, is not as straight or as rigid as gravity; as strict as gravity, the social bond nonetheless makes loops, whorls, twists, and turns. It passes in front, then behind; it stabs in the back, and nobody is ever certain of being behind everybody's back. This is the game: there is never any absolutely master card, nor any side of a die that gives all the money. Scissors cut paper, which covers rock, which breaks the scissors. A bad infinite, which never ends. Sum paid, sum played, sum stolen. Gold circulates along the same vicious paths, vitiated by power, chance, or trickery. There is always someone stronger or cleverer. Thus every discourse and every philosophy that insist on passing behind everyone prove that they are playing a game or seeking power, never the truth. Moral: demarcate an entanglement while fortune-telling. "He who will dance on the tightrope will be alone" [L554-B303].

Magdalene, who has danced too much, is alone. Everyone easily sees the progress of the three women keeping vigil on the path of renunciation, a progress marked by the double light, the death seen full face and from behind, and the nothingness without mirror.[17] But on the path of detachment? An unclasped necklace on the table, open bracelets fallen on the floor, rivers of fire pulled along by themselves. New jewels, not cut by another but willingly undone, placed, secondly, on the edge of the book and below the abject skull, and, additionally, exhibited as images. Third, and to conclude, the three ropes. The penitence belt, around the stomach and extending to the ground, the end of Eve's pride and indicating the fall, the flagellation whip above the cross and lying before the books' edges, vertical discipline, that too, and vector toward the ground, and the big lamp wick. The parable of the wise virgin who keeps the fire going until the bridegroom's arrival. All three ropes treated with the same strands, the same knots, and the same splice. The hemp has replaced the rocks: it girds the solitude and the asceticism, mortifies the three libidos, it burns. And the three ropes are first horizontal, on the fixed end, and then perpendicular, along the free end. All three are level and then delivered over to the necessities of a law. The rope belt falls from the hips, *libido sentiendi;* the lashes fall under the silent folio, *libido sciendi;* the keepsake of an open bracelet, above them, also falls according to the vertical. But the splicing of the wick, parallel and similar to the whip handle, turns about its end and flames upward. *The bond of consumption has reversed its law.* The open and untied string around the carpenter's neck has come too close to the mystic flame. It burns, after coming untied; the consummate detachment consumes itself in flame. An upward gravity, ascension. The ropes are no longer to be sliced, the example of Alexander, the king, the captain; they no longer fall according to the laws of statics, the example of Archimedes, the prince of geniuses; they vanish into an upright incandescence. Their brightness, their luster, in another order. Woven over itself, the cellar rat candle burns under the virgin's hand.[18] The candle is closely woven, ardent. Joy, fire. Detached from everything, the bonds catch fire. Vigil, night. Separated from everything, and everything abandoned, fled, renounced. Total and sweet renunciation. All the ropes burn. Loop, strand, braids, knot, and turns, aligned, pacified together in the vertical blaze. The midwife has just cut the umbilical cord and its turns; she illuminates the first rising after childbirth [*relevailles*].[19] Irene has untied the straps and their turns around the tower where Sebastian was bound; she illuminates the final lying after death [*funérailles*]. In impregnable solitude, in which birth and death meet, end and resurrection, be illuminated only by what has been adored too much, thrown in the fire forever. Enter this night, where every rope burns. Helix of the bond and red swirls: the flame and the chain designate the high point, which is absent, through the conjunction of the straight line and the circle, the tower and the turn.

Wax

The path is apophatic. Space disappears, reference falls. The worldly world is left to a theatrical exterior, a flat plane in front of an empty scene. Few objects, other than some figures, rocks, ropes, books, and candles. A continual purification by negation and death. Only humans. Their bodies received the marks of history over a long time before entering here. Old age, misery, despair, struggle, combat, lie, wrinkles, white hair, sobs, slumping of flesh, distress. An often-improbable anatomy. Faces made profound by misfortune or inexpressive by dissembling. So history ends in the infirmities of old age; the work begins at this very point.

The path then has turned around. The origin is the old man, the old woman, the end of history, and what follows is a procession of the elderly, apostles, Job, Jerome . . . Passing to middle age, moving into adolescence, then extreme youth, all the way to infancy, and the dawn of childbirth, where everything comes to an end, as though in the East. The route seems to reverse apparent time: a sign by which one always recognizes a work that follows the straight grain. Autogenesis from the downstream to the upstream, the inevitable path to the beginning. In the past, Plato described this as the "golden age": a different history of the world, time going backward in relation to its ordinary course, a fabric necessitating productive work, the reversed cycle of the vital fall. A new chronology that can be interpreted at will—as psychic time, by anamnesis; as the time of knowing, by recollection and the quest of reason; as a religious time, by the wait for a Messiah . . . but that is simpler to take as it is, as the real time of production (the word *produce* expresses well that it is led forward) and that is established through praxis, unavoidably.

Apophatic via the Jansenist stripping down and reversed by *the fundamental time of every work,* the path is always tangent to death, which is invisible and weighs heavily upon afflicted old people, which is capitally present with Magdalene and with Jerome, and in person at Irene's knees. Death shapes the bodies. Then it gradually leaves this habitation. It objectivizes itself, exorcised. Hence the transfiguration that makes the body that is hollowed, wrinkled, furrowed, marked, and scraped with its terrible signature into a smooth body, polished, level, and flat. Jerome is right in the middle of this drama: death has just appeared, still half hidden; the body is a death body; the work has not entered the lights of night. The great trilogy seeks a new equilibrium. Magdalene: the candle is lit; the skull comes into evidentness; the old marks are erased from the flesh. Smooth face, even profile, round shoulders, and a head of hair like a drop of oil. As with Dorian Gray, it is the painting, the object, the death's head in the mirror that store the furrows of time. Progressing in the work means objectivizing death, lighting it up full force, giving birth to it. The real body then radiates, unreal. What made its raw opacity was this terrifying internment. The objective expulsion frees it, exorcised. Put this bare, stony, abominable object at its feet, on its lap, and on the table. Hence an unspoken detachment and a new childhood. All that remains of the bodies is wax statues. From improbability, anatomy passes into impossibility. Figurines instead of figures. Not massive objects with relief in the face of the light source or turning their backs to it, for an exact partitioning of shadows, but translucent volumes into which luminosity seeps, maintaining a loving, secret inner relationship with the light. Magdalene has wax hands, and Sebastian a wax body; the faces without any hollows are masks of wax. Amorphous and colorless material in which the trilogy of the body, death, and light is tied and untied. No, it is not a death mask, nor a waxy tint. The hand in front of the flame lets the epiphany be glimpsed.[20] Wax bodies and wax candles, the fire shines the way the body burns, as though the wax catches fire by secret flashes. The wick, the rope, is only black coal; it is the wax that flames, like the body that has become semitransparent. It is less the wax torch that shines than the new body of the new child, newly born from the new mother and who, for his part, has a body, maybe the only true, real body in the entire work, in any case the first child body in history, a living body, freed from death, which, with all its carnal tissue, reflects the light and multiplies it.

The body goes toward rock, or it goes toward wax, according to the time it has chosen. Toward the skull or the translucent hand. Toward the final earth or the radiance. Painting wax is giving light a chance to filter out death across the body. Finding a material that burns and shines: this is reversing the irreversible. In the reversal of the fall into the flame, the wax also intervened. A writer like Pascal forges a dialectic for the reversal of laws: a painter, for a similar project, must discover a material.

Masculine, Feminine

Men and women. The division is exact, surely calculated. Men and women, this is saying too little: it is femininity that is at stake. Femininity does not appear in Pascal and fairly little in the authors of the day. It is proper to La Tour and maybe to Corneille. Man is naive, it seems, by nature; he never completely leaves the state of infancy. Woman has shifted away from this immediacy; she is less of a dupe, cleverer, better defended. She is behind; she moves to the back; she is the thought or motive hidden behind. She opens up less, reserves herself, and guards herself. Hence her distance, her strength, and her cleverness. Her meditative power and her reservoir of morality. She towers over the old man by a head, Job by a chest, Sebastian by an entire body, the newborn child by an anterior life. She deceives, but is not deceived: four gypsies form a chain to fleece the young pigeon, the dark old woman, the young fair one, the mature one, and the pretty brunette; but the courtesan is not duped, her gaze and hand say so, by the ace of diamonds behind the back; the servant girl managed to warn her. The forest of hands in the middle says so. The dissembling of the beribboned, mustachioed man cannot fool anyone, except the big baby-faced naif sitting opposite. Look at Peter's stupid and dumbstruck profile, who resembles his rooster so much: all this for a denial in front of the servant girl with the candle.[21] One always forgets that the story of Peter is the story of a woman. Overwhelmed by the idiotic brawl, exhausted by the lovemaking of the soldiers, dismayed by the death of Sebastian the worshiper, contemplative at the miracle of this newness: she knows that the child of man will recommence, will endlessly repeat his stupidities, trickery, playacting, violence, and despair, without ever learning anything, without ever knowing anything, without finding his distance with respect to this naive and dangerous immediacy, without ever rejoining her. Midwife and wise woman by mothering, candle-bearer, light-bearer, and, by this very fact, occasionally Lucifer, she is an endless and useless protector. Solitude for Jerome and Magdalene: the one solitude filled with sound and fury, whip, rope and discipline, the topsy-turvy cell, disorder and war, spilled blood, cross in the hand and cloak on the arm as in the theater, the open book and scattered rocks, the bones of my mother the earth, the tragic din, the grandiloquence of the incomplete nudity, playacting up close, as close as the big hat, noise, always noise. The holy woman sinner's solitude is in silence, sitting, stable, gathered around herself, without any other movement than an attentive gaze, equilibrium in the nothingness contemplated behind the mirror of the dark light. Motionless wisdom, serene, the center found again. Jerome is only a squirrel in its cage.

Gradation, reason of effects, half-clever people and perfect Christians, and reversal of the *for* into the *against*, according to the light one has [L90-B337]. Thus those of the people immediately have the same idea as the clever ones who have traveled the path twice and who, as a consequence, have returned to the same place. One should be surprised at the admiration of historians for the painter who expressed, through everyday life, the highest spirituality. This law of repetition is a simple idea of the time, which was well codified by Pascal. But, here, femininity is always one trick ahead: half clever with respect to the naif, clever when faced with the half-clever, and perfect Christian with respect to the mediocre Christian. Jerome is doubtless impeccable and only reaches asceticism, beyond knowledge. Magdalene has sinned; she arrives at charity. Even if I should have the languages of men and angels, if I did not have charity, I would only be a brass noisemaker. Women bear light; they are at the very source of this reason of effects.

Hence the discourse of Job's wife to Job, the discourse of any woman to any man in misfortune, and the fact that it does not have to do with the book of Job is of no consequence. Every man in misfortune is Job, and we can do without books. You cry, you moan, you fill space with your clamors and supplication, you want to stop everything, the occupations of your parents, the people passing by, the path of the sun; you want everyone, men and the world, to hear your questioning, yours, your own. Why, why, yes, of course, why? But there is no answer; you know that now, since the week your threnody has been dragging on. Fine, you are in misfortune, but you think yourself the only one; you want to stop the world around you with your pain. You think yourself the center of the world; you think you are the only one to ask the radical question; you think you are the only one to have gone beyond discourse. What a fuss, my philosopher. All this noise to find out what every man knows, every woman, and every crushed being. Every old man, every old woman of the people. Nothing is new under the sun. Solomon and Job knew best and spoke best of human misery. All this jumble, all this indecency, in order to write a book, a song, a psalm, a hymn, in which you proclaim your humility, your fall to the ground, onto the ash heap. If what you say were true, you would entrust yourself to silence. This true knowledge is not spoken. Consequently, go into your room, all alone and uncommunicative, like the young woman Magdalene, and stay silent in the nothingness about the truth of your discourses. Or wipe your nose, get up, and go cut wood, bore into a beam, do something, for goodness' sake. Put your clothes on; that's enough—enough of always seeing naked men, old men without clothes offering the indecent spectacle of their pitiful flesh; us, we do this to give the breast, look for a flea, or give birth.[22] You, it's always for shouting and flagellation. Us, for life; you, for death. That's enough. Pitiful piety and misfortune declaimed to the eight winds of Israel, impotence, complacency. Job disappears from the light; the courageous woman appears in the luminosity she herself produces. Standing, better than standing, leaning over he who has fallen. And, for once in La Tour's work, two beings look at each other. The book of Job, once again, is nothing but vanity. The proper name must be erased. Complacent nothingness is another triumph for oneself. Exacerbated narcissism in one's asceticism. With her gesture, the woman erases the discourses that were so content with themselves. Happy is the art that says without words that unheard-of thing that abolishes words. Not misfortune and its poem, but its universal and pacified consolation, the loss of identity to oneself in the community of others and natural legislation. Spinoza's wisdom: the law of falling rocks, the search for a veritable good capable of communicating itself, the forgetting of personal identity, and the refuge of emotional words in the glacier of geometry. Whom should I love?

A global path on which the mother starts, Eve of the human race standing before the real, a sempiternal path on which the mother ends, and starts again, with the presentation of her newborn. Eva, Ave, a cyclic chain, a continuous scale, a tree of beings, the tower, a procession, a line of women leaning over nothingness, or hope, generalized to the entire work, a woman leaning over that nothing that is the flea, a woman leaning in fact over pregnancy, women leaning over Sebastian, over Job, over the skull, and over the new child, their affair is death and life, rupture and continuity, the end, the thread of time and the beginning, to carry the torch and pass it on, vestals at the fire that never goes out, genesis of humanity, repetition, genealogical tree, its feminine flow, an old mother, a courtesan, a servant girl, a future-telling Romani woman who holds onto a guilty thread, which the Fury, behind, begins to cut, a repentant young woman, a strong woman, a pregnant woman, and the strings have been tied again, a midwife, crying women, a fiancée, a *first rise after childbirth*. Lateral men, outside the chain of beings, adventitious branches of a tree with hardly a leaf, Joseph who incessantly returns, chaste in boring the beams or dreaming of impossible angels,[23] labors and dreams as substitutes, their affair is elsewhere and, as though marginal and unreal, crybaby men, disheveled, gamblers, deceived, deceivers, Peter who incessantly returns, a sham clever man or a sham naif, a paving stone on the ground, fighters, blind men, men in despair, in distress, destined for death, giving their life. The inattentive masculine collapses and dies at every instant; the feminine remains, invariant in history and stable across her misfortunes, the genus of the species, protector of life against obscurity, weaving the cloth and the thread of the work. La Tour in the feminine. Going from the old man to the child via the female invariant. Reversal of laws, reversal of time. Through the woman accompanist.

A Space Plunged in Another Space

The woman at the top, standing, holds her handkerchief in front of her eyes. She remains in the dark—mourning sight. The second woman, lower, bent over, reveals only, under the cold blue veil, a profile with no gaze. The third woman, even lower, stooped forward, has half opened her veil, her hands, and her eyelids. Irene, on one knee, in the lowest position that a woman, here, can tolerate, only lets a tear from her eye be seen . . . and therefore Philip and the hurdy-gurdy player had cried their eyes out; one enters into night and blindness by shed tears; Peter the rooster, among so many others, has taught us this; eyes only see or no longer see except through tears; they are given not for sight or truth but for tears and charity. Sebastian, stretched out, has just entered his final night. The torch scarcely burns for the sake of seeing; it burns like suffering. It burns in the opening, hollowed out in a V, of the fall. The women form a chain; not that horizontal chain of four where the looks cross without meeting, behind the back of the naive dupe, but a chain that plunges, as one advances from right to left, toward the strict vertical.

The absent gazes of each woman toward the one she cries for draws a fan whose ribs close at the execution column. Each woman is a station or step in the fall, a stopping point in the plunge. They draw the staircase of the tomb, the steps of death, the descent, the Jacob's ladder placed either upright or inverted, depending on whether one is trusting to the hope of the flame or the obligation of the mast. The entire work is there, summed up, motionless. Lit and upright, Eve is sobbing; then the neck bows, the shoulder stoops, the legs bend, the body becomes prostrate and spreads out, back to the ground, face at the base of the cross, and the mouth exhales its last flame. Implacable statics has recapitulated its law—all the way to the lowest point, all the way to the dark humility of death, the head of the dead man to the left, the murderer's helmet to the right, all the way to the foot of the tower. Execution column, tree with hardly a leaf, mast of martyrdom, cross of calvary, axis of the world rooted in the center, in the middle, in the most abject and most necessary point, irrepressible vector of beings and things, absolute rectitude of direction without recourse, the tower, the tower itself, La Tour himself. And the path is in the name, a signed work even without a signature, the way the fire of the memorial, seen in ecstasy amid tears of joy, will be the unbearable appearance of the Paschal fire. La Tour, symbolizing verticality. The column and the flame of the lowest descent and the highest hope.

Death has mown down the youth; the feet are all in the same spot. Those of the standing women, of Irene kneeling, and of Sebastian lying supine. Ripe ears of corn and harvested wheat—the old central region of gravity, in the lower right, governs the curve of the heights; it groups the stroke of the scythe. The corpse has lost this site so as to join the bottom of the axis where the personages, as they say, are contemplating it. The center of gravity, of stability, is lost at the foot of the tree and moves toward it. I have mentioned Eve standing in tears; I have mentioned the tree with hardly a leaf; I have mentioned the fall: and this is the original sin. The sin or the lack of love. The middle of world space or of worldly stations, at the center of the stepwise curve, is the lowest point on the right, the feet;

the middle of supernatural space, at the center of the blind gazes, is the lowest point on the left, the root of the tree or the tower, at the base indicated by the hope torch and the day's flying arrow. *A sagitta volante in die, a negotio perambulante in tenebris, ab incursu et daemonio meridiano.*[24] From one center to the other by the stroke of the scythe and the bite of the arrow, from one site to the other by the flatness of death.

Hands clenched around her eyes, which are masked by the shroud handkerchief, hands joined for prayer in front of the blue veil, hands open with pity or grief, on the immense, impeccable dark dress, and hands occupied with holding the torch and Sebastian's wrist, whose hands are lifeless and spread apart, defeated, gasping. Their angle unfolds, little by little, and becomes given. The hands are symmetrical at first, with respect to a mirror plane, skew next, in space, and turned on their axis. To the point of giving life, without restraint or order. A diagram that, roughly, forms a double cone, or a double nappe: Irene and the woman with the veil, Sebastian and the two supernumeraries. They mark out globally, in the upper right, what is called a point of view [*vue*], which is poorly named: it is a dark cell. The source: a dark space, a blind point. Poorly named, since the tears, veils, and eyelids do away with the gaze. It is a real point of view, but absent like a hole, the absurd and senseless point of charity from which tears flow, not sight [*vue*], and from which the painting flows like a nappe and a river. A river of Babylon and a valley of tears, a valley carved in a V on the painting, a dark valley, a river of tears on its less abrupt side, the women cry from seeing flow all the perishable things carried by these torrents; the women wait to rise in the light, a memory of their dear country during the length of their exile. River, torrent, valley, continually opening toward the river mouth, the mouth of the inanimate dead body, waterways stemming from this absent source, from this dark hole, from this invisible center. The high point of the imminent fall, the pole of light in shadow.[25] The dry source of the river.

The center, at the bottom, is designated by the law of gravity and the union of the bases. The center, at the bottom and on the other side, intersects the column and the arrow. Present and defined regions. The center, present, at the top, is dark. The center, at the top and on the other side, is infinitely absent, right where the parallel lines of the fire and the tower would join for the geometer or the believer—for Desargues, the theoretician of pencils of lines of the same order, and for Pascal, who knew how to mark the missing points. The infinite vanishing point of parallel lines: God is absent, vaguely indicated by a weak flame; the point of view in the end, the real one, persists forever outside the working drawing, outside the space where things happen, pass, and fall. If it is there, it is dark, and if it is bright, it is never here. That is to say, here below. Thus everything goes from right to left, as indicated by the staircase, the descent to the tomb, the fall, and the valley, as indicated by the stretched-out body of the young worshiper and the fletched vector. The center of gravity is lost; through death, one rejoins the middle or mid-site of stability through which the world axis passes, where the tree of the cross takes root: the holy women, Irene peace, the pietà, were contemplating this figure of an unrepresentable Christ and, beyond this visible figure, the invisible pole. The point of view, which here below is said to be high, is never, and cannot be, at the sources of light; it is dark; knowledge is useless and vain due to this obligatory shift; what remains is crying charity, burning charity, pacified. The pole where the gaze is the light itself, where the fire sees, is absent; it is at infinity, outside space, dissociated from this world here below. From one to the other, the journey-life fills this distance, passes through the valley of tears, tumbles, and falls at the threshold of death, endlessly burning along the length of the flame tree. Whatever one may do, one is in the night. The nights of La Tour are also night in the sense of the *noche oscura,* the dark night of the soul. I wait for you, the way the blind hurdy-gurdy player hopes for light, the way the hurdy-gurdy player, tired and frail, is on the watch for the dawn.

Space is decentered to such an extent that it is torn apart, into the four corners, by four centers. And by four centers that flee and vanish. The low point of stability gives way by definition; it always tends toward the lowest; it falls, of itself, by nature, physics, and mechanics. A station of gravity, a step of a stairs, the infinite descent of weighty objects. Walk without resting, walk boldly, you fall, the ground gives way. The abyss by your sides, Pascal. The central point of the world where the cross takes root, around which everything rolls, one must die to know this point, even if one is the son of God; it is not much, the height of a body or of the genuflections of women or the length of a martyr, that marks out the stair steps and measures the stations and rungs of this descent into hell. The execution, the death, and the descent into the tomb are only finite stages. The earth, the earth of burial, gives way, here again. *Conceptus, natus* (the woman), *passus* (the execution and the footstep), *crucifixus* (the column), *mortuus et sepultus* (the earth), *descendit ad inferos. Tertia die resurrexit a mortius, ascendi ad caelos.*[26] The point at infinity bursts forth the length of the axis by means of the chimney of the Paschal flame, by its ascent and its verticality; the roof in its turn gives way, and the skies are open. *Sedet ad dexteram patris. Sedet,* sits on a high and secure foundation, outside space. *Mundus patet*, the old Rome said.[27] The point of view, blind, incomprehensible like a black box, the source and origin of the procession for the holy women, is always behind, behind the back of whoever in the procession, the infinite flight of the pole, moving in a series, a sequence, or a chain. The clear-sighted absolute or the charitable without sin, without veil and without fold, interminably withdraws the length of an endless procession of the blind or the half blind. The roof once more gives way by this gradation, lacking a first term.

The painting explodes then, torn by the law-abiding fall and the senseless hope, the view without final point and the incomparable charity; it flees from the four sides, asymptotically; it bursts its frame and amorphous space; it spreads into the dark world, a flight of stairs of the limitless staircase; it has no place, it does not take place, it is the entire place; it is randomly partitioned, here or there, where everything is middle indifferently; it diagonally crosses the two infinities of misery and of greatness by means of the relentless and unceasing procession of mourners and those moved to pity, a procession, a river, a slow irrepressible descent, an ascent indicated by the ladder of Jacob, of all of humanity, and of history, rushing in droves and in order toward death and the helmet, but gently burning to rise, in peace, toward the light. The world is this somber vale, carved with steps, crumbling with tears, a deadly vale, in which shines, darkly, an inextinguishable fire. The painting is its fabric. Why is spatial reference lacking in La Tour? Because demarcating a site in one spot or another makes no difference; the dark world and the valley of tears are everywhere as well as here. Whether middle or elsewhere, the point of gravity (foundation) and God (the point at infinity) are always absent from them. Space is lost, paradise lost, humanity—by the sin and the fall—is lost. A painting is nothing if it has a site, marked personages, historical scenes, and original models—if it is not a figure, a figure in Pascal's sense. What vanity a painting would be that attracts admiration by the resemblance of things whose originals are not admired in the least. So do away with worldly references; let space flee, erase the discernible traits of the individuated body: Sebastian, an endless series of indefinite figurines.

Stroke of the scythe, fall, flight of stairs, all the way to the last of the rocks, at the bottom, to the left, all that is true, roughly, as an initial approach. The geometric order is too marked for attention not to redouble. The rectangle is globally Arguesian, or Pascalian, due to its missing points, its absent references, or, as they used to say, its elements at infinity: a space that's perspective or projective due to the dark point of view and the vanishing flight of parallel lines, a space that's open due to the statics of the lowest point. A mystic quadrilateral, the hexagon has been called "mystic" with less reason.[28] The fact remains that the rectangle is locally Cartesian. This is a second space, here, plunged in the first one, the way the world here below is surrounded by the supernatural. The painting is Cartesian, due to the coordinates that are arbitrarily set, but set exactly with respect to the frame. A pencil of lines parallel to the tree: the flame and the torch, the posture of the women, the folds of the clothing, these are vertical axes; the stretched-out execution victim, the ground, horizontal axes. Here is the big orthonormal trihedral, for which the paving stone at the bottom is a reduced model. The single diagonal arrow is a bisector indicating the origin. The weapon is pointing like a vector. Sagittal mathematics.

That said, nothing is straight; everything is curved. The rope's helix descends along the tree, and the flame vortexes in swirls. On the main diagonal, parallel to the vector, aligning the faces of the young man and the two lit mourners, Irene and her blue shadow draw a curve. It seems to be governed by a very simple law. Let there be two forces, a horizontal one and a vertical one, components of the vector-arrow. Go straight, walk; let yourself go with the fall. I want to head for the tree; an implacable force attracts me. And, therefore, I inevitably go to the point I am not looking for. This is a mechanical curve in Descartes's sense. It is the opposed drama of action and passion, two forces that pull in different directions. The fall is deferred by the force of the soul. But only deferred. La Tour lastly allows an interesting isomorphy to be understood between *The Passions of the Soul* and the geometry of the period. In the final analysis, here below, Job and Sebastian's reasoning is correct over the dutiful women. But at the limits of Cartesian space, Pascal takes up reason again and opens another space: that incomprehensible roof under which Job's wife bows her head.

Peace

No one has ever attained or produced beauty if one wanted it for its own sake. Beauty is superfluous and more or less gratuitous, and encountered moreover in striving toward something other than it. It is an unexpected recompense that arises unexpectedly behind one's back. It is pure modality—an adverb—of a labor, of a process, or of a route. This is why no one has ever been able to discourse about it, since it happens, inexplicably, to the verb and to language. Language turns around well enough to express everything—about other things, about itself, even about its own tropes; it nonetheless cannot say what happens, by chance, behind its turnings around. Beauty: the absent phantom behind the back of the person who moves forward, on the condition that he or she walk toward a different goal. Should he or she turn around, a seer, beauty stiffens into a pillar of salt. Whoever makes art for art's sake, pure painting, pure poetry, or even pure geometry, has never produced anything but a tired, repetitive, bloodless academicism. One sophistry among others, a rhetoric of modality. Making or talking about the beautiful is neither a profession nor a talent: one makes the beautiful, and that is all. Direct aesthetics is devoid of object; beauty is only a modal supplement: the ad-verb of adverbs; becoming either an aesthete or a rhetorician is all you need do to say goodbye to it forever. Rape whomever cannot love you.

I don't know if La Tour sought God in the miserable streets of Lunéville, Rome, and Paris; I don't know if he was a mystic, even though his work, or what remains of it, made some progress that testifies to this. But I am sure, at least, that he sought peace—inaccessible, improbable, impossible peace—in his province at war amid Europe on fire. Peace, solitude, and silence. The peace for which everyone at that same moment thirsted. The peace of Spinoza, the excommunicated, the expelled, the lapidated. The peace of Descartes: "now that I have procured for myself an assured repose in peaceful solitude."[29] The peace of Pascal, in his cell, at Port Royal. The peace of Leibniz, roaming the states of Europe with his irenic projects, Irene's torch in his hand. "I finally resolved to seek whether there might be some object that would be a veritable good, one capable of communicating itself, which would affect the mind singly, to the exclusion of all else, a good whose discovery and attainment would bear the fruit of a continuous and sovereign happiness."[30] La Tour seeks peace, Irene. He immediately enters solitude, before and at the time of the brawl, when the knife is held by the blind man, amid the noise of the idiotic laughter and impotent tears, the brawl of murdered music. He enters silence and his own night, once Jerome's frenzy is pacified, books closed, asceticism surpassed. His virtuosity, itself, becomes pacified; it enters simplicity. The three libidos become pacified, described by a tradition that's almost as refined as our grids. The *libido sentiendi:* Magdalene sitting, alone, in silence. The *libido sciendi:* crouching Jerome flaying the book-man, the sad and scholarly flesh, and the cardinal red. The *libido dominandi:* the helmet fallen at the feet of the dead man, the hat abandoned behind the prelate's back. Wretched is the land of malediction set ablaze by these three rivers of fire rather than watered by them. Flame everywhere. Sitting, crouching, or stretched out, these people were formerly swept along by these rivers. Peace beyond tears. Peace sought during the night and under the trembling fire of the candles and torches. The tower [*la tour*] of quietude and serenity. Of the seriousness necessary for serenity. They don't strip themselves naked in La Tour's work just for show: it has to do with stripping down. The clothes themselves lose their luster: the clothing, little by little, is denuded. The clothing, the faces, the bodies. Statues of wax.

La Tour of solitude and the tower [*la tour*] of silence. Who speaks—emits sounds—from among this rare crowd? The beggar hurdy-gurdy player shouts his lament; the Romani woman tells fortunes; Job listens to his wife scold him; the servant girl with the candle receives Peter's denial. The speech is deceitful or pathetic. All the rest is silence: lips forever closed, broken musical instruments. Keep quiet. Entirely silent paintings. The old Stoicism reinvaded Europe and submerged the Christian bedrock. The public turmoil and the misfortunes of the times had brought it back, after more than a thousand years, as they always do. Keep quiet, close the eyes that have seen too much or cried too much; plug the ears that have heard too much noise, too much vanity, absurdity, and lies. Silence and solitude, suppression of the background, suppression of the noise, suppression of the message. A compact and light world where communication ceases. No longer have ills, so many ills have been had. Cut off the sources of suffering, every source. Nothingness of reception, the ivory tower. There is haughtiness, stiff and proud aristocracy, in this renunciation. The Vulgate is closed; speech is vulgar and vulgarizing. Spinoza himself wrote the book of the deepest misfortune and the highest human consolation in signs that were outside the discourse of divulgation: he engraved them on the walls of the geometry tower. Desperate refusal, haughty, to spread oneself and compromise oneself. Beyond the aforementioned affliction, tower over the book of Job and the *Guide for the Perplexed*. At this acme of solitude, it is inevitable that one encounter death. The malevolent instinct obstructs the path. There death is, at Jerome's feet, who is alone; it is hidden under the book. It wins. There it is, on solitary Magdalene's lap, on her table and under her hand, on the book now, the back of its neck toward the mirror and its face toward her, with dark orbits and hollow earholes; it is stretched out horizontally under Irene's torch. Solitude and silence haunted by the dreadful presence; more, dead solitude and dead silence. Yes, outside, death was committing its ravages, and you rejoin it inside where you had wanted to escape it.

He sought peace, solitude, and silence. Death and despair had not left him. So beauty itself came to seek him. With it having arrived, everything was resolved. Continual beauty, sovereign beauty. Incomprehensible beauty. Newly born from a simple mother and from the respectful midwife. The beauty that sleeps in its swaddling clothes and no longer says anything and will never say anything—except in dreams and during work. This light shines in the darkness. *Et lux in tenebris lucet, et tenebrae eam non comprehenderunt.*[31] John, life, tenderness, and not Peter, rocks, death. Life. The torches have changed hands, from the strong woman to the midwife, and from the accoucheuse to the child. The child who is learning the work from the practiced hands of the carpenter, hand transparent with light, the child who blows on the fire, and the child who launches dreams.[32] The new life radiates with light. "The free man thinks of death least of all things; his wisdom is not a meditation on death, but a meditation on life."[33] The mother, silent in the face of the miracle and the new work. We think and we experience that we are eternal. In ignorance and night. Simple, silent, and tranquil: the wisdom of the woman who does not yet know that she has just given birth. Childbirth in beauty. Peace, lastly, shines, calm.

The East

Thus the paintings are seen from too far away and from too close; there is only one indivisible point that is the veritable site. The newborn. At ten paces, turn around. The light, hidden, flames in the room. A few paces more, it seems to grow. Farther, even farther, its radiation spreads. An absent focus, an unlocatable point of view, *he* is the true site. If the space were given to us, this night object would seem a sun. At the unthinkable extremities of the known and unknown world, he would resemble the dawn.

Lost, Found Again

Of Port Royal, not a rock remains. The abbey was too dangerous, with its conviction that all power is lie and posturing, that institution is theater, and custom farce relative to time and place. Port Royal would die by the hands of the powerful, but also died of its own death instinct. Force was outside and nothingness inside, a skull from a skeleton in each room. Weak torches that desire ash. Of Pascal, only disordered papers remain. The trembling, evident fact that all order is vanity is destructive of everything, and finally of itself. It would be just and salutary for the *Pensées* to remain in disorder; they say this about the world, or they say nothing. Of La Tour, it was inevitable that the name should disappear, for the same reasons, and inevitable that the nameless icons of nothingness, alibi, chance, death, and deceit should end up exploding in space, from the west to the north, by the sixteen winds of a history that wouldn't be able to bear this message without mortally laughing at itself. History had lost them, finally avenged on the icons for having put it in hock. All order, idiotic and cruel, was outside, and nothingness inside. Of this seventeenth century, of the true—radical, revolutionary—it was inevitable that nothing should remain. Above the cavern of anguish, quickly, the Baroque needed to be constructed, a sad and somber order, a well-draped academy, Boileau, the Sun King. Torn-apart Sebastian's torch leaves Louis XIII's chamber in order to hang on the sky's false roof: that sun that Pascal calls but a lamp. The days like the nights.

Historians of art reconstruct La Tour the way Lafuma and others have reclassified the *Pensées*. And now this dangerous milieu of the seventeenth century, in which all of Europe was burning, is becoming close to us—so familiar, so ours, that we are starting, once again, to understand. And now there is no longer any need for theology or metaphysics for nonmeaning to explode, with a great deal of noise. Nonmeaning hangs about in the street, in the clutches of the powerful, in the mouths of the learned, and the Grand Guignol of history. The loaded dice, the master cards behind the back, the eyes elsewhere and the blind gazes, we know. The death that reflects death across the solitude mirror, we know. Irene, peace, with her single tear and hesitant torch, bent stiff and straight over the murdered youth, we are there. The decentered space, the milieu without middle, the vanished reference, the inconsistent time, the undone identity, the erased nature, the claustration in vacillating light, we experience them. No, this is not utopia; it is right here. It was inevitable that he would be lost and inevitable as well that today the painter of *The Newborn Child* would be found again. The hope to recognize, beyond the idiotic misfortune and nameless solitude, the incomprehensible and tranquil birth of Newness.

PS—Irene's torch bears the number 392. The second verse of Psalm 39 of the Vulgate expresses the subject of the painting (he made me climb back up from the deadly pit) and my interpretation (he set my feet on the rock, making my steps firmer).

9

Turner Translates Carnot

In 1784, at the express request of Samuel Whitbread, a brewer of beer, George Garrard, who was then twenty-four years old, executed something like an advertising sign for Whitbread's warehouse.[1] The collection of objects put on display is the *recapitulation* of a perfect world that would soon disappear. Men, horses, tools, ships. We see a wooden warehouse built on a wharf, where a three-master with furled sails has just tied up and is being unloaded: the warehouse exhibits a flawless framework—tie beams, lintels, and rafters—which overhangs and covers the scene. The world of work and commerce: to the left, the owner, among the chests or the trunks (of gold?), is conversing with a client; his workers are bustling about; they are not very numerous. Obviously, it is the equipment that was to be showcased. Hence the recapitulation. For mechanics, work is a force in motion. What are the origins, the sources of this force? There are four of them, and only four: horses, and here they are, two in profile and one full face, harnessed in every manner typical of the time; men, and here they are, one of whom, perched on the wagon, is leaning over to lift up a sack; wind, and here are the ships, hawsers tied to the mooring posts, sails at rest, rigging free and in place, ropes, ratlines, sheaves, straps, mast grooves, snatch blocks, rolling gear for mooring, shackles, tackle, and gantlines. Nothing is missing from the balance sheet, not even the ton sling and its strop. A real treat for the sailor. Water, lastly, and here is the Thames, the immense, dark waterwheel on the left side of the painting. The producers of force: men, horses, wind, and water. The horse first of all, valorized, clarified, magnified, magnificent. To apply the force: collars, harnesses, axles, anchor points, masts, guy wires, and more. To transmit it: pulleys and tackle, wheels, gears, and chains. Simple machines. In front, to the right, one can see an immense scale in its most unbalanced position: one pan on the ground, full of weight, the counterweight to the left, the beam raised. All the weight is on the side of the owner, and on the other side, the side of the workers, even the tray is missing. Which goes to show that justice is a scale, which is to say, a beam used as a scourge. To transport: a wheeled cart for the horse shown in full face, a cask on a sliding strut at the bottom right, and boats, one of which, shown in profile, is being rowed by a group of young men. To lift: derricks, archaic jib cranes, and, once again, pulleys, slings, winches, levers, ropes, and weights. An exhaustive collection of instruments for lifting, packing, and transporting, equipped with their transmission mechanisms, and of sources of force.

It is a matter of a tableau, in the sense of "tabulation." Stating the set of tools and omitting nothing, tabulating all the products of mechanics—static and dynamic: from the framework to the cargo booms, from the wheel to the sail. All this makes a world. A drawn world. A drawable world. In which the chains draw motion, like the ropes and hawsers, and in which the beams and masts draw rest, like the truss and the axles. Lines, points, circles. Geometry. The cask is a volume, as with Sarrus; the trunk is a parallelepiped; the load of Oriental fabrics is unpacked, assessed, unfolded. Geometry, a diagram of mechanical forms, the applied geometry of our relation to the world, the geometry of work. The tools are dominated by form, produced by it. Hence drawn outline dominates the paint, which is tawny, golden, soft, inward, and somber, and in which only a scarlet waistcoat sings out at the left: the owner's waistcoat. The drawing is a graph of the tools and the people who use them. Drawn outline and geometry dominate the paint, the matter. Garrard says something important here: he says, in and by means of drawing, exactly what Lagrange says by expressly denying himself any possible drawing. *Analytical Mechanics* appeared in 1788, contemporary with Garrard's painting. It gives a statics, the theory of rest, and a dynamics, the theory of motion. And its introduction, by means of pulleys and tackle, tells the tableau of the painter. This introduction *recapitulates,* through its story and in its system, a perfect world that would soon disappear, totally overthrown when fire and its power supplant wind and water, horses, and men, as source and origin of force. What Lagrange says is that he must adopt, at the outset, the same set of objects as the set seen by Garrard at Samuel Whitbread's warehouse: levers, scales, winches, hoisting derricks, pulleys, ropes, weights, tackle. He says that in light of this world geometry alone holds sway. Thus what the painter draws Lagrange abstractly deduces from a single principle, that of virtual velocities, but it is the same world. It is the same objective world and the same apprehension of it by means of geometric diagrams. There are no horses, no men, no water, and no wind for the geometer, but rather some unspecified powers. These powers, however, still refer, in fact, to wind, water, men, and horses. Ropes, weights, pulleys; monomials and equations, but this discourse, in fact, designates the networks, whether simple or complex, drawn by machines. Garrard shows what Lagrange deduces. The same thing, and at the same moment.

That is to say, at the end. One always recapitulates when a certain history is coming to a close. Perfect and in its death throes. This history is so old, so old that Jupiter (the church steeple) and Mars (Nelson's Column?) still tower over the warehouse of Quirinus. In front, in the foreground, the watchdog. But the forest of masts in the distance, more numerous than these two spires, is also going to be felled. What is the Industrial Revolution? A revolution operating on *matter*. It takes place at the very sources of dynamics. At the origins of force. One takes force as it is, or one produces it. Descartes and Newton, crowned by Lagrange, belong to the first case: force is there, given by the biotope, the wind, the sea, and gravity. With this force, which only depends on us insofar as men and horses depend on us, but doesn't depend on us when it is a question of heavy bodies, air, and water, one produces motion, work, by the mediation of tools— those mentioned above. This mediation is inscribed in their form: their drawn outline, their geometry. Garrard's form, Lagrange's formal demonstrations. The paths of work, whether practical or virtual. A thunderbolt on the primary elements: fire replaces air and water in order to transform the earth. Fire, which will incinerate *Analytical Mechanics* and Samuel Whitbread's warehouse. It will burn down the wooden building, the wooden ships. The fire that finishes off the horses, strikes them down. The source, the origin of force, is in this lightning bolt, this ignition. Its energy exceeds form; it transforms. Geometry disintegrates, drawn outlines are erased;

matter, ablaze, explodes; the old paint—soft, tawny, golden—is now strewn with bright flashes. The horses, now dead, pass over the ship's bridge in a cloud of horsepower steam. The brig-schooner is in wet dock, disarmed: the new ship, which wins the big prize, is called the *Durande*.[2] Here comes Turner.

From Garrard to Turner, the path is very simple. It is the same path that runs from Lagrange to Carnot, from simple machines to steam engines, from mechanics to thermodynamics—by way of the Industrial Revolution. Wind and water were tamed in diagrams. It sufficed to draw or to know geometry. Matter was dominated by form. With fire, everything changes, even water and wind. Look at Joseph Wright's *An Iron Forge* (1772). It is still the water, the waterwheel, and the hammer, the weight—all of them strictly and geometrically drawn—that triumph over the ingot in fusion. Now comes the time when victory changes camps. Turner is no longer in spectacle mode; *he enters into Wright's ingot;* he enters into the boiler, the furnace, the firebox. He sees matter transform by fire. The new matter of the world at work, where geometry comes up short. Everything is overturned; matter and paint triumph over outline, geometry, and form. No, Turner is not a Pre-Impressionist. He is a realist, literally a materialist. He makes one see the matter of 1844, the way Garrard made one see the forms and forces of 1784. And he is the first to see it, the very first. No one had really perceived it before, neither scientist nor philosopher, and Carnot had not yet been read. Who understood it? Those who worked with fire and Turner. Turner or the introduction of fiery matter into culture. The first true genius in thermodynamics.

Wooden ships are dead and over. *The Fighting Temeraire* is being towed to her last berth to be broken up.[3] Contrary to what the history of glorious events recounts, the true battle did not take place at Trafalgar. The old ship of the line did not die from its victory. It was murdered by its tugboat. Look at the prow, the beam, the sheer—the framework and the geometry; look at the masts and the superstructures of this gray phantom: it is Samuel Whitbread's warehouse, it is Lagrange's primary collection of objects—the forms, lines, points, straight lines, angles, circles, networks, the actualized mechanics of wind, men, and water. The victor towing it to its torture, sitting low in the water, is deprived of this lofty form. The tugboat, red and black, spits fire. Behind it, the white and cold sails of the funeral procession are shrouds. The sun is setting on the black moorings of the final rest. The new fire is master of the sea and of the wind; it defies the sun. And here is the true Trafalgar, the true battle, the true confrontation: the immense division of the heavens and the sea into two zones. One is red, yellow, and orangish, where the hot colors shout, ignited, burning; the other is violet, blue, green, and sea-green, where the cold and icy hues freeze. Within its own matter, the entire world becomes a fire-powered engine between two sources, as defined by Carnot: the cold source and the hot source. Seawater in the tank. Yes, Turner entered *into* the boiler. The 1838 painting is *inside* the tugboat.

Hugo called it the *Durande*—hardly a proper noun, this heavy, clumsy galliot with its long black smokestack that traverses Turner's waters. Here, it is not named. The geometrically drawn ship with timber and sail has a name, a proper noun. The dirty, ill-defined, servile steamer only has a common noun. It is a sign, a signal. A legend. By which one recognizes what must be read, seen, and understood. It carries inside itself a conflagration, and masters and envelops it, from which it draws its force. It carries inside itself fire, air, and water. It is the material microcosm, the model of the world. Look at Turner's *The Burning of the Houses of Parliament* of 1835. At the bottom right, the *Durande* tows a barge almost in place of the signature. And once again, the world is its image, its reproduction, strictly speaking. Turner sees the world in terms of water and fire, as Garrard saw it in terms of figures and motion. Believe me, a ship is always a perfect summary of space as it is and time as it goes—of space, of time, of work, as they are in their day. Of history. Thus London and the Thames are like the steam-powered boat. The conflagration divides the cold canvas in two, with half in the atmosphere and half reflected in the water. An axis of roaring fire on a green volume. On the balance sheet: furnace, water, hot and cold, matter in fusion, drawn line abandoned in favor of random matter, a matter without definition and statistically grouped in packets—in the clouds of ice, on the one hand, and in the clouds of incandescence on the other. Carnot, almost Maxwell, *almost Boltzmann*. Turner understood and revealed the new world, the new matter. *The perception of the stochastic replaces the drawing of form.*

Matter is no longer left in the prisons of diagram. Fire dissolves it, makes it vibrate, tremble, oscillate, makes it explode into *clouds*. From Garrard to Turner, or from the fiber network to the chance-filled cloud. No one can draw the edge of a cloud, the limit site of the aleatory. Where particles waver and melt, at least to our eyes. Where a new time is being cooked. On these totally new edges, which geometry and drawing abandon, a new world will soon discover dissolution, atomic and molecular dissemination. The boiler's fire atomizes matter and gives it over to chance, which has always been its master. Boltzmann will soon understand it, but Turner, in his own domain, understood it before him. Turner entered whole-bodied into the swarming cage of Maxwell's demons. Garrard remained in Poinsot's motion; Turner gives himself over to Brownian motion. He passes from the rationalized real, from the abstract or polytechnical real, to the teeming real that radiates from the furnace. Where edges collapse. And, again, paint-matter triumphs over drawing with geometric edges. There is another *Durande* in *Staffa, Fingal's Cave (1832)*, another reproduction, an enlarged model of its fire-powered engine. How would you explain, supposing I were wrong, the double source of light, so paradoxical at first sight, which divides the cloudy masses in two, with the steam galliot resting between the two? Are there two suns in the Hebrides? Ossian or Mendelssohn would have noticed them. No, it is Carnot who speaks; the Scottish *Durande* says it: its smoke moves from the hot sun to the cold cavern, from one cloudy packet to another. And how would you explain the microscopic red spot on the quarter of the black ship? The microcosm *Durande* wears a sun; at twilight, the entire world functions on two sources. The cosmos is a steam engine, and inversely. There is an analogous division of the sky—a snowstorm in the sunlight, the sun a high, yellow note towering above some foul murder—during the crossing of the Alps by Hannibal's army. The same division of the scene occurs when the keelmen heave in coals by moonlight. The blaze reddens, flames, and roars among the topsails, the rigging, and the spars, in the corner that is the site of a greenish-yellow mass.[4] Wooden ships are truly dead. They are burning. Strictly speaking, they are only wrecks. There are two canvases, here at least, where wrecks float in a raging sea.[5] A monster. Read Lucretius and see how shipwrecks, aplustria scattered in the surf, and decomposed waves are the obsessive metaphors of dissolution, mingling, and exhaustion, for a poet who himself had also entered whole-bodied into teeming matter. The image, perhaps, of the second law of thermodynamics. Its archaic, dreamy, intuited form. Motion on the sea is not perpetual; it dissipates, and the sea absorbs its disintegrated details. Yes, one can die from the sea and from the wind; one can die also from the ice floes where the brig is trapped. Two methods exist for freeing oneself: by hauling oneself out using a fixed point, with boat hooks, grappling hooks, and heaving at the capstan. The static technique has clearly failed. What is left is fire, burning whale blubber. The fire that rescues from the ice. A new fire-powered engine: it triumphs here over rest, over forced immobility. The whole painting is again divided into two cloudy masses: red incandescence and blue-green cold. The ice field is not white; the sun is almost erased. The world disappears; it is man's work that requires the two sources, red fire and green cold. Hope and death.

Fire, the new history, is passing like thunder over the green water where a boat rocks.[6] *The Human Beast* and *The Steam House* were depicted in 1844, well before Jules Verne and Zola.[7] Here, however, there is no relation to humankind, whether it be one of death or one of optimistic confidence. The fusion of work in the real world. Always the object, always matter. A red, rectilinear axis slants off toward the right and pierces a cold gray, bluish, sometimes yellowish mass. The material cloud with its aleatory edges becomes a squall, and the water in the tank, driving rain. For a moment, the engine dissolves into the world that resembles it; it passes like a scourge of time. Man has constructed a thing-nature. The painter lets one see the entrails of this thing: stochastic packets, dualism of sources, flickering fires, its material entrails, which are the very womb of the world—sun, rain, ice, clouds, and showers. The sky, sea, earth, and thunder are the interior of a boiler, and this latter cooks the material of the world. At random.

Turner changed ships. Whalers themselves light fires among the flaw ice (praise be to Melville). Look how he changes studios. In 1797 (the date is important), he painted in watercolor no longer a warehouse in the style of Garrard, and no longer a forge in the style of Wright, but a foundry.[8] Slowly climbing back up the chain of material transformations: wood, iron, hammering, fusion. Heading toward the liquid ingot, heading toward the furnace. Before the geometrized solid, before cold form, was liquid; before liquid was gas, cloud. Hotter and hotter, less and less confined by a boundary. Transition: in 1774, Wright executed in gouache an infernally red *Eruption of Mount Vesuvius* that Turner would soon copy. Volcano, the forges of Vulcan, the foundry of the world (praise be to Verne). From human work to cosmic forces, the sequence is correct. With Fourier, it will be evident that a storm functions like an engine and, with others, that sun and ice are the two sources of the natural motor. That said, let's return to wood and shipbuilders. In Samuel Whitbread's warehouse, the truss is flawless, drawn to perfection; geometry has passed through there, as has the smooth statics of the division of forces. Calm, serene, secure shelter. Yes, a haven. Wright's framework, already, the one that covers the forge, has gaps, reinforcement rings (iron aids wood, which weakens from contact with fire); the ax has passed through there; the rafters are not in finished form. There is an enormous tie beam, twisted braces, and a king post that does not appear to be square. Statics by approximation. A tree more than a beam. As though the blacksmith, arms crossed, with his biceps of steel, were scorning the carpenter of yesteryear, ready to replace him. He knows full well that he will make hulls, masts, ropes, and trusses. Hence the rickety roof at Turner's foundry. Everything about the roof is badly squared, the height of disorder. The cut of the tie beams is never uniform; the vertical line has been lost, as though the plumb line had melted in front of the furnace. The truss is askew; the jumble of the rafters couldn't care less about equilibrium. The wooden framework is dead. Statics is dead. Mechanics, geometry, and drawn outline vanish before the fire. Three states of the roof mark the Industrial Revolution, mark the former and the new attitude toward old wood, our old pro-tector. Under it, in it, the new matter is born. The almond kills the shell.

Wright: there was no furnace in the inferno of his forge. Turner: here is the furnace, the new model of the world. The ingot is right there in the center, handled by three men, luminous as a hole in the middle of a gray-brown-black ensemble, flaming by a white stroke of gouache. There are, however, two centers: the opening of the furnace, to the right, gleams softly, dark radiance, a new sun. One forgets the third, the window in the background. Hence everything you would want: the red and the black, the two sources, the wavering of the cloudy silhouettes, disorder everywhere, and especially in the back of the shop, where other trails of white gouache accentuate the jumble. Theorem: beneath the forms of matter, in the back shop of bodies, stochastic disorder reigns as master. To smelt is to rejoin this major randomness. A furnace is a machine for going back toward chaos. A foundry is where creation starts over at zero. History is recast beginning with primitive matter. But watch out! Remember how, with Garrard, society had its strict order—in front, the watchdog, and behind, the two church steeples of Jupiter and the martial column. Horses, sailors, and men were forbidden to leave the picture. At the bottom left of Turner's watercolor, a new monster, a new watchdog, is crouched: an enormous piece of artillery, black and terrible. It is a product, the product of the furnace, the cold product of fusion. This is not a new history that starts over from zero; it is the same one. Maw of the dog, maw of the furnace, maw of the cannon—the latter ready to rake the foundry and block the exit of the workshops. The men are forbidden to leave the picture. The new society resumes a strict order. They believed they were recreating the world; death, once again, recaptured it. Not death hanging from the masts and gallows of Lagrange, but a lightning death from cannon fire. The science Carnot is the son of the war Carnot.[9]

Garrard paints an exposition, a tabulation. Everywhere dense. Plane by plane, from the foreground to the background. Wright sets out an exposition as well. The forge is still a theater, and the painting could have served as an advertising sign. A work scene, the workers seen from behind—this is no accident; a family scene, where all are seen full face, except the wife—no, this is no accident. The muscular master is glorified; the watchdog is always there. There is no longer any representation in Turner's foundry. The painting is a furnace, the furnace itself. A disordered dark mass with the fiery hearths as centers. From geometry to matter, or from representation to work. From the theater to the furnace. By climbing back up to the sources of matter, the painter has broken the shackles of the fine arts copying each other. No more discourses, no more scenes, no more sculptures with clean, cold edges: the object directly. Without theoretical detours. Yes, we enter into incandescence. At random.

The balance sheet is easy to draw up. Tools: the locomotive, the steamships, the furnace, the foundry. Fire: the blaze, the sun, the trapped ship where whale blubber burns. Ice: Chamonix, the glacier, the whaler, prisoner of the ice field (of icebergs and flaw ice). The two sources: the major division of the spectrum into two zones, one with red dominating, the other with blue; the hot source, the cold source. Falling, the model of energy for Carnot: *The Great Falls of the Reichenbach* (1804), for example. Matter: it is in motion and agitation; it forms into aleatory clouds, the stochastic is essential, the border disappears, opening up a new time. The instant is not statically frozen, planted like a mast; it is an unforeseen state, full of chance, suspended, drowned, melted in duration, dissolved. It will never return—unlike the Indian mail boat at the edge of the Thames—it is irreversible. This balance sheet of the science of fire, of the practical applications of fire, of the world of fire, of matter on fire is almost as exhaustive as the balance sheet of the world of figures and motion, at Samuel Whitbread's warehouse of mechanics.

Within a half century, England knew two worlds. And its painters said it better than anyone else. On the continent, the Academy persisted—history and mythology—bloody and cold, foreign to work and to science. It is true that our neighbors also had the Pre-Raphaelite Boy Scouts.

Fire. The other, the same. Turner never painted anything but cosmic copulations, so obvious that no one saw them. The lovemaking of fire and water, physically *drawn* with precision. Turner—or the old-style riddles: *cherchez la femme*. When the sun rises, who does not like to sail between two promontories?

Part IV

The Land

10

Roumain and Faulkner Translate Scripture

At an appreciable distance from aseptic *toubabs*, sophisticated WASPs, neurotic managers, and theoreticians with their conceptual autopsy, there exists a literature. In which words name the things: hunger, drought, the village divided by hatred, water, the oppressive sun, love. The tall, beautiful woman announced on the road, like a miracle; the naked death that was the high price for a moment of happiness and wasn't too high a price for the future of the land. The low complaint of the peasants.

I have always imagined that the city had invented separation. From which it results that those from the burgs, the bourgeois, travel. To get a change of place or scenery, as they say. Displaced from the start, an admission of their state. From which it results that they learn languages. No one has ever learned anything except in the hollow of a lack. He is never really in foreign lands, the peasant.[1] He doesn't feel the need to travel all over the land, since he inhabits it. A homebody of the universal, speaking his land-based patois. Whether Serbian, Chinese, Greek, Haitian, Turkish, from Carolina or Ukraine, the land, low by the height of a body, demands a relation and gestures that are everywhere the same. An unspoken international class of farmers, the lowly class, the humans of the humus. Soon murdered, without hope, there is no global crisis more serious than that of agriculture. On the Malian banks of the Niger, men and women fish, water tomatoes, and talk endlessly; these are the banks of Garonne. Bambara, I thought you were my brother; you are my father. My bargeman father on our pirogue-gabarre, my father who broke his back sowing corn or millet. Black is not a color, it's a name; the name of the last farmers; the true proper name of my father, and mine, by heredity. Africa, the land, my land, my mother finally found.

For people of cultivation and agriculture, history moves as much and as little as a tree. The genealogical tree. One of the possible meanings of certain miraculous Italian landscapes has lain buried in Columella and Varro for thousands of years. This meaning really only changed in the middle of this century. Due to bulldozers, hillside impoundments, dams. In Tuscany, too, eternity has changed. It has resisted better in Africa. And yet, they don't economize on engineers, geographers, and ethnologists there; they—meaning the city, urban civilization. The land carries the inertias and invariances of time. The land also fairly laughs at history, out of that gentle irony practiced by those who truly speak the patois with regard to the others who have learned it so as to defend it. The land remains curled up, round, like a sleeping dog, inside the aleatory and standardized cyclic returns of the female lunar months, the major sunlight, and the announced water. What endures in the land is the world; what changes is the city.

I have always imagined that the city had invented politics. To my knowledge, this is not imagination; it's the most obvious reading. A reading that also says that it may have invented history. Where is information amassed? Everything happens as though the world rolled along at least two times. The time of accelerations, of dynamic events, which is put, here and there, in a space having inert time. Megalopolis, which is invading the land, uproots the land of its eternity, of its astronomical stabilities. The end of cultures is on the horizon of the end of agriculture. The land had, from time immemorial, invented religion. All religions are agrarian; they constitute the set of peasant knowledge and range of feelings. There has been no new religion for several centuries, not, as Nietzsche seems to say, out of imaginary decadence, but because nothing has fundamentally changed in our relationship to the land since the most recent religion. Should this relationship truly change, as in our times, you will see a new religion blossom. Or not, if industry changes the relation. This is because the Industrial Revolution, by nature, is antireligious: it erases necessity. The massively atheistic humanity dates from then, and with no return. Agriculture is a religious practice; religion is the elective way of talking about peasant practices. Industry is an atheistic rationalist practice; atheistic rationalism is the adequate way of talking about industrial practices. Every crisis in religion is a crisis in agriculture; every religious residue is a way of resisting both the metastases of the city and those of industry: all this is true, all the way up to the converse.

The bourgeois or burghers, then, are those who inhabit the city. There is only one city left, the immense Megalopolis, which covers over the major part of the northern hemisphere with its network. Included on its roads and within its walls is a global class, that of the bourgeois. But Megalopolis is at the end of its history, that adventure begun in the Neolithic. It unconsciously notes the failure of its developmental, economic, cultural, ethical, and ideological models. It lives this failure. It doesn't realize it because it mistakes the speed of its inert momentum for acceleration. It repeats. But repetition is death. Nothing is appearing today—and hasn't for a good century—that can take over the reins to get ahead of this inert momentum and break the spell of these repetitions. The future is in the South.

The danger for the South, the danger for all humanity, would be to imitate Megalopolis's models. The models of a global class that has had its time in history, its time of reason, work, blood, and violence. The new proletarians, the other global class, are the class of farmers from the southern hemisphere. They can, perhaps, use a few means stemming from Megalopolis, which has nothing but means, and which only knows how to repeat them, but they mustn't borrow its models, which have all failed. It is to be hoped, for the sake of the future of the world, that the new Marx will be Black. That he will shift geography and history onto new paths that would be unimaginable anywhere else than in Africa or South America. The third world is the world to come; it is the history to be written; it is the new start of time. The new, new world. May the old one exhaust itself killing.

*

A few means, not the models. In this hope, we read the literature of the so-called third world. Afraid that it will repeat our schemas and try to import them. Hoping that it will banish them and discover something new. Manuel, the hero of *Masters of the Dew*, demonstrates a vital equilibrium, a strength, and a wisdom that promise this new thing. Alas, he is a bearer of the word, three times over. But how does he carry this word?

There is a major equilibrium between what is said, in express words, like a rational theory, an imperative action, and what is recounted about life as it goes, the story. This equilibrium scorns and laughs, with tears in its eyes, at the manifest contradiction between the story and the theory. Manifest for whom? Me, Black, vanquished by the beating of the drum in the most secret parts of the blood that thunders; I dance, dance, dance, and dance the whole night through; I dance my complete fill, and I give myself up, naked, to the mysteries. But when the day comes, I think, reason, debate, argue; I organize the revolt of the poor and the inhabitants' *coumbite*, in the name of a practice that's as reasonable as science.[2] It took hundreds and hundreds of years, and Nietzsche's books and everything that ensued, to again teach the West, which still refuses them and may die from always refusing them, these simple reconciliations lived every day, in the peace of the body, between the arms of the Niger or in the Gulf of Mexico. Reconciliations known to our mother Greece, the daughter, as well, of hunger, and to our peasant fathers below the curves of the Garonne. A wisdom that has no color, but which is given in its entirety by the needs of the earth. A wisdom that unites political reason and the buried tradition of religious emotion. Through the awaited, announced, consummated nuptials of the land and the tree, of the sun and the water. Of Annaise and Manuel.

Something that is written as a theory, something that is induced from the state of things and the relations of forces, as a law, something that is indicated as a rule and announced as a hope. Here is a man with a red scarf;[3] he arrives from Cuba during the burning hot hours of dryness, of hatred, of the separation that delays the rain. For years, he fought against capitalist exploitation. Against the pillaging of poor lands. Rage in the heart: every man loaded, like a gun, up to his eyebrows with his rage [147].⁴ Killing a Haitian, killing a dog. They call us barefoot Negroes, barefooted vagabonds, big-toed Negroes, us shoeless poor people: some day we will take our big flat feet out of the soil and plant them on their behinds, the bastards [141]. He arrives from Cuba, where he had to kill, one night, in order to survive, a man from the rural police. He has gained some distance, he has traveled, he has fought, he has learned, he knows. He knows that this single finger is small and weak, that this other one isn't any stronger, and this last one's standing all alone and on his own behalf: that a clenched fist, alone, is solid, firm, united. The NO uttered by a thousand voices [186]. He returns to his land, at his mother's house, in his hut, and amid his fields. He knows that the millet, bananas, potatoes, and corn will no longer come back to Fonds Rouge if the inhabitants don't, beyond genealogical hatreds, set up a *coumbite* of brothers. The old times had known them; murder has recently made them unravel. This reversal of history must be gotten beyond. A simple dialectic and transformation of the land, everything is in place, clearly: Fonds Rouge and red scarf; black is red.⁵ Law, rule, hope, and express theory.

And here is the problem; it is posed to Manuel. Are there inhabitants in Cuba—*inhabitants,* by this deep word I mean peasants? With a plot of land, poultry, and a few head of cattle? No. The land there belongs to Mr. Wilson, as well as the factory to process the sugar. Opposite him are workers, wage-earners, to cut the cane, while he busies himself with other *toubabs* knocking a white ball back and forth with a washerwoman's paddle [155-56]. Manuel reflects: adapt the rule, the theory, and the law to the traditional agricultural environment. That is the book's subject: how to transport revolutionary practice into narrow parcels on which little owners, exploited by creditors, are dying of hunger, Hilarion and his Florentine. And when the rain delays in coming. This is no small problem: doubtless one of the most vital in the world today. In which the farmers, en masse, are the main people exploited by industry, in which the land is divided up into Megalopolis and rural space, the true border, the abyss. I am not saying that Roumain resolves it; it is even likely that he doesn't resolve it, supposing it to be resolvable like that, on a white page, with words. Roumain is not Renaud Jean⁶ or Mao

Zedong. But if he doesn't resolve it, he at least states its conditions and presuppositions. And the conditions are severe. Exacting.

These conditions touch on the facts of necessity. Industrial practice, as soon as it spreads and becomes the culture's main reference, sets that old agrarian notion into crisis and impedes it. As though there were two physics of the lived world below all active and experimenting physics: the physics of the Stoics, in which a given part of things doesn't depend on *us*, the one that endures, by Descartes, across the foundations of experimental knowledge, and the physics that affirms that *humanity* never poses itself any problems but those it can resolve. The latter physics is industrial; the other one is rural. The latter physics is true from one end to the other and without any other residues than virtual ones in the space of cities, factories, dominated work, and laboratories; it is true by reference to the newly formed systems of efficient reason, of reason as a well-founded superstructure. This physics nevertheless leaves a gap, due to the displacement of the infrastructure, a visible gap in space and agricultural systems. It is possible that this displacement is, for time and the direction of history, quite regressive, oriented toward archaism; the fact remains that, for global space, this displacement is even imposed on three-quarters of humanity. Here, questions arise, often the most worrying ones, primary questions, open and without answer at the scale of the social group, as it is, in its ecological space. Every peasant knew before, from Laplace to Brillouin, reason demonstrated it, every peasant knew, in his hands and by his hunger, that local weather is stochastic within a global system of regularities. There is law, and I can command by obeying it; there is gambling, chance, and randomness, and this is the real, and there is nothing we can do about it. A yawning gap due to the facts of necessity; when I say necessity, I am talking about the needy, about those who are hungry and thirsty, and about the rain that doesn't come, and about the arid soil with its flying dust. A gap in the real that is so yawning it precipitates industrial speech toward a collectivist idealism: as though the world, by the practice of industry, had become the outcome, the result, the resolved thing of the problematic enterprises of the collective in general. When problems have no other residues than their exhaustive solutions, they are, literally, representation. In fact, when the technological environment is complete, continuous, compact, cohesive, without rending like a well-joined roof, it doesn't say anything other than a demonstrable, factual, reliable version of the old saying of the idealist dream: the world is nothing other than representation; a version that makes the site of the subject slip from the individual to his collectivity. The world, this well-formed world, without any fissures, is our representation. Industry, at its birth, required philosophies of transformation. Its triumph having come and its system formed, nobody transforms anything anymore but the already worked on, the semitheoretical. There is no longer any raw material, and there is less and less of it. There are no longer any problems in the things themselves without the paths, drawn in the things, of their solutions. The victorious theoretical traverses the industrially constituted world from one end to the other. Without any gaps, without any defeat except for temporary ones at the level of objects. Hence this universe that is the outcome, the result, the thing virtually without shadow of our representations, of our problems resolved without residue. The victorious West in its realized theoretical sardine tin. This is, indeed, the site of the most classic idealism, which nobody today is able to stand firm against. A ruse is enough to cause one to succumb to it: by defining idealism differently, for example, as the naive belief in another world, defining it by its opposite, the realism of idealities. Thanks to which we install ourselves in the oldest idealism the West has dreamed up, with conveniences like hot water over the kitchen sink, the car, and pharmacy: the world around us is nothing other than us. And this is true, at least here: now there is no longer any problem but the mastery of our mastery, the mastery of the collective. There is no exclusive politope but in the sites of a compact technology.

This is true, here, but not quite elsewhere, where this gap in the real still yawns open. Where matter and material are not at all veiled by the protective roof of reasons that have become real.

An analysis of content is always extremely easy to handle. It is enough to exhaustively inventory the various codings. A teachable and distinct technique, without any obscurity. It is true that the example selected is easy. But why not begin with the simple? Jacques Roumain expressed a global political theory clearly, stemming from Marxism. A theory without refinement or scholasticism, and therefore well adapted. What should we do? What should we be on guard against? Hence a series of solutions, as well as a series of critiques; a reasoned, social, and directly agronomic practice, the elimination of ideologies that obstruct work and the tribal group. Manuel says the theories, he practices them, he has learned them, he applies them. That said, and done, he finds himself in difficulty. It is not quite possible to immediately transport these theories and practices into an agrarian environment, in which determining conditions hold sway: family tradition, which has very rigid superstructures founded on an archaic infrastructure. The transport of the schema reveals, almost the way developing film does, the power of ideologies, and Manuel is going to die as a result of this—Manuel who, nonetheless, achieved a supreme equilibrium between wakeful consciousness or active reason, and the old familial love toward the entire cultural Afro-Haitian bloc; Manuel who knew how to work without dreaming and to voodoo dance until the break of day. The entire story then changes color, like toner does in the development of film: it recounts the passion of a man born a native of the land and come from overseas to redeem his brothers. The religious bloc closes in: the old traditional Christianity of the Antilles reappears. And it reappears, no doubt, because the transfer of the schema has been accomplished without any precautions. It had to do with the sun and the water, and the class struggle lacked an opponent: Hilarion is indeed there to represent the city, the bourgeois, and their police, but he is not very effective. He plays, he cheats, he wins, but he is not really the direct opponent. The facing player, subtle, cruel, doesn't cheat: it's the soil. And here, devoid of strategy, the author and the hero, together, repeat the ancestral gesture of the agrarian relations with the sun and the water. The sociopolitical content of practice and science changes into the content of religious ideologies around this third element, which is the basic narrative, the cosmic lovemakings of the sun and the water, whose product is the fruits of the land. The productions of the social group at work, yes, once it has settled its internal disagreements—but also—and above all—the productions derived from natural conditions.

In the industrial chain, production is controlled, from the initial conditions to the final product, link by link and actively at each stage: without the intervention of work, the hand, humans, or a program, the sequence is broken. For the products of the soil, a finite group of initial conditions can be mastered, and the active interventions are discrete along a continuous process. Regarding this process, no one, to my knowledge, since the Neolithic, has ever been able to do anything. It happens of itself. It is produced without us. You have to wait. The set of discrete interventions can be endlessly multiplied, but the continuous thread of growth nevertheless remains autonomous. One doesn't shake up this residual time without risking killing its product. Hence that unspoken respect the city is ignorant of. In the final accounting and at the end of practices, you have to wait. The sun, the rain, the spring, the wasted fecundation, the ripe grains. Roumain wasn't able to know about the great enclosing of fauna and flora that, nowadays, is bringing the Neolithic to a close, in which the process is optimally controlled. The new history or the time of greenhouses. In which man will be alone among the plant prisons and the animal jails. The generalized subjecting of the biosphere to the disciplinarity of schools. You can't stop progress: it always goes from outside to inside. So yes, we shall no longer talk about anything but politics. Everyone will be in the city. Shut away in his laboratory. But again, greenhouses or not, you have to wait. Even if phytotrons accelerate the thread. Waiting. When reason settles down and the body stops, dreams grab them. Every religion, as well as a few other areas of culture, was born from this, from this waiting. Our good professors must truly have been born from technology, the city, and industry to naively believe that only the dominant classes in the past had the spare time to invent science and everything that ensues from it. They must have been thinking about vacations, about leisure, about those others unceasingly chained to work. They must have been thinking of this new homogeneous time as a human fate. There is no spare time in industrial time, but this appropriation, this theft, is entirely new. Spare time, rustic time, occupies three-quarters of the farmer's time. This is the time of speech. This is how speech was born. It died from the murder of time. And cultures with it. Délivrance awaits the return of her son, and speaks, her mouth full of dust. The whole village waits for the rain and speaks about old times. Annaise waits for her child, and says, "No, Manuel isn't dead." He said, "I will hope for you, Anna." Fonds Rouge waits for the rain, like the Savior. The Savior of yesteryear put in prison and dead. And Roumain, who knows all that, and has for at least thousands of years, thousands and thousands of years of waiting and culture, Roumain the speaker, a master in the art of speaking, a master of human memory, a griot, a sack of words, a scholar in speech, naming, and genealogy, makes him arrive, makes him come back, along the circle of time, the circle of waiting, the circle of the sun. The recommencement.

He doesn't arrive, he comes back. He doesn't die, he stays and rises from the dead. He comes back; here he is, at the elbow of the road, with his red scarf, the dawn. In the deadly dust of desolation. Of insolation and solitude. Délira waited for him, as did Bienaimé, Fonds Rouge, and Annaise. If you have ever waited, truly waited for the dew, you know what the sun is. The sun clock that marks the waiting. The sun furnace that decomposes everything down to ashes. The major sun that censors time, that is time melted into the spectrum of identity. Honor and respect, master sun, rising sun. The Black men salute you. When the sun is absent, foundering behind the woods, darkness drowns these men delivered up to hardship, and then the dawn breaks, the day anew, similar to the other one and without any hope. Old sun, the same one, blind to hope; new sun, the stranger of the returned morning. The dreadful master and the devastator. The mountain is bare, ravaged; the sun has given it a lick with a tongue of fire. It scratched its scorched back with its shining fingernails [162]. It keeps close watch on it with its red and vigilant eye. It hurls sulfur darts into the bleeding sunset [177]. It punishes with its arm, with its gaze, with its mouth, and with its claws. It weighs on the shoulders like a burden [146], the weight of the blinding light [175]: Manuel was walking; his back was bent, as though he were carrying a load [166].

A bad god, a vengeful father, present like a remorse, destroyer of the land. Harsh. *No, the other fire:* he opened his arms; his face was full of sunlight [208]. The ripe oranges are like little suns hanging up in the leaves [257]. The true dawn has returned. Identical and new.

Water is no longer in the sky, where the male is all alone. It is in the secret of the land. In the uterus of the land. The spot, long abandoned, was full of weeds and prickles [203]. It's dark! How dark it is! Vines, the suffocation of plants that must be hacked with a machete. You wouldn't think there was a great sun outside. Here it filters down drop by drop [205]. Digging through. A narrow gully encumbered by creeping vines which fell weeping from the trees. The giant fig tree proudly lifted its powerful trunk: the tree's roots are in the water, an authoritative hand over the ownership and secret of this corner of the earth; its crown is in full sun, its branches in the silvery moss. Water is there, the gentle, the good, the flowing, the singing, the fresh, the benediction, life. He laughs [199]. They laugh.

The sun Manuel makes love to the water Annaise; they have the tree in common. Yes, the oranges swollen with water and honey will be called little suns.

Once upon a time, there were a few aseptic and reasoning toubabs: they invented, without understanding, this imbecilic word: *animism.*

Between the legs of the mountain, that spring flows. A cool ravine because of the branches of the mombin trees that shade it. Ferns are everywhere in its oozing humidity; a mat of watercress and mint wades in its slowed current. The sun delights in playing on the pebbles where the water babbles. The Mistress of the Water is a mulatto woman; she combs her long hair at midnight, a music sweeter than violins. She waits for the one who hears her; she waits, she too, at the edge of the spring, sings, smiles at him, and beckons for him to follow her into the bottomless water from whence he will never return. Annaise, at the spring, is mistress of the water; she looked like a queen of Guinea with her curved hips, her naked breasts, hard and pointed, her skin so black and smooth. She swoons, feels a weakness, at the edge of the water, as she had done last night when he kissed her, when she had felt herself drifting in a burning current whose every wave was a thrill to her body, when her blood gushed from the depths of her flesh. Roselia, with her sharp tongue, is old, her bosom dry and flabby. She looked enviously at Annaise's well-filled breasts, with nipples mauve as grapes. The secret: there'll be reeds by our canal [225-26].

Woman water, woman spring, spring woman, current, wave, blood, grape wine, canal, ravine, humidity. Buried under the foliage. A fountain outlined like the mons Venus, femininity engendered from the waves. Master of the dew, despite appearances, is a feminine name: mistress of the water, divinity. Here, the formation of the myth is caught in its nascent state, at body level, at word level. But the religious word definitely gets the last word: Manuel will never return from the depths of the well. His machete has ruptured the foliage; he has unveiled the secret of the buried dew; the mulatto woman is his mistress: he dies—or dies from it. This is the vengeance of the Mistress of the Water: that's what's dangerous, *oui*, sister, the spirit of the spring [237].

The political theory, express and clear like science, dictates, with a single gesture, a wise practice of agricultural work and an incisive, sound, and permanent critique of ideologies and illusions, religious ones in particular. Manuel never stops driving this home, in front of his mother and his fiancée, and in front of his comrades, who are immersed in a syncretic tradition in which the contributions of Christianity and those of Afro-Haitian cults are mixed together. There's heavenly business and there's earthly business. They're two different things. The sky's the pastureland of the blissful angels, where the banquet continues as long as you like: the white angels just sing like nightingales all day long or blow on trumpets; the black angels do the washing. The earth is a battle day by day; the Lord hasn't got a thing to do with it. No, it's not God who abandons the Black man; it's the Black man who abandons the earth [152].[7] "By the grace of God": a hypocritical resignation that dispenses with work. It is only discouragement: you keep on waiting for Providence and Its miracles, rosary in hand, without doing a thing. Prayers won't make it come. Providence is a Black man's determination not to accept misfortune; it is his determination to tame the earth and the whims of the waters; it is his prudent work as a serious peasant. The miracle is the fruit of his hands [159]. God is here; he is the *coumbite* together. What you said, answers the mother Délira, sounds like the truth, but the truth's probably a sin [152]. However, an entire chapter takes pleasure in exploring voodoo at length. The inhabitants forget hunger and troubles through its rituals. Dancing and drinking anesthetize them—sweep away their shipwrecked consciousnesses to drown in those dubious regions of unreality where the fierce madness and irrationality of the African gods lie in wait [172]. Everything is in place, lucidly: the opium religion, the sinful truth. He is smart, that Aristomène, even when in a hurry, with all his Latin, the ignorant peasants said [248].

So you are going to die, Manuel announced, like straw in a furnace. What have you done? You have cleared the hills of trees and thereby set in motion an irreversible process [184]. You don't need to redress this sin; you need to remedy this error. Brothers have killed brothers. You don't need to absolve this sin, but to erase the account books. What are you doing today to prevent the consequences? One thing only: you sing. You cry about your misfortune to the *loas;* you offer ceremonies so that they'll make the rain fall. So much silly monkeyshines. You substitute an imaginary exchange of gifts for the principle of reason, which organizes praxis. The blood of a rooster or a young goat can't make the seasons change, or alter the course of the clouds and fill them with water like bladders [184]. That is an agrarian cult founded on the idea of a causality that radiates outward in a star shape, with only an oblique effectiveness and without end-to-end linkage. The couple reason–effect finds itself melted into a network of symbols, a collection of illusory personages who give each other presents. You dream of exchange and gifts; you forget the physical sequence of causes, which work links together to its profit. Water is not a grace; it is the fruit of a search, a study, and an excavation. A willed discovery.

A question for Manuel: true though it may be that the blood of a rooster won't precipitate vapor into dew, how, in truth, can we make it rain? In the case of the rooster, it is certain that a causal chain and the efficacy of reason in producing effects are lacking, as well as scientific understanding. But, for Manuel, where is the chain and its practical links? Whence the narrative's best lesson: there's God, he said, heavenly business, and there's also earthly work. They're two different things. The novel doubles the theory with a story, one in which there is heavenly water and there is earthly water. They're two different things: rain clouds and groundwater. Délira and her husband, along with Annaise and her family, wait for the heavens' dew; Manuel acts as a well-digger. The symbol is as clear as the theory is lucid: don't lift your head nor lose it in the clouds—that's where the *loas* and Providence wait for you, as well as the necessary cycles of the seasons, along with their unpredictable earliness and lateness ruining harvests and overwhelming the women. Rain being late is a matter of course. Annaise is expecting a baby. Bend your head, quite the opposite, and dig: the earth will give what the heavens refuse. You are, by work, masters of the earth; you are finally no longer mastered by the dew. And water comes from here below—tough luck for elsewhere. The symbol is clear, but only when there is groundwater. Hence my question: what are you going to do, in truth, when there isn't any?

The narrative's lesson is as deep as you like or can draw from, but it is not universal. The symbol is local, restricted, and temporary. From the story to its meaning, the inference is good. But not conversely, from the theory to the story. When there is no underground water in the surrounding sites, we are forced, again, to lift our heads toward the heavens, toward its norms that suffer from chance ruptures, in which dreams, illusions, African and Asian divinities dwell. Replacing a fantasy with cheating is never to your benefit. For there is cheating, strictly speaking: Roumain gives himself water a league away and six feet down. When it is there, already, the assembled *coumbite* poses itself problems it can resolve. Or rather, if it doesn't settle them, owing to the old politics, only a new politics can do so. From which it results that a change of politics merely allows problems that have already been resolved to be solved. Always beware, just as we beware of cholera, plague, and incurable diseases, of this discourse by politicians, which is as constant as history and as old as the world: if you put us in power, the world will change its course to your advantage. This, too, is a religious discourse. Political idealism, the widespread and false idea that every problem is political, comes from right here, from a confusion between necessity on the one hand and sufficiency on the other. Yes, one sociopolitical organization conceals solutions that some other unveils, after the revolution. But it unveils them when there are solutions. Like it or not, it is the material that commands: the best government in the world can give only what it has. Sometimes it doesn't harbor any water pockets. And the rainy season is late. Hence the title's cheating: masters [*gouverneurs*] of the groundwater, and not of the dew.

Hence the critique, in response, of the critiques of this idealism. This is a law that tolerates no exceptions and which is reciprocal: every idealism talks by means of everything and nothing. When everything is explained by one pole, any proposition stemming from elsewhere is false, absolutely. But there is never, anywhere, everything and nothing. Not even in mathematics. A thousand scientific practices are embryonated, here and there, in the vague, down to and including old wives' tales. It wasn't me who invented this: Leibniz said it a hundred times, and Homer a hundred thousand. And Mao Zedong. The farmers knew, before the experts and agronomists, before Columella and Varro, before Hesiod was born, that you don't clear trees from a hill with impunity. The peasants of the whole earth, black, yellow, brown, or white, have known this since the invention of agriculture. It is the city-dwellers who clear-cut—namely, the newcomers, not the inhabitants. The mistake of Fonds Rouge is improbable. That's not all: when Jean Dessens made it rain, almost twenty years ago, by means of rocks with silver iodide and powerful burners capable of gathering clouds, he was very surprised, when applying his technique in tropical or subequatorial regions, to discover that certain African witch doctors used practices similar to his own. Minus the iodide, of course. All this means that the critique of ideologies that delay science mustn't be carried out like an operation en bloc, but like an attentive and refined filtering. The critique is worth what the science behind it is worth. Either it is crude, unintelligent, and poorly refined, like a dualism in the Iranian mode, or it is pluralist, sharp, and vigilant, like the educated flexibilities of conjectures and rectifications. There is not, nor has there ever been, science on the one side and myths on the other. The share of pertinent knowledge in a given myth, an ancient tradition, or a savage thought is probably as large as the share of mythology a given science envelops within itself. We know something about this—we Westerners, saturated with science for centuries and encumbered everywhere by the farces and traps that have slipped under this term.

Reciprocally, the person who dictates by everything and nothing is invariably idealist. In his acts and by definition: he makes the gesture of division, that of the priests and rituals of all times; he separates the sacred from the profane, the wheat from the chaff, the good apples from the bad, the just from the unjust, the elected from the condemned; the real world is that of his practices, his decisions, and his representations; all the rest must be rejected. Lastly, he forms a second world, since he transports the filtering of the true to the court of the just; moving the practitioner or the scientist to the court is changing spaces as well as changing laws; it is translating accuracy [*justesse*] into justice [*justice*]. Therefore, he is an idealist, twice over de facto and twice over de jure. So the entire philosophy of the true, taking its values from the practices of the real, swings toward judicial authority, as the word *critique* indicates—that is, toward its foundation—power. How this can be avoided, I don't know, but I'm wary of birettas. Whatever their color may be.

He judges and says, "That is only an illusion." He becomes a mythologist. I nevertheless deeply fear that he will soon lapse into mythomania. Here is why. Skillfully cut off the fringe of irrationality attached to knowledge; make this fringe pass through acids, the fire of a blowtorch—subjecting it to every imaginable analysis, corrosive ones, solvent ones, ones that strip. Go behind, underneath, above, and in the holes; don't allow suspicion and doubt to slumber. Trim hard, and more rather than less; cut down to the flesh. You will get, after washing, a product that is pure, aseptic, trans-lucid, and as clean as a well-behaved virgin's room. This chemistry suddenly turns against itself: *this product, purified of all myth, becomes mythical through and through*. The old inhabitants have always known this: you don't clear trees from a hill with impunity. The mania for cleanliness, at the limits, is a suicidal impulse. Knowledge without illusion is an entirely pure illusion. In which everything is lost, including knowledge. This more or less amounts to a theorem: *there is no pure myth but knowledge that is pure of all myth.* I'm not aware of any others, so full are myths of knowledge, and knowledge full of dreams and illusions. What method, on the other hand, can be used to "purify" a myth? In other words, critique wouldn't rectify anything if the imagination (or something that can bear this bad name) hadn't played the first moves. If critique denounces this priority, or imagination itself in its functioning and rights, in its being, then it stops the very motor of knowledge, its acceleration, its force for bushing out, its essence as moving truth. Of knowledge, critique only leaves arrested images, old certitudes, ancient error, myth itself. The duty of critique, in science, comes second in relation to the right of dreaming. This duty is its dependent, its successor, its serving parish priest. An inventor, even a local one, is only an ironist in the shadow of a visionary: the refuter comes long after the maker of hypotheses. I'm talking about the individual, symbolically. There are fecund theories and clean expositions. But fecundity increases with manure, cleanliness with rhetoric. Inventing, teaching. Dreaming discovers, lucidity gives lessons. In the rostrum or the court. And what do they do, the judges?

From which it results that philosophy, reduced to methods or strategies of control, loses the living half of knowledge and becomes involuted into ancient dreams in which one no longer dreams. Critique and pasteurization. Ceaselessly turning around toward the rear to erase phantoms, it only finds pillars of salt before its gaze. The absolute limit to strategies of cleaning is the very function of producing, including errors. It's a monumental misinterpretation of science to believe it is entirely governed by rectification. It would be dead from this, the poor thing. On the contrary: dream boldly, something of it will always remain. What is science? A myth, yes, constantly renewed, which becomes master of itself through self-critique and self-regulation. But who would be master of what if no margin by which to dream existed? Science lives and propagates by this border of nonscience that fecundates and renews it, like trees by the bark. Do away with this margin, and it petrifies.

Thus all critique, exceeding its secondary role and secondary power, is an antiscientific enterprise. History has shown this a thousand times, long ago, recently, and tomorrow morning.

It is possible that you might not take my word for it. It is possible that someone might say that this is not always true. Then I would have to take up history again. And this would be interminable and boring from the repetition. Do you want me to prove it, here and now, regarding the current example? The thing is so clear that it brings about conviction. And so I shall begin again. Manuel divides space with his stick: on the one side, science, praxis, work, *coumbite,* and the earth; on the other, empty hopes, illusions, indolence, dream, and religion: heaven. Roumain holds the end of the stick and, holding the end of the pen, tells his story to show us his theory. But I said just now that, with this division by everything and nothing, one ran the danger of a complete reversal, the danger that the product obtained might become an out-and-out myth. That is indeed what happens: the story is not free; it is not even isomorphic to the theory; it is a religious dream, that very dream both the author and the hero were keen to send definitively packing. Even when read inattentively, the novel is a seamless reprise of the Testaments of the Christian tradition. A projection, a simplified outline of the Holy Scriptures. Let's prove this.

The mother's hand.[8] The beginning: *we're all going to die . . . She plunges her hand in the dust. Old Délira Délivrance plunges her hand in the dust.* The ending: *she took the old woman's hand and pressed it gently against her belly where the new life was stirring.* Death, rebirth of the land. Or of the waters. Death and dust. Dry. *The dust slipped through her fingers, the same dust that the dry wind scattered over the devastated field. The dust swirled up from the highway. On Délira Délivrance's head, a gray frizz sprinkled with dust.* In her hand, amid the sterile countryside, on her hair. *We're all going to die and God has abandoned us.* The dereliction of Fonds Rouge's gardeners is not that of Epicurus or Lucretius, all alone faced with the chaotic dust of the first atoms, while the gods, forgetful, get drunk at the feast; it's that of the ones excluded from the first garden, their heads covered with ashes. She remembers, the woman invaded by dust: *in those days,* at that lost, finished, dried-up, closed, unforgettable moment, at that time that was a long time, whose trace three years without water has erased, as though the other year, the exception, was the leap year, *in illo tempore:*[9] there was harmony, mutual help, corn as much as you wanted, abundance, perpetual banqueting. In that time. We're all going to die, like dust. I work the soil, suffer in childbirth, am hungry and sweat, die: *quia pulvis es, et in pulverem reverteris* [dust you are and to dust you shall return]. The story climbs on board Genesis while the latter is underway, with the abandonment, but tirelessly returns to the lost and promised garden, to the archaic place that had the tree, the mango tree green with promises, where thirst was slaked, where words were things, friendship peaceful, and protection tranquil. Where the sun and water made love so that the village could eat in abundance. Bananas, sweet potatoes, and yams to throw away [142]. Everything has returned to dust.

Three times: lost Eden, the dry and dark waiting, and the arrival of someone who carries the promise and dies voluntarily for reconciliation *so that life can start all over again, so that day can break on the dew. Because what counts,* he said, *is the sacrifice of a man.* The garden is given only for the memory; the future is happy only as work that is to come. And therefore, the story is isomorphic to the Scriptures. It is the Scripture itself, in which the one who carries the promise gives the water of the well, blood, and the drink of immortality. *Because what counts,* he said, *is the blood of a black man. Go, go see them,* he said, *tell them the will of the blood that's been shed* [236]. In exchange for the water discovered. The equivalence of water and blood is the Scripture itself. Christ is Black.

The soil is arid, and the inhabitant waits. He waits for the dew. We need to speak Latin again (my, but he's smart, that Aristomène): *rorate, caeli, desuper, et nubes pluant justum.*[10] That was the traditional metaphor; let the just one descend, like the dew, from the heavens above; let the clouds shower and justice rain down. Goodness, figs, and mangoes indeed rain down. The metaphor engenders the entire story. He arrives, he is just, he is going to give water. The water—precisely—that we call dew. He comes from elsewhere, and he is from here, a double nature; he is an inhabitant, and he comes from the land where there is knowledge. Natal-native, and newly arrived. *Children were following him, fascinated by his great height. To them, he was the man who had crossed the sea, who had lived in the strange country of Cuba. He was crowned with a halo of mysteries and legends* [179]. What is this just man's name? Manuel. This is the name he gives at first to the tall Annaise on the road at the top of the mound where he met her, when she answered him: by the grace of God, all right, *oui* [145–46]. Manuel, Emmanuel, the messiah, the heaven-sent, the son of Délivrance and Bienaimé, himself the son of Josaphat-Joseph, himself the brother of Joseph. The repetitive genealogy shakes up the admissions. Secrets always lie in namings along a family tree.

"Soon I'll tell you some great news, you hear?"
"What news, what event?"
"It's too soon to tell it. But it'll be something to be glad about, you'll see" [193].
The water. My time hasn't come.

She moved toward him. Her breasts were high and firm; the regal motion of her legs; the luscious shape of her body; I greet you, Manuel; I greet you, Anna. She touched his outstretched hand with her fingertips. *You came? I came. I'm listening,* oui. *No man has ever touched me. I trust you. I'm surprised,* she said, *I listen to your words. You have nothing false about you, Anna; you are clear and clean like a spring and like a light.* She laughs like a turtledove. A dove [183–84]. *What would you say, Anna, if the corn grew? Thanks for such good fortune. If the millet was reborn? Thanks for the blessing. Can't you see the clusters, the ears? Yes, I see. The banana trees and their bunches? Yes, yes. Can't you see the ripe fruit? Oui! Oui! Do you want fruit? Yes. But how might this be possible? What do we need, Anna, for the fruit? Water. I will bring you the water, which fecundates. You could do that, Manuel?* He had been revealed to her, as if she were recognizing him for the first time. *You'll be master of the springs, you'll walk,* she said [185]. *You're full of spirit, and you'll be the mistress of that garden. Her face aglow: not the setting sunlight, happiness. Yes, Anna. Yes, my master* [188].

This is the bare story, filtered of the aforementioned critiques. It says no to the express theory. It is recognizable word for word, figure for figure, and nothing is lacking in it, not even its own explanation by the most natural. Go and see it in Filippo Lippi or Ghirlandaio. Go and read it in Luke or Matthew. It is called the Annunciation. Anna.

Délira Délivrance: *man has been abandoned. The Lord is the creator of heaven and earth, and the earth is in pain. So the Lord is the creator of pain, the creator of suffering. My whole body aches, and my whole body gives birth to suffering. I don't need anybody piling damnation on top of that. Her eyes had the light of a spring* [137-38]. Annaise: *Manuel, Manuel, ho! No, God, you're not good. It's not true that you are good. We call on you to help us—you don't hear. Look at our grief! Look at our sorrow! Look at our tribulations! Are you asleep, God? Are you deaf? Are you blind? Have you got no heart, God? Where is your justice? Where is your pity? Where is your mercy?* [238].
The book of Job.

And Charité has gone off, too [195].

That's true, Manuel thought. Life is life! However much you take side roads or make long detours, life is a continual coming back. The dead, they say, come back to Guinea, and even death is only another name for life. The fruit that rots in the ground nourishes a new tree's hope [150].
If a grain dies, it bears much fruit. The reduced model of the story: Manuel dies for Annaise's new fruit. The figure of a circle. Death and resurrection. The sun.

Manuel, it's just like we were on a little island. We're far away, we're at the very end of the world. At the beginning of the world. Because at the beginning of beginnings, there were a woman and a man like you and me. The first spring flowed at their feet, and the woman and the man entered the spring and bathed in life. She walked in the mysterious shade of the giant fig tree. Sacred terror. The tree. The branches laden with silvery moss. You can't see his head. His head's in the sky. His roots hold the water. I greet you, holy water [205].

Eve. Haiti, west of Eden. An island so distant, to the west of the Tigris.

The water carried along within itself a voice that was the tumult of her own blood. I'm going to die! [206]. Water and blood. *The water will wash the blood away* [210]. Manuel's blood purchases the water and redeems the blood. Annaise's blood is the water of the earth. Let it soon be shown that the Gospels are constructed around a cycle of liquid metamorphoses.

The passion according to Manuel. I'm going to bring you living water. The drink of immortality. He appears before the court, at the assembly of the people who hate him. *I have come, brothers. I come with peace and reconciliation. Remember when you were accused of stealing in the garden, and I stepped up and confessed that it was me. And my papa tore the skin off my back with his whip.* From original sin to flagellation. *And I found the peasants divided up. Blood has flowed.* The murder of the father. *Sauveur died and vengeance was gotten. You've sold your honor for a few drops of water. You'd sell yours, all right, for white rum.* Judas Gervilen. *He disappeared in the night. Here is my hand for peace and reconciliation. Take this piece of pine wood. The pine torch cast a bit of light around him.* The garden, the other garden, *a garden of stars.* A mortal blow. *I'm going to die.* The scoundrel.[11] Abandoned. Toward the grave, toward the dust. Thirsty. *I'm thirsty. Tell me the bandit's name.* Mother, forgive him. No, we mustn't repeat the murder story, Sauveur's murder. What counts is the sacrifice of a man. The blood of a black man. *Tell the will of the blood that's been shed—reconciliation—reconciliation—so that life can start all over again, so that day can break on the dew. He had taken her promise with him.* The testament of the new covenant. *She uttered a cry, her body opened its arms, crucified. There was a light on Manuel's forehead* [228-37].

It wasn't Manuel, that great, cold, stiff lifeless body. It was only his likeness in stone. The real Manuel was walking, walking, through the *mountains and the woods in the sunlight* [239]. Or will be reborn from Annaise's womb.

There was a light on your forehead. Not even death could take it away. May this light guide you [247].

That earth that he loved so much and for which he had died [249].

The good news has been transmitted, and the promise of the covenant: *what counts is the sacrifice of a man. The blood of a black man* [236].

He wanted, I now understand, his death to be the beginning of life for us [253].

No, he isn't dead [258]. *He will return.*

For once, the question of knowing whether or not an author is clear about what he in reality writes, hardly so interesting in the majority of cases, is decidable. Does the author distance him- or herself from their production? Yes, this distance exists; it is measurable with sufficient exactness. Before evaluating it, let there be a parallel text: another agrarian story, not very far off in time or space, in which the Synoptic Gospels are in play precisely regarding negritude. William Faulkner recomposes them in *Light in August.* American literary criticism has reconstructed the dictionary, term for term; it has located the traces of the projection; it has gathered the set of keys—laid flat as if they were the pieces of a jigsaw puzzle. It gives the characters their second names, the episodes their second frameworks, the discourses their double intentions. As though a narrative in the normal degree existed behind the narrative in the zero degree. This consists in reading what is projected on the basis of the terminal points of the extension lines. One plays a guessing game; one decodes what is disguised. But nothing has really been done if one hasn't set into place the laws of transformation, the complete system of its references, and the regulated set of the operations of transcription. The thing is not very easy, but it is possible nevertheless. Having Joe Christmas, for example, be Christ himself hardly presents any difficulties: but he is both the son and the father, since his first name is Joseph, and Mary, pregnant, travels, abandoned; he is Black and white, Negro-white; he is the same and the other; he is, in fact,

Christ and Antichrist. It is not hard to suspect Roumain of having rigorously attempted the same adventure. *Light in August*'s scientific projection is not simple, cylindrical, or conic, as they say in geometry; it is not, on the other hand, a simple inversion, the one that was missing in the Haitian story. In the latter, the fire sun, mentioned on almost every page, God, father, male, fecundator, and punitive, preserves its natural course, and its cosmic lovemakings with the water of the earth, which is female and buried, have their natural end: Manuel in Annaise's arms, rending, embrace, deliverance, and fecundity. The translation is almost mundane, a linear projection. In the former, and Faulkner says this in express words, "the sun had not set but instead had turned in the sky before reaching the horizon and retraced its way,"[12] and Christmas is castrated. Time turns in the inverse direction. August is in the dark of night; winter is bright: perhaps the book should be titled "Darkness in December." So this is the Antiscripture Scripture, this is the Black Gospel. But again, things are not that simple, and the inversion isn't enough: this is because the projection preserves and contraposes at the same time; it multiplies the reversals and intersections; I have defined this transformation elsewhere as a caustic. In short, it is so complex and sophisticated, so delicate to handle in its outline, that it required much more than clear consciousness, the reasoned attention of each moment. The distance taken to the production is measured in the mediate lengths of the deduction, in the thickness of the translation's intermediaries. Faulkner's Antichrist-Christ has the complexity of a multiple reflection on a Greek and Nietzschean myth, the circle, the eternal return, Atreus's sun, sickness, and normality, et cetera; Roumain's Christ has the transparent simplicity of the Marxist model, the mirror with two images, real and virtual, science and ideology, vibrating only because of the agrarian transposition. What unites them is manifestly the project and the consciousness they have of it, and the critique, fierce on both sides, but different in its modalities. What unites them is Freud, but not the same Freud. And this is the distance, so easily measurable, in *Masters of the Dew*.

The projection in it is so transparent that the distance to the production cannot be assessed on the outline itself or on the critique's counterimage, but on the very way of drawing it. The drawing, at some point, hesitates and reveals shakiness. The Testaments are not always the origin of the image, the object of transcription. The object sometimes is not the scriptural text but its interpretation, its analytical interpretation. It is in and by this distance that the author reveals himself. I would bet a thousand to one he has read *Totem and Taboo, The Future of an Illusion, Moses and Monotheism,* and the like. This is because he reduces the grand ancestral gesture reconstructed by Freud regarding the same Scriptures to the ultrashort genealogical interval, within the scope of individual memory: the discord between brothers of the same father, the first murder, from which all history, mythology, and human suffering ensue. The religious tone of the novel at a stroke reveals what, to the eyes of the author, makes this discord possible and engenders guilt. The persistent presence of father sun confirms the hypothesis.

It's an old story. Blood was shed. He was called General Longeannis, a well-mannered Negro, a patriarch. They don't come like that any more. Through him, we were all related, more or less. He had so many children you can't count them. He died. And the division happened because of the murder. And it was Sauveur who killed [164–65]. Fratricide or parricide?

Three contents are clearly distinguished. The sociopolitical theory and its doublet, the critique of ideologies: the inhabitant is the sole master of the land by and through his work within the collective. The agrarian infrastructure and the immediate bushing out of its myths: honor, mistress of the water, respect, master sun. The projection of the Scriptures, doubled with its key to analysis: Longeannis, a patriarch, a rich peasant, a general, they don't come like that any more, and his descendant, Jean like him, at the end of the genealogical tree: *in truth, in truth, your boy was a real Negro, an inhabitant to the roots of his soul; we won't see another like him soon* [253]. So goodbye, Chief. Manuel Jean-Joseph, ho, mighty Negro, *hého* [257]. Three systems of mastery coded onto three contents. The masters are no longer Hilarion and his Florentine, the people of the city and of money, but us, the *coumbite*, the proletarians. Yet mastery is at the sources of energy: the liquid spring and the chief of fire. Mastery is in the hands of those of the lineage who leave a mark on their time and are recognized: the great common ancestor and the son of the son of his son. Systems that are analogous in their formality but so different as to be contradictory. Decide, who is the master? You can die from hesitating to answer. So Roumain answers all the above and keeps the three threads together: the true sun has returned, water has been found again, the son of Bienaimé returned and was resurrected, the *coumbite* of the old days has been reformed. The contradictions subside into an equilibrium that, under other skies, would be called syncretism. Manuel is political chief, sun master, and sacrificed savior. The structure is no longer formal; here it is realized. His scarf is red: the red of the revolution, the sun, and blood. The reason for this unexpected alliance?

The reason for it is the master of masters, which is to say, time and its historical form.

Délivrance: I sew, I sew and I stitch together the old days and the new [256]. Whereupon everyone repeats the old song of the spinners, of the weavers on the sidewalks, and the clothes menders of the thread. Manuel, for example, at the summit of knowledge: naturally, the day comes when each man must enter the earth, but life itself is a thread that doesn't break, that can't be lost. Do you know why? Because every Negro ties a knot in it during his lifetime with the work he does—that's what keeps life going through the centuries—man's usefulness on this earth [203].

They think the thread is broken and there are two times. Here is the governor of the dew: the person who fills the rendings. He or she sews, he or she ties a knot with the thread. A mending together [*raccord*]. Roumain brings the masteries into accord by resewing the threads of time. Manuel's departure—his hidden life—leaves a hole in his mother's boubou: he has returned; on the hill shaped like a cranium, he contemplates the desert, a gap without any water. Discord and murder have divided the genealogical tree with a machete. The murdered dead haunt the village, like ghosts. The bad sun punishes with every dawn. It is necessary to stitch back together; it is necessary to unstitch. Cut off the frayed borders, reattaching at the point where the fabric is good. Undo the discords and reconnect with the old time of abundance, the time that was a long time. Rediscover the deep old water, the water that slumbers and is not dead, and, through it, renew the old sun. Stitch back together the time of the world and the time of men, generation. To the mother without a son, give again a son, a daughter, and then a son to this daughter. Even if, again, the father has to be struck down by this; even if the son has to be murdered. The women remain, the stitchers. The annunciation in the Garden of Eden. Stitch back together the end and the beginning, the promised future to the beginning of beginnings, beyond the hole of time, a gap or tear, beyond misfortune, the desert, the failed harvests, death, thirst, thirst and suffering. The structure is sewing. Catching the good thread once more, finding the good cycle again, cutting off the bad one, doing away with the fringes around this margin. The good thread: the meaning of history, and not the other meaning, a countermeaning, the thread of water, a slender silver strip that runs in the plain, the thread of songs, simidor, the thread of generation, of sons and filiation.[13] Life.

Separated by the distance of the sea from reasonable reasonings, Roumain says this, which is easy as pie: the three codes, together, are structured like filters, specifically time filters. They separate two histories, the one that must be unstitched and the one that must be restitched, the bad time and the good time, before and after Manuel, the meaning and the countermeaning, the action and the reaction, the old and the new, the implacable sun and the generating fire, the cursed water one dies from and the water that gives. Filters, divisions, critiques, and returns. Everything begins again, following the thread of the straight grain. Is it truly inevitable, when speech judges, that it only engenders myths, in the sunlight?

By the way, why do people come and talk to me about myths or reasons when it is a question of drinking or dying of thirst, of being hungry or having a full stomach?

Bamako, February 29, 1972

These lines finished, a geologist discovers some groundwater under the Bandiagara Escarpment. That cliff from which the dawn is the beginning of the world.

And his wife gives birth a few days later.

Notes

Preface

1. [*Déduit* is related to *déduction*, but also means a pleasurable occupation or pleasures of the flesh.—Trans.]
2. [This neologism, "pantopian," is constructed from the Greek words *pan*, all, and *topos*, place.—Trans.]

1. Translations of the Tree

François Jacob, *The Logic of Life: A History of Heredity*, trans. Betty Spillman (Pantheon Books, 1973). [I have inserted page references at times. My insertions are in square brackets; Serres's references are in parentheses. All such insertions in this chapter refer to this work, even when other authors, such as Claude Bernard, are being discussed.—Trans.]

1. Many of Jacob's pages are written in precisely Leibnizian language: the places where he talks on his own account are pages 285-86, 288, 290-91, 292-93, 299-300, 305-7, 314-15, and 317-18. And therefore, the only criticism to be made about his book centers on Leeuwenhoek: when the latter saw the animalcules, the theory able to welcome them already *existed*, extremely close to our theory.
2. ["The other location was in the sun, whose heat could directly activate the elements, earth, water, and all kinds of debris to produce vile beings: 'serpents, grasshoppers, worms, flies, mice, bats, moles, and everything that is born spontaneously, not from seed, but from putrid matter and filth,' said Fernel."—Trans.]
3. [In *De arte combinatoria*, "complexion" is Leibniz's general term for combination. The word is also used by Boltzmann and Planck. In physics, it has been superseded by "microstate."—Trans.]
4. [For *combinatorics*, the Spillman translation has "combinative system." —Trans.]
5. ["'The apparent organization of foliated or layered Stones,' specified Charles Bonnet, 'such as Slate or Talc, that of fibrous stones or those composed of filaments, such as Asbestos, seem to constitute transitional stages between solid brute Beings and organized solids'" (34). "A sponge—who can say it is a plant or an animal? Coral—is it really a rock? 'Just as zoophytes resemble both animals and plants,' said Cesalpinus, 'so do mushrooms belong both to plants and inanimate objects'" (23).—Trans.]

6. [The Spillman translation has "Each plant can be represented as a collection of elements in a given number and proportion. Each of these can vary *ad infinitum* and each variation join with the others in infinite combinations. Botany becomes a kind of combinative system with almost unlimited possibilities."—Trans.]
7. [The "great principle," as stated on Jacob's page 34, runs as follows: "This was true of the bone structure of animals and their body size which, as Galileo said, cannot be increased indefinitely, 'neither in art nor in nature' without destroying the unity and hampering the normal functioning of organs. 'I believe that a small dog could carry two or three dogs of the same size on its back, but I do not believe that a horse could carry even a single horse of the same size.'"—Trans.]
8. Claude Berge, *The Theory of Graphs* (Dover Publications, 2001), chap. 16, "Trees and Arborescences," 152-64.

2. Life, Information, Second Law

Jacques Monod, *Leçon inaugurale* (Collège de France, 1967); and Jacques Monod, *Chance and Necessity,* trans. Austryn Wainhouse (Knopf, 1971).

1. The term "phenomenology" is used in three senses, two of which are important: the astronomical sense in the manner of Johann Heinrich Lambert, and the energy sense, imposed by the anti-Boltzmannians so as to return to . . . positivism.
2. [The title of chapter 1 of Monod, *Chance and Necessity.*—Trans.]
3. [In *Chance and Necessity,* Monod defines teleonomy, at the level of individuals, as "*objects endowed with a purpose or project,* which at the same time they exhibit in their structure and carry out through their performances" (9). At the level of species, he defines it as follows: "We shall arbitrarily choose to define the essential teleonomic project as consisting in the transmission from generation to generation of the invariance content characteristic of the species. All the structures, all the performances, all the activities contributing to the success of the essential project will hence be called 'teleonomic'" (14).—Trans.]
4. [See Monod, *Chance and Necessity,* 95. The Wainhouse translation has "blossoming firework": "At each stage more highly ordered structures and new functions appear which, resulting from spontaneous interactions between products of the preceding stages, reveal successively, like a blossoming firework [a multistage fireworks rocket], the latent potentialities of previous levels."—Trans.]
5. [Comte classified the sciences according to increasing complexity and decreasing generality: mathematics, astronomy, physics, chemistry, biology, and sociology.—Trans.]
6. [Monod, *Chance and Necessity,* 20-22.—Trans.]

7. [See Gaston Bachelard, *The New Scientific Spirit,* trans. Arthur Goldhammer (Beacon Press, 1984), 139, which states "[modern science tries] to read the real complexity of things beneath the simple appearance." See also Jean Perrin, *Atoms,* trans. Dalziel Hammick (Van Nostrand, 1916), vii, which reads "explain the complicated and visible by the simple and invisible."—Trans.]
8. [Monod, *Chance and Necessity,* chap. 5.—Trans.]
9. Claude Berge, *The Theory of Graphs* (Dover Publications, 2001), 107ff.; Claude Berge, *Programmes, jeux et réseaux de transport* (Dunod, 1962), 173ff.
10. [See Monod, *Chance and Necessity,* chap. 1.—Trans.]
11. [In Descartes's *Geometry,* he distinguishes geometrical curves and mechanical curves. Geometric curves can be constructed from algebraic equations or using the continuous motions of ruler and compass, whereas mechanical curves cannot. For Descartes, the former were geometrically exact, while the latter were not.—Trans.]
12. [Antoine Cournot defined "chance" as the encounter of two independent causal series. For instance, the chain of events leading to the tile falling from the roof and the chain bringing the man beneath it, where he is struck on the head. Antoine Cournot, *Exposition de la théorie des chances et des probabilités* (Hachette, 1843), 73.—Trans.]
13. [The French *cas* does not change in the plural.—Trans.]
14. [See Monod, *Chance and Necessity,* 113-14.—Trans.]
15. [See Francisco Goya's *Fight with Cudgels* (ca. 1820-23).—Trans.]

3. Betrayal

1. Robin Clarke, *La Course à la mort,* trans. Georges Renard (Seuil, 1972). [I haven't succeeded in ascertaining the English original of this work, but it is probably *The Science of War and Peace,* published in 1971. The French title translates to "The Race to Death." The book deals with nuclear weapons, space militarization, naval armament, the exponential growth of war, environmental destruction, and related issues.—Trans.]
2. ["Ward No. 6" is a short story by Anton Chekhov about the psychological decline of a doctor in charge of a hospital that includes a bleak ward for psychiatric patients.—Trans.]
3. [In the thought of Gaston Bachelard, recurrent history is one in which the past is understood in the light of the present.—Trans.]
4. [A reference to Honoré de Balzac's novel *The Wild Ass's Skin,* involving a magical shrinking piece of shagreen leather.—Trans.]
5. [A reference to Hippasus of Metapontum, a Pythagorean philosopher from the fifth century BCE.—Trans.]
6. [Léon Brillouin, *Science and Information Theory,* 2nd ed. (Academic Press, 1962), 293-94.—Trans.]

282 NOTES

7. [Carl Friedrich Gauss, an influential German mathematician and scientist. Regarding his conception of the infinite, in an 1831 letter Gauss wrote, "As to your proof, I must protest most vehemently against your use of the infinite as something consummated, as this is never permitted in mathematics. The infinite is but a figure of speech; an abridged form for the statement that limits exist which certain ratios may approach as closely as we desire, while other magnitudes may be permitted to grow beyond all bounds." Quoted in *Number: The Language of Science*, by Tobias Dantzig (Penguin, 2005), 220. The contrast is between a completed infinite, such as an actual set that contains infinity, and a potential infinite (Gauss's), which is better described as a potentially infinite process, such as iterative counting or approaching a limit asymptotically.—Trans.]
8. [An obscure word in French, meaning "emergence" or "rising."—Trans.]
9. [The third person plural form of Nero's "Qualis artifex pereo!" as quoted in Suetonius. Instead of "What an artist dies in me!" Serres writes, "What artists die in them." "Munitions pyrotechnicians" translates *artificiers*, which is, of course, very similar to the Latin plural for "artists," *artifices*.—Trans.]

4. Descartes Translated into Statics Language

1. [Chain = *chaîne*, which can also refer to a production line.—Trans.]
2. ["Hyperbole" derives from the Greek for "to throw beyond."—Trans.]
3. [High = *haut*, derived from the Latin *altus*, which Serres, as will become evident in the next paragraph, associates with verticality.—Trans.]
4. [*More geometrico* = following a geometric manner. *More statico* = following a statics manner.—Trans.]

5. Leibniz Retranslated into Mathematical Language

1. [For Leibniz, a *calculus ratiocinator* is a universal logical calculation framework.—Trans.]
2. [In Vitruvian architectural drawing, an "ichnography" is a ground plan, whereas a "scenography" is a drawing that takes perspective into account. For Leibniz and Serres, "scenography" means the view of an object from a particular point of view, whereas "ichnography" means a view free of perspective, ultimately, a view that would encompass all possible scenographies. Strictly speaking, this ichnographic view is accessible only to God.—Trans.]
3. [Dietrich Mahnke wrote a book titled *Leibnizens Synthese von Universalmathematik und Individualmetaphysik* (Frommann-Holzboog, 1964).—Trans.]
4. [G. W. Leibniz, *Philosophical Essays*, trans. Roger Ariew and Daniel Garber (Hackett, 1989), 40. Emphasis added by Serres.—Trans.]
5. [Unity = *unité*, which can mean "unit," "unity," or "oneness." The term will

be translated as all of these at various times, depending on the context, or in combination when multiple senses are simultaneously relevant. Unlike in English, where "one" and "unity" appear less visibly connected etymologically, the French *un* is visibly embedded in *unité*.—Trans.]

6. ["Il y en a qui croient que *Dieu fait tout*, d'autres s'imaginent qu'*il ne fait que conserver la force qu'il a donnée aux créatures*. . . . Or puisque les actions et passions appartiennent proprement *aux substances individuelles*, il serait nécessaire d'expliquer ce que c'est qu'une telle substance." My emphasis. The Ariew-Garber translation (Leibniz, *Philosophical Essays*, 40) has "some believe that God does everything, while others imagine that he merely conserves the force he has given to creatures. . . . And since actions and passions properly belong to individual substances, it will be necessary to explain what such an individual substance is." A more exact but clumsier version to fit the context: "Some believe that God does [or makes] everything; others imagine that he only makes the force he has given to creatures be conserved."—Trans.]

7. [The Ariew-Garber translation has the following: "It is indeed true that when several predicates are attributed to the same subject and this subject is attributed to no other, it is called an individual substance; but this is not [enough]" (40-41).—Trans.]

8. [The first quote below refers to first group of words cited in this sentence of the main text; the second quote to the second group. The Ariew-Garber translation reads, "An accident, on the other hand, is a being whose notion does not include everything that can be attributed to the subject to which the notion is attributed. Thus, taken in abstraction from the subject, the quality of being a king which belongs to Alexander the Great is not determinate enough to constitute an individual and does not include the other qualities of the same subject, nor does it include everything that the notion of this prince includes," and "We can say that the nature of an individual substance or of a complete being is to have a notion so complete [*accompli*, "consummate," as I have rendered it] that it is sufficient to contain and to allow us to deduce from it all the predicates of the subject to which this notion is attributed" (41).—Trans.]

9. [In paragraph 4 of "Principles of Nature and Grace" (*Philosophical Essays*, 208), Leibniz distinguishes "apperception" from "perception," the former being "reflective knowledge" of the representation, whereas some perceptions are not so consciously perceived, such as noises our hearing has filtered out. Leibniz terms these "minute perceptions."—Trans.]

10. [For "homogon," see note 18 of this chapter.—Trans.]

11. [This essay has been translated as "On the Ultimate Origination of Things" in Leibniz, *Philosophical Essays*, 149-55. For the Latin phrases in this section, I shall include the Ariew-Garber translations and page references in brackets.—Trans.]

12. [Part of the Leibnizian lexicon, the term "geometral" designates a point of view on an object that would include every possible point of view, thereby delivering a complete, ideal perspective on the object. God alone is capable of this.—Trans.]
13. [Leibniz, *Philosophical Essays*, 213, paragraph 3 of "The Monadology."—Trans.]
14. "A Vindication of God's Justice," *Monadology and Other Philosophical Essays*, ed. and trans. Paul and Anne Martin Schrecker (Bobbs-Merrill, 1965), 116.
15. [In the very first sentence of "On the Ultimate Origination of Things," we find the phrase "there is some One Being." In Latin, the phrase is *datur Unum aliquod*. This sentence could more literally be translated as "Some One Being is given."—Trans.]
16. [G. W. Leibniz, *Sämtliche Schriften und Briefe,* ser. 6, vol. 4 (Akademie-Verlag, 1999), 1426.—Trans.]
17. [The source for this citation and the one a few sentences below is G. W. Leibniz, *Leibnizens Mathematische Schriften,* ed. C. I. Gerhardt, vol. 7 (Olms Verlag, 1971), 18.—Trans.]
18. ["Homogon" and "homogen" are somewhat obscure Leibnizian terms. Citing a translator's note from *Hermes I,* trans. Louise Burchill (University of Minnesota Press, 2023), "Underlining that pairs of homogons, such as that of the limit and the bounded, are not to be confused with homogeneous terms, Belaval explains . . . that what defines homogons is the transformation, by continuous change, of a 'genus' (such as a limit, a curve, time, space, and so on) into what might be termed its opposite 'species' or a 'species of its contradictory kind'" (344–45).—Trans.]
19. ["Terrain" derives from the Latin *terrenum,* land or ground. The form of the word Leibniz's text uses is *terreno,* plot of ground, which, of course, would presuppose the broader concept *terrenum*. But even this *terrenum,* as we shall see, is necessarily bounded. The passage Serres is commenting on runs as follows: "The plot of ground on which the most pleasing building possible is to be built" (Leibniz, *Philosophical Essays,* 150).—Trans.]
20. [A play on Leibniz's famous quote *Dum Deus calculat, fit mundus* (while God calculates, the world is made).—Trans.]
21. [For this passage, see Leibniz, *Philosophical Essays,* 150. In proportion to = *en fonction de,* which can also mean "according to" or "as a function of."—Trans.]
22. [Leibniz, *Philosophical Essays,* 150.—Trans.]
23. [Leibniz, *Philosophical Essays,*150. The Ariew-Garber translation reads, "An equilateral triangle would be drawn" (151).—Trans.]
24. [Leibniz, *Philosophical Essays,* 151.—Trans.]
25. [Savage ethics = *éthique sauvage,* which recalls Claude Lévi-Strauss's notion of *pensée sauvage,* a wild thinking or mind, or perhaps untamed. Savage mind uses whatever means it has at its disposal and is to be contrasted with the civilized mind, which uses strict methods and tries to change the world to fit

its aims. Lévi-Strauss goes to great pains to inform the reader that the term "savage" does not exclusively apply to "primitive" peoples. Such thinking also exists in the "civilized" mind.—Trans.]
26. "Discourse on Metaphysics," in Leibniz, *Philosophical Essays*, 47.
27. [The one who benefits from it is the one who committed the crime.—Trans.]

6. Auguste Comte Self-Translated in the Encyclopedia

1. ["The law of three states" is translated as "the law of three stages" in English, but I shall keep to the more literal translation for reasons that will become clear below.—Trans.]
2. [Respectively, Jean Richer and Nicolas-Louis de Lacaille. In this piece, the French word *voyage* is translated as "voyage" in some instances and as "journey" in others.—Trans.]
3. [As a young man, Comte had been Henri de Saint-Simon's secretary.—Trans.]
4. [Translation = *translation*, which signifies "translation" in the sense of motion. Serres also uses the word *traduction* in this essay, which would also be rendered as "translation" (i.e., translating into different languages). To avoid confusion, in this chapter, I will put *traduction* in brackets when "translation" is meant in the sense of rendering into a different language, except in cases where the context makes this unnecessary.—Trans.]
5. [In the second lesson, Comte distinguished a historical procedure for discussing a science and a dogmatic procedure. The historical procedure sets out the knowledge of the science in the order it was historically acquired. The dogmatic procedure sets out this knowledge more logically and coherently from the standpoint of the contemporary researcher.—Trans.]
6. [See note 25 in chapter 5 of this work. Again, *pensée sauvage* recalls Lévi-Strauss's book and conception, though here the pejorative notion of "primitive," may also be in play.—Trans.]

7. Ambrosia and Gold

Johannes Vermeer, *Woman Holding a Balance* (ca. 1662–63), and Nicolas Poussin, *The Feeding of the Child Jupiter* (ca. 1650), National Gallery of Art, Washington, D.C. [The Poussin painting is also known as *Nymphs Feeding the Child Jupiter* —Trans.]

1. ["Punctual" is being used in its scientific and mathematical sense of related to a point.—Trans.]
2. [The name Callirhoe derives from Greek words meaning "beautiful flowing."—Trans.]
3. ["Unanimous" should be understood in its etymological sense of one soul or mind.—Trans.]

4. ["Stigmatic" should probably be understood in the etymological sense of *stigma*, "mark of a pointed instrument."—Trans.]

8. La Tour Translates Pascal

An exhibition of Georges de La Tour's work at the Musée de l'Orangerie, Paris, May–September 1972.

1. [References to Pascal's *Pensées* include both Lafuma (L) and Brunschvicg (B) numerations, the two standard systems for identifying fragments. Since these systems are independent of specific editions, no particular edition is cited. Entries are listed in brackets in this text as L##-B##. The translations are mine.—Trans.]
2. [In Latin, "alibi" means elsewhere.—Trans.]
3. [See La Tour's *Old Man* (ca. 1618-19).—Trans.]
4. [La Tour was born in Vic, Lorraine.—Trans.]
5. [See *The Hurdy-Gurdy Player* (ca. 1620-25).—Trans.]
6. [See *Saint Jerome at Prayer* (Stockholm version, ca. 1642). Also, the French original reads "dihedral" instead of "trihedral."—Trans.]
7. [See *Job Mocked by His Wife* (ca. 1620-50).—Trans.]
8. [The hurdy-gurdy players in La Tour's paintings are called *veilleurs*, individuals who are either up all night or serve as night guards.—Trans.]
9. [For this paragraph, see *Saint James the Minor*, *Saint Philip*, and *Saint Jude Thaddeus* (all ca. 1620).—Trans.]
10. [See *Saint Jerome Reading* (1621-23).—Trans.]
11. [Luminosity = *clarté*, which can mean clarity or light, but usually in a sense less intense than sunlight: room lighting, lamplight, or moonlight.—Trans.]
12. [See *The Musicians' Brawl* (ca. 1620-30).—Trans.]
13. [See *Saint Sebastian Tended by Saint Irene* (ca. 1649).—Trans.]
14. [See *Saint Joseph the Carpenter* (ca. 1642-44).—Trans.]
15. [See *The Fortune Teller* (ca. 1630)—Trans.]
16. [See *The Card Sharp with the Ace of Diamonds* (1636-38).—Trans.]
17. [See *Magdalene with Two Flames* (ca. 1640), *Magdalene at a Mirror* (ca. 1635-40), and *Magdalene with the Smoking Flame* (ca. 1640).—Trans.]
18. [See the version of *Young Virgin Mary* (ca. 1640) exhibited at the Detroit Institute of Arts.—Trans.]
19. [See *The Newborn Child* (ca. 1645-48).—Trans.]
20. [See *The Newborn Child* (ca. 1645-48).—Trans.]
21. [See *The Denial of Saint Peter* (1650) and *Saint Peter Repentant* (1645).—Trans.]
22. [See *The Flea Catcher* (1630s-40s).—Trans.]
23. [See *The Dream of Saint Joseph* (ca. 1628-45).—Trans.]
24. [From Psalm 91:5-6: "(You shall not be afraid) of the terror by night, nor of the arrow that flies by day, nor of the pestilence that walks in darkness, nor of the destruction that lays waste at noonday" (NKJV).—Trans.]

25. [Pole = *pôle*, which does not mean a "pole" in the sense of a telephone pole, but rather the pole of a magnetic or conceptual field. This is true for every instance of "pole" in this work.—Trans.]
26. [Serres is quoting from the Apostles' Creed. Here is my translation of the Latin as it appears in this sentence: "Conceived, born, suffered, was crucified, died and was buried, descended into hell, rose again from the dead on the third day, ascended into heaven." Two sentences below, the Latin reads, "And is seated at the right hand of the Father."—Trans.]
27. [The Latin translates as "the world is open" and refers to an ancient Roman ritual in which the *mundus cerialis*, a pit supposedly leading to the underworld, was opened.—Trans.]
28. [Pascal's theorem is also called the *hexagrammum mysticum theorem*.—Trans.]
29. [See Descartes's *Meditations on First Philosophy*, "First Meditation." My translation.—Trans.]
30. [See the first paragraph of Spinoza's *Treatise on the Emendation of the Intellect*. My translation.—Trans.]
31. [John 1:5: "The light shines in the darkness, and the darkness did not comprehend it." (NKJV)—Trans.]
32. [See *Boy Blowing at Lamp* (ca. 1640).—Trans.]
33. [Spinoza's *Ethics*, part 4, prop. 67. My translation.—Trans.]

9. Turner Translates Carnot
English Romantic Painting, Petit Palais, Paris, January–April 1972.
1. [See George Garrard's *Mr. Whitbread's Wharf* (1788).—Trans.]
2. [The *Durande* is the steamship in Victor Hugo's *The Toilers of the Sea* (1866).—Trans.]
3. [See J. M. W. Turner's *The Fighting Temeraire, Tugged to Her Last Berth to Be Broken Up* (1839).—Trans.]
4. [See, respectively, Turner's *Snow Storm: Hannibal and His Army Crossing the Alps* (1812); *Keelmen Heaving in Coals by Moonlight* (1835); and *Whalers (Boiling Blubber) Entangled in Flaw Ice, Endeavouring to Extricate Themselves* (1846).—Trans.]
5. [Presumably, by "here," Serres means the Turner exhibition he visited, mentioned in the unnumbered note for this chapter.—Trans.]
6. [See Turner's *Rain, Steam, and Speed: The Great Western Railway* (1844). —Trans.]
7. [Railroads figure prominently in both Émile Zola's *The Human Beast* and Jules Verne's *The Steam House*.—Trans.]
8. [See Turner's *The Interior of a Cannon Foundry* (1797-98).—Trans.]
9. [Carnot's father, Lazare Carnot, was a mathematician and also an organizer of French military operations during the Revolutionary Wars.—Trans.]

10. Roumain and Faulkner Translate Scripture

Jacques Roumain, *Masters of the Dew,* trans. Langston Hughes and Mercer Cook, in *The Collected Works of Langston Hughes* (University of Missouri Press, 2003), 16:137–258.

1. [Peasant = *paysan.* "Country" or "land" is *pays* in French. Hence peasants are intrinsically tied to the land. City-dwellers are *dépaysés.* Hence they are "decountrified" or "displaced," as I have rendered it here. Besides *pays,* "land" in this essay is also used to translate *terre.*—Trans.]
2. [A *coumbite* is an act of collective agricultural work.—Trans.]
3. [Hughes translates *foulard* (scarf or kerchief) as "handkerchief."—Trans.]
4. [Serres often quotes Roumain's text without attribution, and not always precisely. I will include page references in brackets for all but the most trivial of references. I will occasionally change the translation. The translation in this instance renders the phrase as "armed to the teeth with being mad—like a gun."—Trans.]
5. [*Fonds Rouge* roughly translates to "red land" or "farm."—Trans.]
6. [Renaud Jean (1887–1961), French writer and leader of a farming union during the interwar period. He was also the first communist deputy from the agricultural world in 1920.—Trans.]
7. [The Hughes translation has "It's not God who betrays us. We betray the soil." "Black man" here translates *nègre,* which would be translated as either the N-word or as "Negro." Hughes often rendered this term as "Negro," but more frequently opted for a neutral equivalent, choosing more general words such as "we" and "man." I will translate it as "Black man" and occasionally "Negro."—Trans.]
8. [For the remaining pages of this essay, quotations from *Masters of the Dew* are written in italics and Serres's comments are in plain font. I shall follow the Hughes translation, but when there are discrepancies between the French and the English editions, I shall follow the French version.—Trans.]
9. [*In illo tempore,* in that time, a phrase used by Mircea Eliade to designate the time of origin of divine acts.—Trans.]
10. [Isa. 45:8.—Trans.]
11. [The French original has *El desgraciado* in Spanish for "The scoundrel," but Serres writes it as "El des*gracia*do," highlighting "grace."—Trans.]
12. [William Faulkner, *Light in August* (Chatto and Windus, 1922), 316.—Trans.]
13. [Simidor is a character in *Masters of the Dew* who is a good singer and often the song-leader for work parties. A *simidor* is also the lead singer in a Haitian voodoo ceremony.—Trans.]

POSTHUMANITIES
Cary Wolfe, *Series Editor*

42 *Creaturely Love: How Desire Makes Us More and Less Than Human*
Dominic Pettman

41 *Matters of Care: Speculative Ethics in More Than Human Worlds*
Maria Puig de la Bellacasa

40 *Of Sheep, Oranges, and Yeast: A Multispecies Impression*
Julian Yates

39 *Fuel: A Speculative Dictionary*
Karen Pinkus

38 *What Would Animals Say If We Asked the Right Questions?*
Vinciane Despret

37 *Manifestly Haraway*
Donna J. Haraway

36 *Neofinalism*
Raymond Ruyer

35 *Inanimation: Theories of Inorganic Life*
David Wills

34 *All Thoughts Are Equal: Laruelle and Nonhuman Philosophy*
John Ó Maoilearca

33 *Necromedia*
Marcel O'Gorman

32 *The Intellective Space: Thinking beyond Cognition*
Laurent Dubreuil

31 *Laruelle: Against the Digital*
Alexander R. Galloway

30 *The Universe of Things: On Speculative Realism*
Steven Shaviro

29 *Neocybernetics and Narrative*
Bruce Clarke

28 *Cinders*
Jacques Derrida

27 *Hyperobjects: Philosophy and Ecology after the End of the World*
Timothy Morton

26 *Humanesis: Sound and Technological Posthumanism*
David Cecchetto

25 *Artist Animal*
Steve Baker

24 *Without Offending Humans: A Critique of Animal Rights*
Élisabeth de Fontenay

23 *Vampyroteuthis Infernalis: A Treatise, with a Report by the Institut Scientifique de Recherche Paranaturaliste*
Vilém Flusser and Louis Bec

22 *Body Drift: Butler, Hayles, Haraway*
Arthur Kroker

21 *HumAnimal: Race, Law, Language*
Kalpana Rahita Seshadri

20 *Alien Phenomenology, or What It's Like to Be a Thing*
Ian Bogost

19 *CIFERAE: A Bestiary in Five Fingers*
Tom Tyler

18 *Improper Life: Technology and Biopolitics from Heidegger to Agamben*
Timothy C. Campbell

17 *Surface Encounters: Thinking with Animals and Art*
Ron Broglio

16 *Against Ecological Sovereignty: Ethics, Biopolitics, and Saving the Natural World*
Mick Smith

15 *Animal Stories: Narrating across Species Lines*
Susan McHugh

14 *Human Error: Species-Being and Media Machines*
Dominic Pettman

13 *Junkware*
Thierry Bardini

12 *A Foray into the Worlds of Animals and Humans, with A Theory of Meaning*
Jakob von Uexküll

11 *Insect Media: An Archaeology of Animals and Technology*
Jussi Parikka

10 *Cosmopolitics II*
Isabelle Stengers

9 *Cosmopolitics I*
Isabelle Stengers

8 *What Is Posthumanism?*
Cary Wolfe

7 *Political Affect: Connecting the Social and the Somatic*
John Protevi

6 *Animal Capital: Rendering Life in Biopolitical Times*
Nicole Shukin

5 *Dorsality: Thinking Back through Technology and Politics*
David Wills

4 *Bíos: Biopolitics and Philosophy*
Roberto Esposito

3 *When Species Meet*
Donna J. Haraway

2 *The Poetics of DNA*
Judith Roof

1 *The Parasite*
Michel Serres

MICHEL SERRES (1930–2019) was an author of more than sixty books, including *Biogea, Variations on the Body,* and *The Parasite.* He was widely known for his poetic prose and interdisciplinary form of thought.

RANDOLPH BURKS is an independent scholar interested in the phenomenology of the body, environmental ethics, philosophy of nature, and philosophies with a realist bent. He has previously translated ten works by Michel Serres, including *Hermes II: Interference* (2025), *Variations on the Body* (2012), and *Biogea* (2012), all published by the University of Minnesota Press.

www.ingramcontent.com/pod-product-compliance
Ingram Content Group UK Ltd.
Pitfield, Milton Keynes, MK11 3LW, UK
UKHW010654090126
466806UK00004B/93